Laboratories of Terror

LABORATORIES OF TERROR

The Final Act of Stalin's Great Purge in Soviet Ukraine

Edited by

LYNNE VIOLA
AND MARC JUNGE

OXFORD
UNIVERSITY PRESS

OXFORD
UNIVERSITY PRESS

Oxford University Press is a department of the University of Oxford. It furthers
the University's objective of excellence in research, scholarship, and education
by publishing worldwide. Oxford is a registered trade mark of Oxford University
Press in the UK and certain other countries.

Published in the United States of America by Oxford University Press
198 Madison Avenue, New York, NY 10016, United States of America.

Library of Congress Cataloging-in-Publication Data
Names: Viola, Lynne, editor. | Junge, Marc, editor.
Title: Laboratories of terror : the final act of Stalin's great purge in
Soviet Ukraine /edited by Lynne Viola and Marc Junge
Other titles: Final act of Stalin's great purge in Soviet Ukraine
Description: New York, NY: Oxford Unitersity Press, [2023] | Includes index.
Identifiers: LCCN 2022042426 (print) | LCCN 2022042427 (ebook) |
ISBN 9780197647547 (hardback) | ISBN 9780197647554 (paperback) |
ISBN 9780197647578 (epub) | ISBN 9780197647585
Subjects: LCSH: Soviet Union. Narodnyĭ komissariat vnutrennikh del. |
Political purges—Ukraine—History—20th century. | Political
purges—Soviet Union—History. | Ukraine. Narodnyĭ komisariiat
vnutrishnikh sprav. | State-sponsored terrorism—Ukraine—History—20th
century. | Soviet Union—Politics and government—1936-1953.
Classification: LCC DK508.833 .L33 2023 (print) | LCC DK508.833 (ebook) |
DDC 947.70842—dc23/eng/20220906
LC record available at https://lccn.loc.gov/2022042426
LC ebook record available at https://lccn.loc.gov/2022042427

DOI: 10.1093/oso/9780197647547.001.0001

1 3 5 7 9 8 6 4 2

Paperback printed by Lakeside Book Company, United States of America
Hardback printed by Bridgeport National Bindery, Inc., United States of America

This book is dedicated to Memorial and all its tireless work for human rights and for history.

Contents

Acknowledgments

THE PROJECT FROM which this volume derives began in 2010 at a conference on Stalinist terror, convened by James Harris in Leeds, UK.[1] Lynne Viola presented a paper on the general subject of perpetrators. In response, Marc Junge noted the existence and accessibility of key sources on NKVD perpetrators in the Ukrainian SBU archives. Subsequently, in 2011, Viola and Junge made an initial foray into the Kyiv archives. The volume of materials was so vast that they enlisted a team of experienced scholars from Ukraine, Russia, Moldova, Georgia, and the United States to join them in this research. These scholars included Valeriy Vasylyev, Roman Podkur, Vadym Zolotar'ov, Serhii Kokin, Andrei Savin, and Aleksei Tepliakov. At a later stage, they were joined by Ol'ga Dovbnja, Igor Casu, Timothy Blauvelt, and Jeffrey Rossman. The team published four volumes of archival documents, as well as an anthology of articles, each in Ukrainian and in Russian.[2] Although we completed the main body of our work before the Russian invasion of Ukraine in February 2022, the project's success was based on Ukrainians, Russians, and others working together. The current, unprovoked war against Ukraine in no way detracts from our successful collaboration, but it is a reminder of the dangers, still, of dictatorial regimes. The chapters presented here are English translations of the final results of this collective work, covering events in the Ukrainian

1. Conference proceedings were later published in James Harris, ed., *The Anatomy of Terror: Political Violence under Stalin* (Oxford: Oxford University Press, 2013).

2. The published documents are in Marc Junge, Lynne Viola, and Jeffrey Rossman, eds., *Ekho bol'shogo terrora* v 3 tomakh (Moscow: Probel-2000, 2017–2019) and, in Ukrainian, *Vidlunnia velkogo terror* v 3 tomakh (Kyiv: Vidavets' V. Zakharenko, 2017–2019). The anthologies were first published in *Z arkhiviv VUChK-GPU-NKVD-KGB*, nos. 1–2 (2015) and then in Russian as Marc Junge, Lynne Viola, Jeffrey Rossman, eds., *Chekisty na skam'e podsudimykh* (Moscow: Probel-2000, 2017).

*oblast*s (or regions) of Kiev (Kyiv), Zhitomir (Zhytomyr), Odessa (Odesa), Vinnitsa (Vinnytsia), Nikolaev (Mykolaiv), and Kharkov (Kharkiv). The pages that follow use the Russian versions of Ukrainian place names given that Russian is the language of the documents.

The editors are pleased to take this opportunity to thank the following institutions for their continued support over the years of this project: the German Research Foundation; the American Council of Learned Societies; the Harry Frank Guggenheim Foundation; the Social Science and Humanities Research Council of Canada; the University of Erlangen, Germany; the University of Toronto, Canada; and the University of Virginia, US. We are especially grateful to the State Archive of the Security Services of Ukraine (Haluzevyi derzhavnyi arkhiv Sluzhby bezpeky Ukrainy) and its fine and professional staff. In particular, we would like to take this opportunity to thank Mariia Panova, who worked tirelessly with our team; Georhii Smirnov; and the administrator-historians of the archive: Serhii Kokin, I. M. Kulyk, Andrei Kogut, and Vitalii Lytvynenko. We thank the book's translators (from Russian and German to English), Simon Belokowsky, Aaron Hale-Dorell, and Caroline Cormier, for their excellent work on the project. Peter Solomon also played a key role at the outset of this project. Finally, thank you to Susan Ferber and Oxford University Press for their fine work on this project.

Chapter 5 adapts material originally published in *Stalinist Perpetrators on Trial: Scenes from the Great Terror in Soviet Ukraine* by Lynne Viola, and has been reproduced by permission of Oxford University Press.

Contributors and Translators

Simon Belokowsky defended his Georgetown University doctoral dissertation *Youth Is to Live in the City!: Rural Out-Migration in the Black Earth Region under Khrushchev and Brezhnev* at Georgetown University. He is also the author of "Laughing on the Inside: Gulag Humour as Evidence for Gulag Society," *Journal of Social History* 52, no. 4 (Summer 2019): 1281–1306.

Caroline Cormier is a PhD candidate in the Department of History at the University of Toronto. Her dissertation is entitled "Spaces of Displacement: The History and Commemoration of Jewish Homes and Judenhauser in Nazi Berlin."

Aaron Hale-Dorrell is an independent scholar, adjunct instructor, translator, and stay-at-home parent. He is the author of *Corn Crusade: Khrushchev's Farming Revolution in the Post-Stalin Soviet Union* (New York: Oxford University Press, 2018) and "Deserters from the Labour Front: The Limits of Coercion in the Soviet war economy," *Kritika* 20, no. 3 (2019): 481–504 (with Oleg Khlevniuk).

Marc Junge is a Senior Researcher at the Department of History, Eastern European History section, at the University of Erlangen, Germany. His work includes *Stalin's Mass Repression and the Cold War Paradigm* (New York: Kindle, 2016) and *Stalinistische Modernisierung: Die Strafverfolgung von Akteuren des Staatsterrors in der Ukraine 1939–1941* [Stalinist modernization: the purge of state terror agents in the Ukraine 1939–1941] (Bielefeld: Transcript-Verlag, 2020).

Serhii Kokin is a Senior Researcher at the Institute of Ukrainian History of the Ukrainian Academy of Science, Kyiv, Ukraine, and former director of the State Archive of the Security Police of Ukraine (Haluzevii derzhavnyi arkhiv Sluzhbyi bezpeky Ukrainy). He is coeditor of *Radians'ki orhany derzhavnoii bezpeky u 1939–chervni 1941 r.: dokumenty HDA SBU Ukrainy*

[Soviet state security agencies in 1939–June 1941. Documents of the Special State Archive of the Security Service of Ukraine] (Kyiv: "Kyivo-Mohylianska akademiia," 2009); and the author of "Nimets'ka operatsiia NKVS v suchasnii istoriografiii," in *"Velykyi teror" v Ukraini: Nimets'ka operatsiia 1937–1938 rokiv. Zbirnyk dokumentiv* ["The NKVD German operation in modern historiography," in *The "Great Terror" in the Ukraine. The German Operation 1937–1938*] (Kyiv, 2018), 42–80, 81–121.

Roman Podkur is a Senior Researcher at the Institute of Ukrainian History of the Ukrainian Academy of Science, Kyiv, Ukraine. His work includes *"Velykyi teror" 1937–1938 rr. na Donbasi* ["The Great Terror": 1937–1938 in the Donbass] (Kyiv: Institut istoriii Ukrainy NAN Ukraine, 2016) and (as coeditor) *Reabilitovani istoriieiu: Chernihivs'ka oblast'* [Rehabilitation by History: Chernihivs'ka oblast'] (Chernihiv: Vidavets' V. Lozovyi, 2018).

Jeffrey J. Rossman is Professor of History and Director of the Center for Russian, East European, and Eurasian Studies at the University of Virginia. He is the author of *Worker Resistance under Stalin: Class and Revolution on the Shop Floor* (Cambridge, MA: Harvard University Press, 2005).

Andrei Savin is a Senior Researcher at the Institute of History of the Siberian Branch of the Russian Academy of Sciences, Novosibirsk, Russia. His work includes *Die Sibiriendeutschen im Sowjetstaat. 1919–1938* [The Siberian Germans in the Soviet State] (Essen: Klartext, 2001) (with Detlef Brandes) and *Unter dem wachsamen Auge des Staates: Religiöser Dissens der Russlanddeutschen in der Breschnew-Ära* [Under the watchful eye of the state: religious dissent of Russian Germans in the Brezhnev era] (Wiesbaden: Harrassowitz Verlag, 2019) (with Victor Dönninghaus).

Aleksei Tepliakov is Associate Professor at the Novosibirsk State University of Economics and Management, Department of Philosophy and Humanities, Russian Federation. Among his works are *Mashina terrora: OGPU-NKVD Sibiri v 1929–1941 gg.* [Machine of terror: OGPU-NKVD of Siberia in 1929–1941] (Moscow: Novyi Khronograf; AIRO-XXI, 2008) and *Deiatel'nost' organov VTsK-OGPU-NKVD. 1917–1941: Istoriograficheskie aspekty* [Activities of the Cheka-GPU-OGPU-NKVD. 1917–1941: historiography] (Moscow: Rosspen, 2018).

Valeriy Vasylyev is Professor of History and Senior Researcher at the Institute of Ukrainian History of the Ukrainian Academy of Science, Kyiv, Ukraine. His work includes *Politychne kerivnytstvo URSR i SRSR: Dynamika vidnosyn* *tsentr-subtsentr vladi, 1917–1938* [Political leadership in the Ukraine and Soviet Union: dynamics of center-periphery relations, 1917–1938] (Kyiv: Institut istorii Ukrainy NAN Ukraine, 2014) and *Radians'ki karateli: Spivrobitnyky NKVS—vykonavtsi "Velykoho terror" na Podilli* [Soviet perpetrators: the NKVD and the implementation of the "Great Terror" in the Podillia region] (Kyiv: Vydavets' V. Zakharenko, 2017) (with Roman Podkur).

Lynne Viola is University Professor at the Department of History at the University of Toronto. Her work includes *The Unknown Gulag: The Lost World of Stalin's Special Settlements* (New York: Oxford University Press, 2007) and *Stalinist Perpetrators on Trial: Scenes from the Great Terror in Soviet Ukraine* (New York: Oxford University Press, 2017).

Vadym Zolotar'ov is Associate Professor at the Kharkiv National University of Radio Electronics, Ukraine. His works includes *Sekretno-politychnyi viddil DPU USRR: spravy ta liudy* [The Secret-Political Department of the State Political Administration (GPU) of the Ukrainian Soviet Socialist Republic: events and people] (Kharkiv: Folio, 2007) and « *Gil'otina Ukrainy* »: *narkom Vsevolod Balitskii i ego sud'ba* [The "Guillotine of Ukraine": People's Commissar Vsevolod Balitskii and his fate] (Moscow: Politicheskaia entsiklopediia, 2017) (with Iurii Shapoval).

Glossary

aktiv	Activists; the most politically active segment of an organization or group
All-Union	Federal level of the Soviet Union
ark. (arkush)	Folio(s), page(s) (of an archival file)
Arkhiv USBU po Odesskoi oblasti	Archive of the Security Service Administration of Ukraine for Odessa Oblast
A GUVD U KhO	Archive of the Main Administration of Internal Affairs of Ukraine in Kharkov Oblast
Article 54	Charge for counterrevolutionary crimes in the Ukrainian criminal code, equivalent to Article 58 in the Russian criminal code
Article 206-17	Charges for violations of socialist legality, malfeasance, crimes of office in the Ukrainian criminal code, equivalent to Article 193-17 in the Russian criminal code
ASSR (Avtonomnaia sotsialisticheskaia sovetskaia respublika)	Autonomous Soviet Socialist Republic
Bund	Prerevolutionary League of Jewish Workers in Russia and Poland, founded in 1897
chastina	part
Cheka (VChK, or Vserossiiskaia Chrezvychainaia Komissiia)	All-Russian Extraordinary Commission (the state security police from 1917 to 1922; superseded by the GPU)
Chekist	Member of the cheka
DAKhO	State Archive of Kharkiv Oblast
DAVO	State Archive of Vinnytsia Oblast

dekulakization	Shorthand for the process of the "liquidation of the kulaks as a class"—the expropriation, deportation, and, in some cases, executions of peasants labeled as kulaks that accompanied wholesale collectivization in the early 1930s
d. (delo)	File(s) (archival)
dvoika	Two-person panels, charged with sentencing in the national operations, to be confirmed in Moscow
f. (fond)	collection (archival)
FSB	See TsA FSB
GARF	Gosudarstvennyi arkhiv Rossiiskoi Federatsii (State Archive of the Russian Federation)
GPU	See OGPU
GULAG (Glavnoe upravlenie ispravitel'no-trudovykh lagerei)	Chief Administration of Corrective-Labor Camps
HDA SBU (Haluzevii derzhavnyi arkhiv Sluzhbyi bezpeky Ukrainy)	State Archive of the Security Police of Ukraine
interdistrict operational group	NKVD operational group during the Great Terror that united a series of districts (raions) within each region (oblasts)
KGB (Komitet gosudarstvennoi bezopasnosti)	Committee of State Security, from 1954
kharakteristika	Certificate or document providing a political and social profile of an individual
Komsomol (Kommunisticheskii soiuz molodezhi)	Communist Youth League
KNS (kontrol'no-nagliadova sprava)	Control and Supervisory File. The final volume of the file (delo) with documents about the destination of the files and any other documents later added to the file.
krai	Territory
kulak	Literally, a "fist"; a prosperous peasant who exploits hired labor; often used as a term of political opprobrium against opponents of the collective farm and other state policies (see dekulakization)

l. (list)	Folio(s), pages (of an archival file)
MGB (Ministerstvo gosudarstvennoi bezopasnosti)	Ministry for State Security, March 1946–March 1953
Mensheviks	The non-Leninist wing of the Russian Social Democratic Party that emerged after the 1903 schism of the Russian Social-Democratic Party; its nemesis, the Bolsheviks, also formed at this time
militsia	Shortened name for regular police force
militsioner	Regular police personnel
MTS	Machine-Tractor Station
MVD (Ministerstvo vnutrennykh del)	Ministry of Internal Affairs, renamed successor to the NKVD from March 1946; superseded by the KGB (Komitet gosudarstvennoi bezopasnosti) in 1954
nachal'nik	Boss
NKGB	People's Commissariat of State Security, February 1941–March 1946
NKVD (Narodnyi komissariat vnutrennykh del)	People's Commissariat of Internal Affairs of the Russian Republic, 1918–1930; All Union Commissariat of Internal Affairs, 1934–1946; later the MVD
NKVD Order 00447	Major mass operation of state repression, inaugurated by the decree of 30 July 1937, aimed against former "kulaks," recidivist criminals, and other "antisoviet" and "socially dangerous" elements.
ob. (oborotnaia storona)	Verso (reverse side of an archival document)
oblast	Region
obvinitel'noe zakliuchenie	Indictment
OGPU (Ob"edinennoe gosudarstvennoe politicheskoe upravlenie)	Unified State Political Administration (the state security police from 1922 to 1934; 1934 dissolved into the NKVD)
okrug	County
op. (opis')	Archive group within a fond
o.s. (osobova sprava)	Personnel file (in Russian, lichnoe delo)

Osoboe soveshchanie (Special Assembly)	Highest Sentencing Board of the NKVD
otdel	Department
otdelenie	Sector
OUN	Organization of Ukrainian Nationalists
Petliura	Ukrainian nationalist and civil war leader who led Ukraine's struggle for independence after the 1917 Revolution
Petliurists	Supposed or real followers of Petliura, civil war leader in Ukraine
Politburo	Political Bureau of the All-Union Communist Party (Bolshevik)
politotdel	Political department
Procuracy	Legal agency responsible for the conduct of prosecutions and the supervision of legality
Procurator	Legal official responsible for the conduct of prosecutions and the supervision of legality
PSZ (Protokol sudebnogo zadedaniia)	Stenographic records of court hearings
raion	District
Red Partisans	Partisans who fought for the Bolshevik side in regions held by the White forces during the Russian civil war.
RGASPI	Russian State Archive of Social and Political History
RO NKVD	Raion or district branch of the NKVD
Right Opposition	The last semi-public opposition to Stalin, led by N. I. Bukharin and A. I. Rykov; the Right Opposition crystallized around the issue of extraordinary measures in grain requisitioning in the late 1920s
sel'sovet	A village soviet or council
shtatnye witnesses	"Official" witnesses
Socialist Revolutionary (SR)	Member of prerevolutionary political party representing the peasantry
soviet	A council or administrative unit, found on various regional levels, from village (rural soviet) and city levels to district, provincial, and central levels

Special Departments	Special departments within factories (and other organizations) that included an NKVD operative as deputy head
spravka	Official certificate, usually testifying to an individual's political and social status
spr. (spravka)	File (archive)
SRs	See Socialist Revolutionary
stoiki	Prolonged, forced standing
tom	Volume
troika	A committee consisting of three individuals, most often used in this book to refer to the important NKVD extrajudicial panels that issued sentences in mass operations of repression and including the heads of the NKVD, party committee, and procuracy at the specific regional level
TsA FSB (Tsentral'nyi arkhiv Federal'noi sluzhby bezopasnosti)	Central Archive of the Federal Security Bureau (successor institution to the Cheka-OGPU-NKVD-MVD-KGB)
TsDAHO	Central State Archive of Public Organizations of Ukraine
uchet	NKVD surveillance registration system
UGB	Upravlenie gosudarstvennoi bezopasnosti (Administration for State Security)
UMVS	Departmental Archive of the Ministry of Internal Affairs of Ukraine in Zhitomir Oblast
upravlenie	Administration
UNKVD	District- or oblast-level NKVD administration
UPA	Ukrainian Insurgent Army, a Ukrainian nationalist paramilitary and later partisan formation.
VChK	see: Cheka
vydvizhentsy	"Socially pure" workers and peasants who were sent to schools of higher education or promoted directly within the Communist Party and government administration
Whites	The main adversaries of the Bolsheviks (Reds) in the civil war, representing the forces of the old regime
zakliuchenie	See obvinitel'noe zakliuchenie
zv. (zvorotnyi bik)	Verso (reverse side of an archival document)

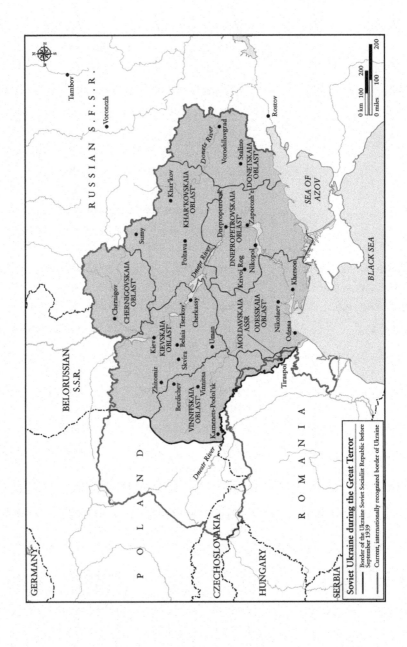

Soviet Ukraine during the Great Terror

Oblasts in the Ukrainian SSR

Khar'kovskaia oblast' (Khar'kov)
Poltavskaia oblast' (formed 22 September 1937) as an administrative division within Khar'kovskaia oblast') (Poltava)

Kievskaia oblast' (Kiev)
Zhitomirskaia oblast' (formed 22 September 1937 as an administrative division within Kievskaia oblast') (Zhitomir)

Vinnitskaia oblast' (Vinnitsa)
Kamenets-Podol'skaia oblast' (formed 22 September 1937 as administrative division within Vinnitskaia oblast') (Kamenets-Podol'sk)

Donetskaia oblast' (Donetsk)
Stalinskaia oblast' (formed 3 June 1938 as administrative division of Donetskaia oblast') (Stalino)
Voroshilovgradskaia oblast' (formed 3 June 1938 as administrative division of Donetskaia oblast') (Voroshilovgrad)

Odesskaia oblast' (Odessa)
Nikolaevskaia oblast' (formed 22 June 1937 as administrative division within Odesskaia oblast') (Nikolaev)

Dnepropetrovskaia oblast' (Dnepropetrovsk)

Chernigovskaia oblast' (Chernigov)

Moldavskaia ASSR (Tiraspol)

Laboratories of Terror

Introduction

Lynne Viola and Marc Junge

LABORATORIES OF TERROR explores the final chapter of Stalin's Great Terror. On November 1938, the Communist Party Central Committee and the Council of People's Commissars of the USSR issued a directive halting mass operations in repression and liquidating the infamous troikas that had served as the main extrajudicial bodies in charge of the fate of hundreds of thousands of Soviet citizens.[1] This directive served not only to end the mass operations, but also led to the release of large numbers of mainly Communist purge victims whose cases remained incomplete.[2] At the same time, it resulted in the "purge of the purgers" or the "Beria Thaw," named after the newly appointed head of the NKVD, L. P. Beria, who oversaw this operation. This episode in the history of the Soviet Union remained hidden from view for decades in the largely closed archives of the Soviet security police. The opening of the Ukrainian security police archives (HDA SBU) in the 2010s allowed historians for the first time to begin to excavate this chapter in the Great Terror.

Laboratories of Terror illuminates the world of the NKVD perpetrator and the mechanisms and logistics of the terror at the local level, two subjects previously opaque. NKVD perpetrators are at the center of this story. The documentary materials on the purge of the purgers derive largely from their criminal files. The criminal files contain verbatim records of the closed trials of NKVD operatives at republican, oblast, district (*raion*), and city levels, along with original arrest warrants, documentation on searches, biographical information offered up in standard forms as well as autobiographical statements from the accused, interrogation transcripts of the accused and of witnesses,

Lynne Viola and Marc Junge, *Introduction* In: *Laboratories of Terror*. Edited by: Lynne Viola and Marc Junge, Oxford University Press. © Oxford University Press 2023. DOI: 10.1093/oso/9780197647547.003.0001 petitions for mercy, sentencing and appeal documentation, and a variety of other types of materials. NKVD operatives' personnel files (*lichnye dela*) and the stenographic reports of NKVD Communist Party meetings from late 1938 and early 1939 provide additional materials and contextualization for understanding this final phase of the Great Terror.

———

The Great Terror (1937–1938) in the Soviet Union has long occupied a central role in the history of Stalinism. During a sixteen-month period, the Stalin regime arrested and convicted over 1.5 million of its own citizens, largely on trumped-up charges of "counterrevolutionary," "antisoviet," or "socially harmful" activity. Half of those convicted were summarily executed; the rest ended up in the Gulag, where they became victims of forced labor, daily abuse, and premature death. The majority of victims of the Great Terror were ordinary people, caught up in two large "mass operations" launched in these years—one against former "kulaks," recidivist criminals, and other "antisoviet" and "socially dangerous" elements, and the other against a series of non-Russian ethnicities.[3]

The mass operations came largely in the wake of the elite, or nomenklatura, purges, spreading the terror far and wide through the vast territories of the Soviet Union. Mass operation 00447, dated 30 July 1937, was entitled "the operation to repress former kulaks, criminals, and antisoviet elements." Although this operation has come to be known in the literature as the "kulak operation," this is a misnomer. The kulak or former kulak figured prominently in this operation but was not the sole socio-political category subsumed. Nor should the figure of the kulak be confused with an objective socioeconomic category. The kulak was mostly a political construct, defined oxymoronically as a "capitalist peasant" during collectivization and, later, by earlier repression in exile or in the labor camps, so-called biological factors, such as a parent or grandparent who was a kulak or other socioeconomic enemy, and largely subjective political criteria including participation in anti-collectivization protests.[4]

In addition to the kulak, mass operation 00447 included as targets of repression former members of "antisoviet" political parties, a series of old regime elites falling under the category of *byvshie liudi* (or "former people," such as tsarist officials, gendarmes, village elders, and clergy), fugitives from repression, and a range of recidivist petty criminals. These already elastic categories would expand according to regional specificities that led to additional enemy categories. Mass operation 00447 also included "the most hostile and active participants" of "cossack white-guard insurrectionary organizations, fascist, terrorist, and espionage-diversionary formations."[5]

Following a month of preparations, including canvassing of lower-level NKVD organs on the numbers of "antisoviet elements" in their domains and a 16 July 1937 meeting of regional NKVD representatives in Moscow, the all-union NKVD compiled a set of control figures for the number of people to be arrested in the course of mass operation 00447.[6] The total numbers of planned arrests was 268,950, divided between a first "most dangerous" category (75,950) and a second "less dangerous" category (193,000). First-category subjects were to be executed by shooting; second-category subjects were to be confined in the Gulag for periods of eight to ten years.[7] With some exceptions, the operation was set to begin on 5 August 1937, starting with the arrest of first-category subjects, and to end in four months.[8]

NKVD investigations of arrested suspects were to occur "quickly" and "in simplified order," with an eye to establishing the "criminal connections" of those arrested.[9] Upon completion of the investigation, the accused were sent on to an extrajudicial troika, generally consisting of the leaders of the relevant regional NKVD, Communist Party committee, and Procurator's office.[10] The troika passed judgment on the accused, sentencing them either to time in the Gulag or death.[11] An NKVD memo of 8 August 1937 ordered the troikas not to announce death sentences to those assigned to the first category, most likely as a precaution against unrest at the time of execution.[12] The troikas generally worked at night. They also worked at great speed. One troika in Leningrad condemned 658 Solovetskii Island prisoners in one night; another, in Omsk, "reviewed" fifty to sixty cases per hour.[13]

The number of arrests quickly surged beyond the NKVD's initial control figures, reaching as many as 555,641 by the end of December 1937.[14] Although the original NKVD order strictly forbade any lower NKVD organ from independently increasing its arrest numbers, it did allow these organs as well as regional party committees to petition for larger numbers, and Stalin and the Politburo seldom refused.[15] The deadline for the completion of mass operation 00447, moreover, was repeatedly extended, first to 10 December 1937, then to 1 January 1938, and finally to 15 March 1938.[16] After that last date, with the exception of Ukraine, the capital cities, and certain key penal regions such as Siberia, the kulak operation gave way to the so-called national operations.[17]

After the confirmation of the kulak operation, at the end of July 1937, the NKVD produced a series of operational orders against specific ethnicities— Poles, Germans, Finns, Latvians, Estonians, Greeks, Romanians, Chinese, and others. On paper, none of these orders called for targeting an entire ethnicity, but for the arrests of national "elements" supposedly engaged in espionage. In fact, at its worst, the national operations swept up thousands based only on ethnic indicators.[18] To take the Polish operation (00485), for example, candidates for arrest included all those who could be said to belong, or to have belonged, to the Polish Military Organization (POV); this was a largely nonexistent organization within the Soviet Union at this time that was said to have infiltrated the Polish Communist Party, the Red Army, the NKVD, and other institutions. Also targeted were Polish POWs from the 1920 Soviet-Polish war, Polish political émigrés, former members of a series of Polish political parties, and the most active local "antisoviet and nationalist elements" from territories with Polish populations.[19] However, anyone with a Polish or Polish-sounding name could be arrested. The Poles suffered the heaviest losses (105,485), followed by the Germans (75,331).[20] As a rule, most ethnicities targeted represented diaspora nations, which, in Stalin's eyes, raised the risk of dual loyalties, particularly in the vulnerable border zones where these populations often lived.

The primary administrative difference between the kulak and national operations was that, instead of the troika, a dvoika, or two-man team consisting of the heads of the relevant regional NKVD and procuracy organs, sat in judgment, condemning individuals and groups to either the first or the second category of punishment. After judgment, the dvoika's lists were sent to Moscow for confirmation by the so-called Great Dvoika, composed of Nikolai Ezhov, NKVD Commissar for the USSR, and A. Vyshinskii, state procurator of the USSR. (From 17 September 1938, the dvoika was replaced by the national or special troika, formed on the basis of NKVD Order 00606.[21]) Another singularity of the national operations, especially the Polish operation, was that they were far deadlier than 00447, with an imprisonment to execution ratio of one to three, versus that of one to one for 00447.[22] Initially, the national operations were to be completed within three months; the deadline was subsequently and repeatedly postponed, with a final date set for 1 August 1938 in most regions.[23] In practice, the kulak and national operations overlapped temporally and could share similar targets; in Ukraine, in 1938, the implementation of the two operations often lacked clear demarcations, with categories of enemies shifted between different NKVD departments.

The number of arrests for both operations skyrocketed far beyond the original control figures. In the Soviet Union as a whole, by 1 July 1938, roughly 1,420,711 people had been arrested; of these, 699,929 were apprehended in the course of the kulak operation, including 376,207 "former kulaks," 121,963 recidivist criminals, and 201,860 "miscellaneous counterrevolutionary elements." The totals for both operations listed some 522,774 "former kulaks," 191,384 *byvshie liudi*, 168,286 "elements" without a defined occupation, 45,009 clergy, and 229,957 white-collar employees; out of these, a "mere" 99,188 were Communist Party members and 15,088 were members of the Komsomol.[24] From the 681,692 executions of the Great Terror, some 90 percent were caught up in these mass operations.[25] In Ukraine, at a minimum, 267,579 people were arrested and 122,237 of them executed in 1937 and 1938.[26]

Stalin publicly proclaimed the Great Terror to be a success. At the 18th Party Congress in March 1939, he claimed that the nation's purge had resulted in the "final liquidation of the exploiting classes [okonchatel'naia likvidatsiia ostatkov ekspluatotarskikh klassov]." He forcefully contested what he called the foreign press's contention that the purge had weakened the Soviet state, labeling that kind of talk "banal gossip" (*poshlaia boltovnia*). Instead, he claimed that the purge had created a new *edinorodnost'*, or internal unity, of the Soviet people that made the Red Army stronger than any other nation's army.[27] This is an important point because at no time in the 1930s or later did Stalin renounce what has come to be known as the Great Terror.

Instead, Stalin renounced those Soviet officials, mainly in the NKVD, who had violated socialist or revolutionary legality in the conduct of mass operations. His renunciation led to the destruction of important clientele or patronage networks within the NKVD. In Ukraine, NKVD boss A. I. Uspenskii's fall cleared the way for the arrest of his subordinates, just as NKVD commissar Ezhov's downfall prompted Uspenskii's flight as well as the destruction of Ezhov's clientele network throughout the Soviet Union.[28] Although the NKVD had been subject to purges earlier in 1937 and 1938 as new NKVD leaders brought in their "tails" and destroyed preexisting clientele networks, this particular purge was different. It did not feature accusations of Trotskyism or counterrevolution, as in earlier NKVD purges, but served instead to scapegoat the NKVD—or, publicly, elements within the NKVD— for "violations of socialist legality" in the Great Terror.[29] The NKVD purge also resulted in what some historians call a "cadre revolution" in the NKVD following the arrests of NKVD personnel who were, in turn, replaced with a new clientele network—Beria's—that would more or less remain in office until Stalin's death in 1953.[30]

This purge of the purgers resulted in a series of trials of NKVD operatives under the jurisdiction of military tribunals that occurred throughout the country. These trials proceeded under the aegis of Soviet justice, an often oxymoronic designation in those times. Yet they had little in common with the staged, show trials of the 1930s and nothing whatsoever in common with the assembly-line troika processing of the victims of the mass operations. Instead, these trials more closely resembled the wartime and postwar trials of World War II collaborators and war criminals within the Soviet Union. Scholars who have studied these later trials have concluded that, despite their political and ideological imprimatur, they were, as Alexander Prusin writes, held in full accordance with juridical norms and provided "relatively accurate descriptions" of the war in the Soviet Union. According to Tanja Penter, the wartime and postwar trials "served the Stalinist regime for its own legitimation inside Soviet society and abroad," with pedagogical and symbolic meaning. The trials of NKVD cadres at the end of the 1930s also revealed a wealth of valuable information about the Great Terror as well as serving pedagogical and disciplinary purposes in spite of the fact that there was scant mention of them in the press.[31]

The NKVD trials were meant to have a disciplinary impact on the NKVD. The relatively wide participation of NKVD operatives in these trials made it highly likely that the substance of the trials was known among its cadres. Their participation as witnesses and signalers meant that they knew what was occurring at these trials locally. Certainly, they discussed these events with other NKVD colleagues at the late 1938/early 1939 NKVD Communist Party meetings and likely elsewhere outside of the trials given the frequent violations of their secrecy agreements. The trials made it clear, above all, that the NKVD, whether due to "institutional interests," "clans" (i.e., clientele networks), or a few "bad apples," must be brought under the control of Stalin and the Communist Party. Above all, they were intended to demonstrate that Stalin was not to blame.

The trials also sent a message to the Communist Party. Stalin cast the Party as the main victim of the Great Terror. Party members and other elites played a prominent role in the trials, mainly as victims, sometimes as victimized witnesses. The Party was given a key role to play in "correcting" the violations and seeking out the transgressors in the NKVD.[32] The Communist Party would also hereafter serve, along with its youth wing, the Komsomol, as the main recruitment pool for the new NKVD cadres brought in to replace their disgraced predecessors.[33] The trials were part of an emerging narrative of Communist victimization in the terror, followed by the "restoration" of Party control, a narrative traditionally associated with Khrushchev and his 20th Party Congress "secret speech" in 1956. The narrative pitted the NKVD against the Communist Party, airbrushing away the majority of the Great

Terror's victims, who were neither Communist nor elite, and, importantly, ignoring the central role of the leadership of the Party in the Great Terror. The trials were Stalin's symbolic gift to the Party, serving to relegitimize its authority and its power following two years of its supposedly diminished status.[34]

Stalin was well aware of the devastating impact of the Great Terror. He certainly knew about its legion of victims as well as the extent to which the terror was undermining local, especially Communist, authority. The victims were not silent, either during or after the mass operations. They and their relatives inundated higher authorities with literally hundreds of thousands of letters of complaint. On 22 February 1938, USSR Procurator Vyshinskii complained to Molotov that the USSR Procurator's office was unable to handle the volume of written complaints, noting that in the first twenty days of February alone, it had received 40,000 of them.[35] In 1938, as a whole, the Procurator's office received some 600,000 complaints related to the terror.[36] The Russian republic Procurator's office was also overwhelmed, receiving 700 to 800 complaints daily, and from February 1938, 50,000 to 60,000 monthly.[37] The Ukrainian RepublicProcurator's office received some 170,855 complaints between 1 January 1939 and 1 January 1940, of which 46,695 went to the republican offices of the procurator and 124,160 to their oblast offices in sixteen Ukrainian oblasts. The Kiev oblast procurator received 21,278 in the same period.[38] These complaints represented the proverbial tip of the iceberg as victims and their relatives also besieged the offices of Stalin, Ezhov, and a large range of other individuals and institutions at all geographical-administrative levels. Needless to say, not all these complaints came from Communists. Stalin, therefore, was fully aware of the pushback against the mass operations.

The 17 November 1938 directive opened up a second floodgate of complaints. News of the directive very quickly reached the prison cells of the NKVD. Many prisoners, whose cases had not yet been completed, rescinded their confessions at this time. This phenomenon was fairly widespread, according to NKVD complaints, and continued into 1939. As a result of the November directive, unfinished cases were transferred to the courts and possibly as many as 110,000 people, mainly Communists, were freed.[39] In addition, some 77,000 purged Communists were reinstated into the Party.[40] At the least, these transfers of cases and releases relieved the deadly prison overcrowding of 1938 and the huge backlog of unfinished cases. At most, they may have served to cover up old wounds and to further strengthen the narrative of victimized Communists.

Stalin may also have been troubled by reports that news of the mass operations had breached the information security perimeters of the NKVD. Although at this point the evidence is far from conclusive, it is clear that there was considerable "leakage" of the terror into the public domain. The trials demonstrated the ways in which the sheer "noise" of terror reached the streets from the NKVD prisons. Another type of leakage came with the appearance of executed victims' clothing at local markets as the wives of NKVD execution squad members tried to benefit from their self-proclaimed hard and dirty work. NKVD operatives also lived at least for a time in the same general areas as their victims, often leading lonely bachelor lives and residing in shoddy Soviet hotels due to local housing shortages and frequent transfers. In the town of Uman in Kiev Oblast, for example, the hotel became a center for NKVD carousing and drunkenness. Here, there were also reports of NKVD interrogators sleeping with prisoners' wives in exchange for the privilege of access to a loved one.[41] In Moscow, according to Russian historian A. Iu. Vatlin, the solution to the housing shortage was for NKVD operatives to move into the victims' former dwellings; outside of Moscow, this may have been a less attractive prospect given the dismal state of the housing stock.[42] Occasional reports of "demonstrations" by prisoners' wives also surface in the Ukrainian documents, providing further possible evidence of "leakage" and suggesting that some brave souls may have attempted to protest more publicly.[43]

The precise dimensions of public knowledge about the terror cannot be demarcated. Still it is clear that there was leakage and Stalin must have known and been worried about news of the terror leaking out. News of the mass operations had also leaked out abroad. In the republican NKVD offices in Kiev, there was near panic when the Munich agreement was reached in the fall of 1938.[44] That agreement raised grave doubts in Stalin's mind about the willingness of the West to fight Hitler. Hedging his bets, Stalin may have realized that war was approaching and it was time to end the mass repressions. The irony here is that Stalin's war against a supposed Fifth Column likely strengthened rather than weakened his sense of international danger.

In any case, it is likely that Stalin utilized these trials to address the grievances of selected audiences, mainly but not only elite audiences, while transferring the blame for their grievances away from himself and on to designated groups and individuals within the NKVD. Perhaps he recognized that in pursuit of the destruction of the much-touted Fifth Column, the terror had begun to create seedlings for new columns. Perhaps he only cared about the damage done to the Party's credibility. Initially, Stalin had asked Vyshinskii, the Soviet chief Procurator, to organize an open trial of leading NKVD workers before evidently reconsidering.[45] The open and extremely revelatory reactions of provincial and local NKVD workers at their trials may have influenced him in this reconsideration. Ultimately, though, Ezhov, Uspenskii, and the past leadership of the NKVD would be condemned for treason, on the grounds of attempting to undermine the Soviet government and crush the Communist Party, while middle- and lower-level personnel were condemned for their violations of socialist legality.

Stalin's scapegoating of officials of various stripes for violations in policy implementation removed the blame from him. It permitted him to explain away "violations" and "excesses" in policy implementation as the work of a relatively few "bad apples." A face-saving measure both for Stalin and his policies, it was not unlike similar practices used by other governments to avoid blame.[46] It was also an established practice that Stalin used to distance himself from the worst of policy practices once a radical breakthrough was achieved. He first deployed it in the violent 1930 collectivization campaign, publishing his famous article, "Dizziness with Success," that led to the scapegoating of (largely) lower-level Communist Party and Soviet government officials for "excesses" in policy implementation. Stalin was clearly not interested in justice per se; his goal to purge Soviet society of its supposed Fifth Column, if not exactly fulfilled, had gone as far as it could and a policy of scapegoating served to paper over social grievances.

In 1939, the purge of the purgers, or the Beria purge, resulted in the turnover of some 7,372 NKVD operatives at all levels of its bureaucracy. The NKVD purge effectively led to the removal of 22.9 percent of its operational staff.[47] The figure of 7,372 is somewhat deceptive, however. An NKVD information report (*spravka*) from 23 March 1940 surveyed the movement of NKVD operative cadres. In all, 937 operatives were arrested and sent to court (according to incomplete data: 91 from the central apparatus of the NKVD, 674 from lower-level NKVD administrations, 91 from the DTO [Dorozhnoi-transportnyi otdel, or the NKVD's Transportation Department], and 92 from the OO VO [Osobyi otdel voennogo okruga, or the NKVD's Special Department in the Military]). In total, 3,342 cadres were fired (375 from the central apparatus of the NKVD, 2,532 from lower-level NKVD administrations, 304 from the DTO and 131 from OO VO). Another 1,164 were placed in reserve, 1,830 were transferred to other work outside state security, and 99 died. From these numbers, some 66.5 percent were fired for violations of socialist legality (*dolzhnostnye prestupleniia*, crimes of office), counterrevolutionary activity, and various types of "compromising material." The largest percentage (41.7 percent, or 2,639) were fired for compromising material; 17.4 percent (974) were fired for violations of socialist legality, and only 2 percent (108) were fired for counterrevolutionary activity.[48]

Although it is difficult to disentangle the official reasons for these firings, these figures demonstrate that, unlike in earlier years, fewer operatives were fired for so-called counterrevolutionary activities in comparison with the period from October 1934 to fall 1938. During that time period, 2,273 NKVD operatives were arrested, of whom 1,861 (82 percent) were arrested for counterrevolutionary activity and 411 (17 percent) for violations of socialist legality. For the period from fall 1938 to 1943 (and it is important to note that arrests continued in the purge of the purgers after 1939), the correlation reversed, with greater numbers being charged with violations of socialist legality. And, in 1939, of the total 1,190 individuals who were dismissed for violations of socialist legality or counterrevolutionary activity, 937 were arrested and handed over to the courts. It is this last number that figures in the purge of the purgers, with the charge of violations of socialist legality dominating over counterrevolutionary activity.[49]

Unfortunately, precise figures exist only for the year 1939 and only spotty figures for Ukraine itself.[50] Arrests of NKVD operatives for violations of socialist legality continued into the early 1940s. Notably, in December 1941, Beria sent an appeal to Stalin requesting that 1,610 NKVD employees, who had mainly been convicted of violating socialist legality, be sent to the front given the shortage of (presumably security) cadres there. However, this figure omits those who had been executed for their part in the violations and those who were prosecuted in 1942 and 1943. Despite the problems of uncertain and incomplete data, 1939, the key year of this purge, resulted in a large turnover of NKVD personnel at all levels of its bureaucracy. Some 22.9 percent of its operational staff turned over and resulted in the recruitment of some 14,506 new cadres (who would constitute 45.1 percent of all operative workers), individuals who would more or less remain in office until Stalin's death in 1953.[51]

It is important to note that the NKVD was in permanent flux through the 1930s and especially during the Great Terror. Indeed, it underwent a demographic shift in these years. As endemic transfers, mobilizations of new cadres, and purges escalated within the ranks, the age and social profile of leading operatives changed. The NKVD became younger, with most rank-and-file workers in their thirties, more plebeian and less educated, with larger numbers of operatives of working-class or peasant social origins. Moreover, the NKVD experienced shortages of operative cadres during the mass operations of the Great Terror, leaving it no choice but to expand its cadre of personnel in the very course of operations. Students from the NKVD preparatory schools were mobilized to help staff the NKVD organs. The NKVD also made use of extensive auxiliaries directly in arrests, interrogations, and executions—a motley crew of semiliterate regular police (*militsionery*), NKVD couriers, chauffeurs, accountants, firemen, postal workers, and others.

In Ukraine, the NKVD underwent two purges before the final rout of November 1938—following the removal of earlier NKVD Ukraine commissars V. A. Balitskii and I. M. Leplevskii, who fell in May 1937 and January 1938, respectively. These purges entailed removing the leaders as well as their "tails," or clientele networks, generally under the accusation of counterrevolutionary activity. When Uspenskii took over the helm of the NKVD in Ukraine, he too brought his clients, many of them extremely young, into the leadership of the NKVD's territorial units. Almost all of the leaders of oblast NKVD administrations from about March 1938 were clients of Uspenskii. When Uspenskii fell, the purge of his minions followed.

This constant turnover testifies to the extreme instability within the NKVD. The purge of the purgers was only the final episode of this phenomenon. Its significance resides less in the numbers of NKVD operatives removed or tried in court than in its function as a break on the Great Terror. The purge of the purgers put an end to the existence of clan warfare in the NKVD. Although one "clan" remained—Beria's—Stalin remained firmly in control of the NKVD, while insisting after November 1938 that the Communist Party would remain the predominant authority in the Soviet Union. Some scholars have also suggested that this purge may have resulted in the strengthening of the Procuracy, the chief Soviet agency responsible for ensuring the observation of legality.[52] While much still remains unclear about the causes and consequences of the Great Terror, two things are clear: Stalin remained in full control until his death in 1953 and there was never a mass purge of the Communist Party again. At the same time, it is important to note that mass violence against civilians continued, especially during World War II and its immediate aftermath.

———

In the last two decades, scholars inside and outside the former Soviet Union have been at work attempting to understand the dynamics and scope of the Great Terror. Historians have carried out a series of valuable studies on the prehistory of the terror, the machinery of repression, and the local and social dimensions of the terror.[53] Among the most contentious issues has been the degree to which Stalin exerted control over the terror's implementation. While some scholars have argued that the terror was a closely controlled mass operation, others have highlighted the local dimensions of the terror, center-periphery conflicts, and societal input.[54] Although the final word on this issue is not in and may never be, it is clear that when Stalin called for an end to what he labeled "violations of socialist legality," the machinery of terror came to a grinding, if sometimes reluctant, halt.[55]

Until recently, much about the Soviet perpetrator has remained fairly opaque. Who participated in the violence of the 1930s? Who was complicit and who benefited? This raises complex and broad issues that have not been adequately studied. However, the research for *Laboratories of Terror* highlights one particular group of perpetrators—mid-level NKVD operatives in Soviet Ukraine. The greatest "gift" of this episode in the Great Terror is the documentation that it bestowed upon historians. Although we can glean valuable information about perpetrator motives and individual personalities from the interrogation materials and trials, it is necessary to use these sources with a great deal of care when discussing perpetrator motives. These sources are clearly *perpetrator* documents; the voices of the real victims rarely surface.[56] However, in the course of their own, often lengthy investigations, the NKVD perpetrators detailed the story of the Great Terror in all its horrors. As such, these sources present unique perspectives not just on perpetrators, but importantly on the mechanisms of repression, how the terror traveled from Moscow to the republic and from the republic to the oblasts and districts. The chapters in this book cast in fine relief the local and regional workings of the terror in Ukraine, especially in 1938, but often with a look back into 1937 as older cases were brought to bear against NKVD operatives.

The NKVD perpetrators arrested at the end of the Great Terror constituted the leadership of the NKVD at the republic, oblast, district, and city levels. The leaders of the NKVD administrations, along with their deputies and the individual heads of key NKVD departments, tended to be the primary targets for arrest. Individual chapters in *Laboratories of Terror* examine cases in the oblasts of Vinnitsa, Odessa, Nikolaev, Kharkov, Kiev, and Zhitomir, as well as in the important NKVD Transportation Department of the Northern Donetsk Railway. As Chapters 1 and 2 show, many of the officials from these offices were targeted by their own former victims, almost exclusively Communists and other elite victims released in early late 1938 and early 1939. Significantly, they were charged not with counterrevolutionary or Trotskyist activities as happened in earlier NKVD purges, but with the "violation of socialist legality" or crimes of office. It is important to be clear, however, that "everyone was guilty," a claim repeated many times by purged NKVD officials. Although it is possible that some of the arrested NKVD operatives had indeed violated specific directives or had drawn attention to themselves through particularly brazen acts, the NKVD, to quote the head of the Kiev Oblast NKVD, A. R. Dolgushev, had acquired a "taste for torture" and other violent interrogation practices.[57]

The true motivations of NKVD perpetrators are difficult to ascertain, but we can see how they justified their actions, at their trials and particularly in their "last words" to the court. Most denied that they had committed a crime. Among these, some claimed to be following superior orders; others believed that they were acting against real enemies—"I believed and could not not have believed in the authority of Uspenskii."[58] Those who admitted guilt said they acted no differently from anyone else at that time—"We are all guilty in this."[59] Many of those caught up in this stage of the purge were young *vydvizhentsy* (or recently promoted workers of sterling social character), who claimed that they were afraid not to follow orders. And, indeed, operatives were punished for being "liberal," for not obtaining the requisite number of confessions, for not using force. At the NKVD operational meetings, NKVD leaders castigated these cadres. At the same time, they praised those who were most reckless, feeding into the pride and ambition of those who routinely beat their victims into submission. In the words of one man, "At the meetings which were then held in the department, they poured shame on the workers of the Fourth Department, who did not use physical methods of influence . . . they set me up as an example to others [in the use of torture]. And, I, fool, was proud of this."[60] The testimony of witnesses (both actual victims of the purges and NKVD colleagues) used words like "sadist," "careerist," and "power hungry" to describe NKVD interrogators. Alcohol also played a role in some interrogations and most executions, whether as lubricant, bonding mechanism, or after-the-fact celebration: executioners routinely drank in the same room where they had shot their victims.[61] Finally, venality characterized those NKVD and other officials who fought over the shoddy material remains left behind by the very people they had executed.

All these motivations constitute the usual panoply of perpetrator motivations seen in other cases of state violence and genocide. However, situational factors were also at play, serving to create certain conditions that dictated practice. For example, G. N. Petrov, a member of the local militia seconded to the NKVD to assist in the processing of victims, maintained that he had no choice but to use force; otherwise, he stated, he would not have been able to keep up with his assigned task of obtaining 100 preliminary confessions a day.[62] The very scale and scope of the mass operations determined many of its practices. Although Moscow created the infrastructure of terror through policy and the intense pressure put upon NKVD subordinates, it was up to the NKVD on the local level to implement the terror. To be sure, NKVD perpetrators acted with an agency constrained by certain parameters, but one which allowed for "creativity" in fulfilling orders that most, in fact, believed would destroy real enemies. As Oleg Khlevniuk has written, "Just because the center controlled the operations that made up the Great Terror (and other similar operations) does not mean, however, that 'elemental factors' and local initiative did not play a role in shaping them."[63] None of them, moreover, were "ordinary men" in the sense of Christopher Browning's descriptions of members of the German order police.[64] Soviet perpetrators were instead trained military operatives long accustomed to strict hierarchies and the use of violence and shaped by radical Stalinist ideology.

———————

This book presents a series of regional microhistories that endeavor to document the mechanisms of the Great Terror in Soviet Ukraine, as well as to illuminate its mid-level perpetrators. At a granular level of detail, these chapters illuminate the darkest corners of the terror—the prison cells, the interrogations rooms, and the execution chambers. They document the NKVD operational and Communist Party meetings where operatives discussed process and procedure and, after November 1938, criticized their bosses. Individual chapters present detailed biographical information about NKVD leaders, including their activities, arrests, and trials, as well as their sentences and later fate when possible. The authors suggest various determining factors for the actions of NKVD perpetrators, including ambition, fear, authoritarian personalities, belief in Stalinist ideology, the culture of the cheka, the need to "follow orders," and a variety of situational factors. Several chapters also explore the causes and consequences of this final purge of the NKVD.

In Chapter 1, Valeriy Vasylyev and Roman Podkur explore the activities of the Vinnitsa Oblast NKVD during mass operations. The focus of their attention is on Uspenskii-appointed Ivan Mikhailovich Korablev, who led the Vinnitsa UNKVD from May 1938 until his attempted suicide in January 1939, as well as his assistants Anton Iakovlevich Prishivtsyn, Aleksandr Mikhailovich Zaputriaev, and Nikolai Stepanovich Butenko. Vasylyev and Podkur document Koroblev's activities and motivations as a chekist "convinced that [he] was executing serious Party business." Following their arrests, the main characters of this story are first sentenced to death, followed by a commutation of their sentences to ten years in the Gulag. None of them served their terms; instead, they were mobilized to the front in 1942, like many other incarcerated NKVD operatives, and lived fairly normal lives after the war. Vasylyev and Podkur also present information on the second wave of arrests of perpetrators after Stalin's death in the 1950s. In that phase, the case against the Vinnitsa NKVD perpetrators was reopened, but ultimately dismissed, showing the limited effectiveness of the "purge of the purgers." The authors demonstrate, importantly, that many Communist Party victims of the purges, whose cases were incomplete at the time of the November 1938 directive, played a key part in the investigations of the NKVD in Vinnitsa by sending waves of telegrams, petitions, and complaints to the authorities.

In Chapter 2, A. I. Savin and A. G. Tepliakov further investigate the importance of the role of released Party and other elites in the NKVD purge. Based on materials from Odessa Oblast, they argue that "the main share of convicted NKVD workers found themselves under prosecution as a result of complaints from victims who survived and were freed after the 17 November 1938 directive." These freed victims were largely members of the Party with connections and status. The authors also note that the NKVD victims of the Beria purge tended to be precisely from among those NKVD operatives who worked specifically in the repression of Communist Party members. According to Savin and Tepliakov, the Great Terror had resulted in an imbalance "below" among mid- and lower-level NKVD workers who came to perceive themselves as above the Party. Focusing on the criminal files of important Odessa Oblast NKVD leaders like V .F. Kaliuzhnyi and S. I. Gaponov and their subordinates, these historians view the purge of the purgers as a rebalancing of power between Party and NKVD, while at the same time never losing sight of the role of the highest levels of the Party in the Great Terror. They see the Beria purge as a tool to discipline the NKVD and follow the story of their main characters through and beyond the war years.

Marc Junge's focus in Chapter 3 is on Nikolaev Oblast, where there were six trials of NKVD operatives for the violation of socialist legality. Junge explores what arguably was the most important of these trials, that of P. V. Karamyshev, the head of the Nikolaev UNKVD, along with three of his associates. The story centers on a fire in one of Nikolaev's sensitive defense-related shipbuilding factories, which were under intense scrutiny in 1938, and the two trials that followed Karamyshev's arrest. Junge examines the Nikolaev defendants' defensive tactics at their trials, their self-image as "good

Stalinists," the role of witnesses, and, ultimately, the death penalty served on Karamyshev.

In Chapter 4, Vadym Zolotar'ov details the career of D. A. Pertsov who, like many of the UNKVD leaders in Ukraine at this time, was a client of Uspenskii. Pertsov was an expert in interrogating detained NKVD operatives both in NKVD Ukraine and in the Kharkov Oblast UNKVD. He led by example, frequently walking in on interrogations to threaten and torture those who hesitated to confess. He also worked in the Polish operations. He ended up working in the Naval Department of the Odessa Oblast NKVD before he was arrested in November 1938. He was sentenced to fifteen years and died in a logging camp in 1948, having been charged anew with counterrevolutionary crimes, an unusual sentence during this NKVD purge, following an earlier more lenient sentence of four years for "violations of socialist legality." The chapter, like many others, demonstrates the importance of personal connections among different groups of NKVD workers.

Lynne Viola, in Chapter 5, examines the case against O. S. Fleishman, the head of the Skvirskii district NKVD in Kiev Oblast, and M. M. Krivtsov, a district-level regular policeman mobilized to work in the NKVD during the mass operations. The chapter offers a view of the Great Terror at the district and village levels, demonstrating the role of "witnesses" and the use of regular policemen in mass operations. Fleishman, who did not admit guilt, claimed to be following orders, as did the policemen working under him who declared that they did everything "under the dictation of Fleishman." Tried in August 1940, Fleishman was sentenced to eight years and Krivtsov to six years in the Gulag.

In Chapter 6, Serhii Kokin documents the unfolding of the Great Terror in Zhitomir Oblast, following the cases of a series of mid-level NKVD operatives purged before and after the November 1938 directive curtailing mass operations. In this oblast and more widely, the mass operations developed at a pace and scope that almost predetermined the use of torture to obtain what were fake confessions within a compressed period of time. Here as elsewhere, NKVD operatives were charged with looting at the place of execution and the removal of gold teeth from victims. Kokin surveys the results of the arrests of NKVD leaders Grigorii Viatkin and Grigorii Grishin and speculates as to the different sentences for various leaders, suggesting that the harshest sentences were dealt to mid-level NKVD operatives, that is, the people directly responsible in various operations. Kokin offers a reminder that, despite the arrest of these NKVD operatives in the Beria purge, no one ever questioned the Great Terror.

In Chapter 7, Jeffrey Rossman focuses on the investigation and trial of Georgii Kocherginskii, who served as the head of the Transportation Department (DTO) of the Northern Donetsk Railway NKVD. This study of a little-known, but important, agency within the NKVD argues that situational factors served as a primary context for the activities and motivations of Kocherginskii and his colleagues. Fear of punishment and the habit of "following orders" combined with ambition and the desire to please superiors to explain the motivations of these NKVD operatives. Additionally, Kocherginskii clearly believed that class enemies permeated the Soviet Union, making him a typical example of a "true believer" in Stalin's Soviet Union.

Each chapter presents its own laboratory of terror, exploring how the Great Terror unfolded regionally. Although many questions remain surrounding causation and consequence, what is clear about this remarkable episode in the history of the Great Terror is that the purge of the purgers was not about justice. No one questioned the Great Terror, no one questioned the Communist Party, no one questioned Stalin. The vast majority of victims were common people caught up in the mass operations. Seldom were they released. "Justice" was a very limited benefit in this time, obtainable only by some elite victims. The most these individuals could hope for was release, reinstatement to the Party, and the punishment of individual interrogators. Still, the purge of the purgers brought to a halt the Great Terror. Moreover, this episode at the end of the Great Terror generated tens of thousands of documents that would re-emerge in legal and Communist Party tribunals in the mid-1950s when victims, mainly Communists, once again attempted to reclaim their innocence.

Notes

1. "Postanovlenie SNK SSSR i TsK VKP (b) 'Ob arestakh, prokurorskom nadzore i vedenii sledstviia,'" in *Tragediia Sovetskoi Derevni: Kollektivizatsiia i raskulachinvanie. Dokumenty i materialy, 1927–1939* v 5 tomakh, ed. V. P. Danilov, R. T. Manning, and L. Viola (Moscow: Rosspen, 1999–2006), tom 5, kn. 2, 307–311 (further cited as *TSD*). The troika generally consisted of the leaders of the relevant republic or regional NKVD, Communist Party Committee, and Procuracy, though at times the subordinates of each could substitute for their bosses. For further information on the troiki, see *TSD*, tom 5, kn. 1, 335–336.

2. Oleg Khlevniuk, "Party and NKVD: Power Relationships in the Years of the Great Terror," in *Stalin's Terror: High Politics and Mass Repression in the Soviet Union*, ed. Barry McLoughlin and Kevin McDermott (New York: Palgrave Macmillan, 2003),

27; and V. N. Khaustov, V. P. Naumov, and N. S. Plotnikova, eds., *Lubianka: Stalin i NKVD-NKGB-GUKR "Smersh" 1939–mart 1946* (Moscow: Materik, 2006), 564n11.

3. The statistics are from V. P. Popov, "Gosudarstvennyi terror v Sovetskoi Rossii, 1923–1953 gg. (istochniki i ikh interpretatsiia)," *Otechestvennye arkhivy* 2 (1992): 28.

4. *TSD*, tom 5, kn. 1, 330–37. At the 18th Congress of the Communist Party in March 1939, the Central Committee noted the widespread use of the "biological approach" in 1937 and 1938, and condemned it as having nothing in common with Marxism. See *XVIII s'ezd vsesoiuznoi kommunisticheskoi partii (b). 10–21 marta 1939 g. Stenograficheskii otchet* (Moscow: OGIZ, 1939), 523. Also see Mark Iunge, Gennadii Bordiugov, and Rol'f Binner, *Vertikal bol'shogo terrora* (Moscow: Novyi Khronograf, 2008), 128–30, on arrest lists in Vinnitsa including those who had been involved in the collective farm disturbances of 1930.

5. *TSD*, tom 5, kn. 1, 330–37.

6. On the 16 July meeting, see Iunge, *Vertikal'*, 19–26; for other preparations behind the directive, see *TSD*, tom 5, kn. 1, 319–27.

7. *TSD*, tom 5, kn. 1, 331–33.

8. *TSD*, tom 5, kn. 1, 331–34.

9. *TSD*, tom 5, kn. 1, 335.

10. On the *troika*s, see *TSD*, tom 5, kn. 1, 335–36; and J. Arch Getty and Oleg V. Naumov, eds., *The Road to Terror* (New Haven, CT: Yale University Press, 1999), 470.

11. *TSD*, tom 5, kn. 1, 335–36.

12. *TSD*, tom 5, kn. 1, 340. On 7 July 1937, NKVD First Deputy M. P. Frinovskii had issued an earlier order to this effect. See A. G. Tepliakov, *Protsedura: ispolnenie smertnykh prigovorov v 1920–1930-kh godakh* (Moscow: Vozvrashchenie, 2007).

13. Iunge, *Vertikal'*, 52–53; A. G. Tepliakov, "Organy NKVD Zapadnoi Sibiri v 'kulatskoi operatsii' 1937–1938 gg.," in *Stalinizm v Sovetskoi provintsii, 1937–1938 gg. Massovaia operatsiia na osnove prikaza no. 00447*, ed. M. Iunge and R. Binner (Moscow: Rosspen, 2009), 560.

14. Iunge, *Vertikal'*, 162; and *TSD*, tom 5, kn. 1, 387–93.

15. On orders not to increase regional control figures independently, see *TSD*, tom 5, kn. 1, 333; on the center seldom refusing, see Iunge, *Vertikal'*, 141–42. In the historiography, there has been controversy over the exact meaning of "*limity*," translated variously as "quotas" or "limits," with scope for regional initiative. See, for examples, J. Arch Getty, *Practicing Stalinism: Bolsheviks, Boyars, and the Persistence of Tradition* (New Haven, CT: Yale University Press, 2013), chapter 7; Getty, "'Excesses Are Not Permitted': Mass Terror and Stalinist Governance in the Late 1930s," *Russian Review* 61, no. 1 (2002): 112–37; Oleg V. Khlevniuk, *The History of the Gulag: From Collectivization to the Great Terror*, trans. Vadim A. Staklo (New Haven, CT, and London: Yale University Press, 2004), 148–49.

16. Iunge, *Vertikal'*, 150, 277.

17. Iunge, *Vertikal'*, 285; Iunge et al., eds., *"Cherez trupy vraga na blago naroda": "Kulatskaia operatsiia" v Ukrainskoi SSR, 1937–1941 gg.: 1938–1941 gg. Vtoroi etap repressii. Zavershenie Bol'shogo terrora i vosstanovelnie "sotsialisticheskoi zakonnosti"* v 2 tomakh (Moscow: Rosspen, 2010), tom 2, 23–25.

18. See Nikita Petrov and Arsenii Roginskii, "The 'Polish Operation' of the NKVD, 1937–8," in *Stalin's Terror*, ed. McLoughlin and McDermott, 154. For a copy of the directive on the Polish Operation, see V. N. Khaustov, V. P. Naumov, and N. S. Plotnikova, eds., *Lubianka: Stalin i glavnoe upravlenie gosbezopasnosti NKVD, 1937–1938* (Moscow: Materik, 2004), 301–3, and, for the official view on "Polish enemies" in the Soviet Union, 303–21. The German "national operation" was not a part of the national operations per se, but began earlier, from 25 July 1937. See Mark Iunge and Bernd Bonvech, eds., *Bol'shevistskii poriadok v Gruzii* v 2 tomakh (Moscow: AIRO-XXI, 2015), tom 1, 205n21.

19. Petrov and Roginskii, "The 'Polish Operation,'" in *Stalin's Terror*, ed. McLoughlin and McDermott, 154–55. See Timothy Snyder, *Sketches from a Secret War* (New Haven, CT: Yale University Press, 2005), for information on the POV and Polish attempts, largely unsuccessful, to infiltrate Soviet Ukraine with a spy network.

20. *TSD*, tom 5, kn. 2, 163 (data for the period from 1 January 1936 to 1 July 1938).

21. The "special troikas" were established by Directive No. 00606, replacing the dvoika used earlier in the National Operations. See "Prikaz No. 00606 Narodnogo komissara vnutrennykh del SSSR 'Ob obrazovanii Osobykh troek dlia rassmotreniia del na arrestovannykh v poriadke prikazov NKVD SSSR No. 00485 i drugikh,' 17.09.1938," in *Bol'shevistskii poriadok v Gruzii*, ed. Junge and Bonvech, tom 2, 165–67. See also Khaustov, Naumov, and Plotnikova, eds., *Lubianka. Stalin i glavnoe upravlenie gosbezopasnosti NKVD, 1937–1938*, 549.

22. Barry McLoughlin, "Mass Operations of the NVKD, 1937–8: A Survey," in *Stalin's Terror*, ed. McLoughlin and McDermott, 141.

23. Petrov and Roginskii, "The 'Polish Operation,' in ibid., 161.

24. *TSD*, tom 5, kn. 2, 156–63.

25. McLoughlin, "Mass Operations of the NVKD," in *Stalin's Terror*, ed. McLoughlin and McDermott, 141. For sentencing statistics, see Khlevniuk, *The History of the Gulag from Collectivization to the Great Terror*, 290.

26. George O. Liber, *Total Wars and the Making of Modern Ukraine, 1914–1954* (Toronto: University of Toronto Press, 2016), 187.

27. *XVIII s"ezd vsesoiuznoi kommunisticheskoi partii (b). 10–21 marta 1939 g. Stenograficheskii otchet* (Moscow: OGIZ, 1939), 16, 26–27.

28. On the eve of the November 1938 directive, when it became clear that Stalin was about to bring down Ezhov, several key NKVD regional leaders fled or committed suicide. Uspenskii fled on 14 November 1938 and remained a fugitive until his arrest in mid-April 1939. For further information, see Lynne Viola, *Stalinist Perpetrators on Trial: Scenes from the Great Terror in Soviet Ukraine* (New York: Oxford University Press, 2017), 162–65.

29. Violations of socialist legality, or crimes of office, fell under Article 206-17 of the Ukrainian Penal Code. Point "A" of the article dealt with minor offenses and could result in imprisonment for a period of no fewer than six months; Point "B" was more serious and could result in the death sentence. The equivalent article in the Russian Republican Penal Code was Article 193-17.

30. Aleksandr Kokurin and Nikita Petrov, "NKVD: struktura, funktsii, kadry," *Svobodnaia mysl'*, no. 7 (1997): 111; and Khlevniuk, "Party and NKVD," in *Stalin's Terror*, ed. McLoughlin and McDermott, 30.

31. For mention of the trials against NKVD workers in Moldova, see *Kommunist* (Ukraine), 30 December 1938; 31 December 1938; and 1 January 1930. On the war and postwar trials, see Alexander Victor Prusin, "'Fascist Criminals to the Gallows!': The Holocaust and Soviet War Crimes Trials, December 1945–February 1946," *Holocaust and Genocide Studies* 17, no. 1 (2003): 17, 21; Ilya Bourtman, "'Blood for Blood, Death for Death': The Soviet Military Tribunal in Krasnodar, 1943," *Holocaust and Genocide Studies* 22, no. 2 (2008): 258–59; Tanya Penter, "Local Collaborators on Trial: Soviet War Crimes Trials under Stalin (1943–1953)," *Cahiers du monde russe* 49, no. 2 (2008): 361.

32. Khaustov, Naumov, and Plotnikova, *Lubianka: Stalin i glavnoe upravlenie gosbezopasnosti NKVD 1937–1938*, 663–64n92.

33. See Khlevniuk, "Party and NKVD," in *Stalin's Terror*, ed. McLoughlin and McDermott, 30, indicating that of 14,500 new NKVD workers in 1939, over 11,000 were recruited from the Communist Party and Komsomol.

34. For more on this argument, see Viola, *Stalinist Perpetrators on Trial*, 166–71.

35. Iunge, *Vertikal*, 299.

36. "Zapiska komissii prezidiuma TsK KPSS v presidium TsK KPSS o rezul'takh raboty po rassledovaniiu prichin repressii i obstoiatel'stv politicheskikh protsessov 30-kh godov," *Istochnik*, no. 1 (1995): 84.

37. S. V. Mironenko and N. Werth, eds., *Istoriia Stalinskogo Gulaga: Konets 1920-kh-pervaia polovina 1950-kh godov v 7 tomakh* (Moscow: Rosspen, 2004–2005), tom 1, 327–28.

38. Iunge et al., eds., "*Cherez trupy vraga na blago naroda*," tom 2, 489, 511–13.

39. Khaustov, Naumov, and Plotnikova, *Lubianka: Stalin i NKVD-NKGB-GUKR "Smersh" 1939–mart 1946*, 129–32, 564n11.

40. Khlevniuk, "Party and NKVD," in *Stalin's Terror*, ed. McLoughlin and McDermott, 27.

41. For examples, see Viola, *Stalinist Perpetrators on Trial*, chapter 5.

42. A. Iu. Vatlin, *Terror raionnogo masshtaba* (Moscow: Rosspen, 2004), 85–87.

43. E.g., Haluzevyi derzhavnyi arkhiv Sluzhby bezpeky Ukrainy (State Archive of the Security Services of Ukraine, further HDA SBU), f. 16, spr. 322, ark. 248–52.

44. HDA SBU, f. 5, spr. 43626 (sledstvennoe delo Grabaria), tom 3, ark. 297–98 (Protokol zakrytogo partiinogo sobraniia partorganizatsii osobovo otdela KOVO, sostoiavshegosia 2 dekabria 1938 g.), tom 5, ark. 585, 595.

45. Khaustov, Naumov, and Plotnikova, *Lubianka: Stalin i NKVD-NKGB-GUKR "Smersh" 1939–mart 1946*, 9; David R. Shearer and Vladimir Khaustov, eds., *Stalin and the Lubianka: A Documentary History of the Political Police and Security Organs in the Soviet Union, 1922–1953* (New Haven, CT: Yale University Press, 2015), 228–29.

46. The same "bad apples" approach to punishment is apparent in the US government's actions in My Lai during the Vietnam War and at Abu Ghraib during the Iraq war.

47. Kokurin and Petrov, "NKVD: struktura, funktsii, kadry," 111; and Khlevniuk, "Party and NKVD," in *Stalin's Terror*, ed. McLoughlin and McDermott, 30. Many thanks to Andrei Savin, Aleksei Tepliakov, Vadym Zolotar'ov, and Wladislaw Hedeler for their assistance in clarifying this issue. Thanks also to anonymous reader 2, who encouraged us to disentangle this figure.

48. These terms, particularly "counterrevolutionary activities," should be taken with a grain of salt. The data are from "Spravka Otdela kadrov NKVD SSSR o dvizhenii operativno-chekistskikh kadrov organov NKVD za 1939," published in Mironenko and Werth, eds., *Istoriia Stalinskogo Gulaga*, tom 2, 173–77.

49. In N. V. Petrov and K. V. Skorkin, eds., *Kto rukovodil NKVD, 1934–1941: Spravochnik* (Moscow: Zven'ia, 1999), 501, the editors make reference to a document in the FSB archives that apparently V. M. Chebrikov made use of when he made the incorrect claim that some 20,000 NKVD operatives had been repressed. This document, somewhat unhelpfully, includes data (not dissected) not only on NKVD operatives, but on other state security staff, including firemen, members of the *militsia*, Gulag workers, and others. This data shows that in 1933, 738 state security workers were "repressed"; in 1934, 2,860; in 1935, 6,249; in 1936, 1,945; in 1937, 3,837; in 1938, 5,625; and in 1939, 1,364, totaling 22,618 over these years. The figure for 1939 seems to be an anomaly; it does not square with the figures presented in our text concerning *only* NKVD operatives workers, and we have no way to check these figures. It should be noted, however, that the editors of this volume also indicate that 7,372 "sotrudniki" (or 22.9 percent of the operative chekist staff) were let go (*uvoleno*) in 1939.

50. For a first attempt, see V. Zolotar'ov "Represii sered spivrobitnykiv derzhavnoi bezpeky URSR u 1936–1941 rr. Personalizovano-statystychnyi analiz," *Z arkhiviv VUChK-GPU-NKVD-KGB*, no. 2 (1998): 156–217. Data are available for the Mykolaiv (Nikolaev) Oblast of Ukraine. Here, a total of six trials for violation of socialist legality took place between 1939 and 1943. In these trials, 13 NKVD workers were sentenced, 4 (31 percent) to death and 9 (69 percent) to camp imprisonment. Not a single one was brought to justice for counterrevolutionary activity. Since the Mykolaïv (Nikolaev) NKVD administration had about 171 operative members, 8 percent of this apparatus was thus affected by the persecutions. In addition, and as elsewhere, many operational staff were interrogated but ultimately not charged. (M. Iunge [Junge], *Chekisty Stalina: Moshch' i bessilie. "Berievskaia*

otepel'" v Nikolaevskoi oblasti Ukrainy [Moscow: AIRO-XXI, 2017], 148–189, 203, 255).

51. See Kokurin and Petrov, "NKVD: struktura, funktsii, kadry," 111; and Khlevniuk, "Party and NKVD," in *Stalin's Terror*, ed. McLoughlin and McDermott, 30.

52. See, for examples, Peter H. Solomon Jr., *Soviet Criminal Justice under Stalin* (Cambridge: Cambridge University Press, 1996), chapters 7 and 8; and Immo Rebitschek, "Lessons from the Terror: Soviet Procurators and Police Violence in Molotov Province, 1942 to 1949," *Slavic Review* 78, no. 3 (Fall 2019): 738–57.

53. For a sampling of the English-language secondary sources, see Getty and Naumov, eds., *The Road to Terror*; J. Arch Getty and Oleg V. Naumov, *Yezhov: The Rise of Stalin's "Iron Fist"* (New Haven, CT: Yale University Press, 2008); Wendy Z. Goldman, *Terror and Democracy in the Age of Stalin* (Cambridge: Cambridge University Press, 2007); Goldman, *Inventing the Enemy: Denunciation and Terror in Stalin's Russia* (Cambridge: Cambridge University Press, 2011); Paul Hagenloh, *Stalin's Police* (Baltimore: Johns Hopkins University Press, 2009); Igal Halfin, *From Darkness to Light: Class, Consciousness, and Salvation in Revolutionary Russia* (Pittsburgh: Pittsburgh University Press, 2000); Halfin, *Intimate Enemies: Demonizing the Bolshevik Opposition, 1918–1928* (Pittsburgh: Pittsburgh University Press, 2007); Halfin, *Stalinist Confessions: Messianism and Terror at the Leningrad Communist University* (Pittsburgh: Pittsburgh University Press, 2009; Halfin, *Terror in My Soul: Communist Autobiographies on Trial* (Cambridge, MA: Harvard University Press, 2003); James Harris, *The Great Fear: Stalin's Terror of the 1930s* (Oxford: Oxford University Press, 2016); Marc Jansen and Nikita Petrov. *Stalin's Loyal Executioner: People's Commissar Nikolai Ezhov, 1895–1940* (Stanford, CA: Hoover Press, 2002); McLoughlin and McDermott, eds., *Stalin's Terror*; David R. Shearer, *Policing Stalin's Socialism* (New Haven, CT: Yale University Press, 2009).

54. E.g., Getty, "Excesses Are Not Permitted"; and Oleg V. Khlevniuk, *Master of the House: Stalin and His Inner Circle*, trans. [stet Nora, her first name] Seligman Favorov (New Haven, CT: Yale University Press, 2009), 183.

55. *TSD,* tom 5, kn. 2, 308.

56. For a discussion of the sources, Lynne Viola, "New Sources on Soviet Perpetrators of Mass Repression: A Research Note," *Canadian Slavonic Papers* 60, nos. 3–4 (September–December 2018): 592–604.

57. Viola, *Stalinist Perpetrators on Trial*, 49.

58. Ibid., 138.

59. Ibid., 48.

60. Ibid., 67–68. "Physical methods of influence" was the NKVD euphemism for torture.

61. On the use of alcohol during the mass shootings of the Holocaust in the east, see Edward B. Westermann, *Drunk on Genocide: Alcohol and Mass Murder in Nazi Germany* (Ithaca, NY: Cornell University Press, 2021).

62. For more on Petrov, see Viola, *Stalinist Perpetrators*, 109–10.
63. Khlevniuk, *Master of the House*, 183.
64. Christopher R. Browning, *Ordinary Men: Reserve Police Battalion 101 and the Final Solution in Poland* (New York: HarperPerennial, 1992).

I

"The Party Will Demand a Full Reckoning"

KORABLEV AND THE VINNITSA NKVD

Valeriy Vasylyev and Roman Podkur
Translated by Simon Belokowsky

FROM THE FIRST days of the Nazi occupation, Vinnitsa's citizens began to approach the occupation authority requesting that it investigate the secret burials carried out by the NKVD in 1937 and 1938 during the Great Terror. However, it was only after their defeat at Stalingrad in 1943 that the Nazis began their investigation, unleashing a wide-reaching propaganda campaign accusing the Communist regime of the mass killing of Ukrainians. In this, they sought to discredit Soviet power in the eyes of the local population, hoping that it could be mobilized as a source of resistance to the approaching formations of the Red Army. This was happening at the same time that Hitler's forces were themselves guilty of mass shootings and genocide in Ukrainian, Belarusian, and Russian lands.

In April 1943, an international commission of experts examined the mass burial sites of Polish prisoners of war executed in the Katyn forest near Smolensk by the NKVD. The next month, mass exhumations began in Vinnitsa. Ernst Kaltenbrunner, the head of the Reich Main Security Office (Reichssicherheitshauptamt), brought together a group of criminal investigators to work in Vinnitsa. From 24 May to 3 October 1943, four commissions examining mass graves operated in the city, three German ones and one international commission made up of experts in criminal forensics

Valeriy Vasylyev and Roman Podkur, *"The Party Will Demand a Full Reckoning"* In: *Laboratories of Terror.*
Edited by: Lynne Viola and Marc Junge, Oxford University Press. © Oxford University Press 2023.
DOI: 10.1093/oso/9780197647547.003.0002

from Belgium, Bulgaria, Finland, France, Italy, Croatia, the Netherlands, Romania, Sweden, Slovakia, and Hungary. In all, 95 graves containing 9,439 corpses were exhumed.[1]

Newspapers in Ukraine and many other European countries devoted significant attention to these events, labeling them a "frightening depiction of Bolshevik inhumanity."[2] Moscow offered a different assessment. On 12 August 1943, the newspapers *Pravda* and *Izvestiia* published a statement from the Soviet Information Bureau: "Berlin provocateurs are currently announcing supposedly 'accidental' discoveries of mass graves, attempting to attribute their own monstrously evil deeds to the Soviet authorities. In Vinnitsa, the Hitlerites are staging an odious and shameless comedy over the remains of its own victims. The killers, whose hands are stained with the blood of innocents, are digging up the corpses of the people they have annihilated and putting on farcical inspections of their graves. The world has never before seen such atrocities and hypocrisy."[3]

When Soviet troops entered Vinnitsa in March 1944, witnesses to the exhumations who had been quoted in occupation newspapers or who simply told their neighbors about them were persecuted.[4] In the course of the Nuremberg trials, Soviet representatives did all they could to avoid the dissemination of information about the events in Vinnitsa.

During the Cold War, information about the tragedy in Vinnitsa periodically appeared in the Ukrainian émigré press. The diaspora preserved the memory of the tragedy, discussing it in terms of crimes against the Ukrainian nation, genocide, or a "forgotten Holocaust." Occasionally, the monstrous crimes of the Soviet regime in Vinnitsa garnered attention in connection with political developments. In September 1959, for example, the US House of Representatives held hearings on the events in Vinnitsa in 1943. It was no accident that these hearings directly followed Nikita Khrushchev's visit to the United States; the relevant report was published under the title "The Crimes of Khrushchev."[5] In Ukraine, the first newspaper articles revealing the mass killings of 1937 and 1938 in Vinnitsa were published only in 1988. The tragedy was referred to as the "Vinnitsa Kurapaty," referring to a wooded tract on the outskirts of Minsk where mass graves were uncovered, also in 1988, containing the remains of those executed by the NKVD during the Great Terror. Only recently has the rich documentation on the Great Terror contained in the State Archive of the Security Services of Ukraine (HDA SBU) enabled the unlocking of the secrets of the Great Terror in Vinnitsa.[6]

"In Ukraine, Entire Antisoviet Ukrainian Nationalist Divisions . . . Roam Underground"

The early stages and mechanisms of mass repression in 1937 are now relatively clear. By the beginning of 1938, some 159,573 people had been arrested in Ukraine.[7] The Soviet leadership, however, was unsatisfied with the scale of repression in Ukraine. In the opinion of the Commissar of Internal Affairs of the USSR, Nikolai Ezhov, the Commissar of Internal Affairs of the Ukrainian republic NKVD, Izrail' Leplevskii, had not shown himself to be sufficiently active in uncovering "enemies of the people." The next phase of repression required new leaders. To replace Leplevskii, Ezhov appointed the thirty-five-year-old head of the Orenburg Oblast NKVD Administration, Aleksandr Uspenskii, a Chekist distinguished by his great fervor in carrying out repression.

In November 1937, Ezhov sent Uspenskii a secret wire (shifrovka): "If you think that you are going to be sitting in Orenburg for five years or so, then you are mistaken. It will most likely be necessary to promote you to a position of greater responsibility in the near future." Later on, Uspenskii recounted under interrogation that "in January 1938 I traveled to a session of the Supreme Soviet of the USSR in Moscow. Ezhov summoned me unexpectedly. I came to see him at his office. He was completely drunk. A bottle of cognac stood on his desk. Ezhov said to me: 'Well, you are going to Ukraine.'" It was subsequently explained to Uspenskii that Leplevskii had lost the trust of the Central Committee of the Communist Party on account of "crude, clumsy actions [grubye, neumelye deistviia]."[8] On 25 January 1938, Leplevskii was appointed to lead the Transportation Department of the Main Administration of State Security of the USSR; he was arrested on 26 April and shot on 28 July.[9]

In 1937, nearly the entire membership of the Politburo of the Communist Party of Ukraine and the Council of People's Commissars of Ukraine was repressed. At the recommendation of the Politburo of the Central Committee of the Communist Party, Nikita Khrushchev was elected First Secretary of the Communist Party in Ukraine during a plenum of its Central Committee on 27 January 1938.[10] Aleksandr Uspenskii traveled to Ukraine with Khrushchev and by 27 January had already taken on his responsibilities as Commissar of the Ukrainian republic NKVD.[11] Almost simultaneously, on 31 January, the Politburo of the Central Committee in Moscow accepted Ezhov's proposal "regarding the approval of a supplementary number of former kulaks, criminals, and active antisoviet elements as subject to repression." In Ukraine it was planned to execute an additional 6,000 people. The work of the extrajudicial troikas was extended. The operation was to conclude by 15 March 1938. Simultaneously, the Politburo in Moscow extended the national operations until 15 April 1938.[12]

In mid-February 1938, Ezhov traveled to Kiev in order to jump-start this new wave of repression in Ukraine. At an NKVD operational meeting, he announced that it was necessary to execute 30,000 people in Ukraine, an initiative approved by Stalin. On 17 February 1938, the Politburo sanctioned the new target as well as extending still further the work of the extrajudicial troikas.[13] Ezhov encouraged the heads of oblast NKVD administrations (UNKVDs) in Ukraine to submit petitions for further increases in "quotas." One attendee at the meeting in Kiev, the head of the Poltava UNKVD, A. Volkov, later recalled that Ezhov "characterized all previous work as superficial and [limited to] individual arrests, and noted the failure to uncover the supposed antisoviet underground. He emphasized in particular the extremely weak efforts aimed at the uncovering of the Ukrainian, Polish, and German antisoviet nationalist undergrounds, and talked about how in Ukraine there remained Petlurists and Makhnovites [remnants of the opposing sides from the Russian civil war] and other antisoviet cadres."[14]

On 26 February and 3 March 1938, Ezhov promulgated decrees removing all heads of oblast NKVD administrations in Ukraine. New, mainly younger people were appointed to these posts. In Vinnitsa, Ivan Mikhailovich Korablev became the head of the Vinnitsa UNKVD.[15] Korablev was born in 1899 to a peasant family in the village of Misino in Pskov gubernia. In 1911, he completed a village school and until 1915 worked as a coachman for a landowner (*pomeshchik*). At age sixteen, he moved to Petrograd (now St. Petersburg) where he worked at a lumberyard and later as a turner's hand at the New Lessner plant and a presser at a cartridge plant. In January 1918, he went to the village of Ponizovskoe in Tiumen Guberniia. He was able to avoid being drafted into Kolchak's forces and entered the ranks of the Red Army in October 1919.

In November 1920, Korablev began his service in the state security organs, in the Cheka in Tiumen. He later served as a plenipotentiary in the counterespionage department of the Transvolga Military District. After graduation from the Higher Border Service School of the OGPU USSR, he served in various senior positions in the OGPU in the Middle Volga Krai. Following the murder of Sergei Kirov in late 1934, he was transferred to the Leningrad Oblast NKVD Administration. In 1937, he was assistant to the Chief of the Third (Counterespionage) Department of the Leningrad UNKVD. Ivan Korablev's report to Nikolai Ezhov dated 16 May 1937 testifies to the manner in which he operated. Within it, Korablev notes bitterly that a series of cadres within the Leningrad NKVD Administration had received promotions, but the author had been "skipped over" even though he had "uncovered" a multiplicity of cases of espionage and sabotage in the city in 1935. Korablev declared that he deserved a promotion.[16] Naturally, such an ambitious "specialist" caught Ezhov's attention.

On 3 March 1938, the decree appointing Korablev to Vinnitsa was formally promulgated.[17] Ezhov received Korablev in Moscow. Ezhov's attention to the new Vinnitsa UNKVD boss was no accident. On 5 March, the Politburo had discussed NKVD matters in Ukraine. In the western oblasts of the republic, the Politburo established a controlled border zone that included three districts of Vinnitsa Oblast. The Politburo envisaged exiling the families of those repressed for spying, sabotage, terrorism, rebellion, banditry, wrecking, illegal border crossing, and contraband activity alongside the families of those individuals who had fled across the border at various times, as well as the "entire politically suspect and criminal element."[18]

At a meeting with Ezhov, Korablev asked for a cancellation of the decree appointing him to Vinnitsa. The Commissar asked why, to which Korablev responded that he was afraid that he was not up to the task. Ezhov consoled him: "There is no sense in discussing it; go and start your work.

FIG. 1.1 I. M. Korablev, from March 1938 to January 1939 head of the Vinnitsa Oblast NKVD. Prison photo from 1940, HDA SBU, f. 5, spr. 66927, tom 1, ark. 11. By exclusive permission of the State Archive of the Security Services of Ukraine.

There, in Ukraine, entire antisoviet Ukrainian nationalist divisions created by Liubchenko and Balitskii roam underground; you must go and destroy these detachments." In Kiev, Uspenskii gave instructions to Korablev, declaring that "all Germans and Poles living on the territory of Ukraine are spies and saboteurs" and "75–80 percent of Ukrainians are bourgeois nationalists."[19]

On 7 September 1938, Uspenskii appointed Anton Iakovlevich Prishivtsyn as Korablev's deputy.[20] Born in 1905 in Mariupol to a Ukrainian family, Prishivtsyn graduated from a railroad school with a primary education. In 1927, he became an apprentice, serving as assistant operative plenipotentiary of the Informational Department of the Active-Investigatory Department of the Lugansk Okrug Department of GPU Ukraine. This same year he entered the party. It is entirely plausible that he excelled in his work because he was quickly appointed plenipotentiary and then head of the Rovenki District Division of the GPU. Interestingly, within the character assessment contained in his personnel file (*kharakteristika*), the following negative trait was noted: extreme ambition "to quickly be promoted," an excessive desire "to move quickly into management," and "an overly hasty attempt to master operative work." Between 1933 and 1935, Prishivtsyn served as head of the Secret Political Department of the Kramatorsk City Division of the GPU; between 1935 and 1937, he was assistant to a division chief of the Fourth (Secret Political) Department of the Donetsk UNKVD; and, between 1937 and 1938, he was a sector chief within the Fourth Department. In 1937, he participated in the uncovering of "sabotage-insurrectionary" groups among special settlers (Germans from the western oblasts of Ukraine), which were supposedly led by agents from the German consulate. In June 1937, he led an investigatory group in Mariupol targeted at uncovering "fascist groups" in the southern districts of the Donbas. Here, three hundred people were sentenced to be shot (according to reports sent to Moscow).[21] Subsequently, Uspenskii indicated that he did not know Prishivtsyn well, but did not have his "own people" in Vinnitsa. According to Uspenskii, he knew that Prishivtsyn "concocted many fabricated cases," while the head of the Stalino UNKVD, P. Chistov, characterized him as a "jack-of-all-trades."[22] On this basis he was sent to assist Korablev and appointed on 5 June 1938 as acting head of the Fourth Department of the Vinnitsa UNKVD.[23] In September, he was appointed acting deputy head of the Vinnitsa UNKVD.[24]

Another colleague of Korablev in Vinnitsa was Aleksandr Mikhailovich Zaputriaev, whom he had come to know through their service together in Leningrad. In 1935, this particular Chekist had been suspected of Trotskyite connections, for which two of his acquaintances had been arrested. Zaputriaev filed a report concerning the incident, but he was expelled from the party and only reinstated after his transfer to Ukraine.[25] Compromised politically, he was ready to fulfill any assignment from Korablev. In May 1938, Zaputriaev was appointed deputy head of the Third Department of the Vinnitsa UNKVD and from 3 July to 22 October 1938 served as chief of the Department.[26]

In May 1938, Nikolai Stepanovich Butenko—who in 1930 had gained significant experience uncovering "counterrevolutionary kulaks" in Velikii Tokmak District (in the Dnepropetrovsk area)—also worked with Korablev. Between 1934 and 1938, he served as Chief of the Teplik District Department of the Vinnitsa UNKVD. In 1937, he demonstrated great zeal in unmasking "enemies of the people" and especially "the uncovering" of group cases. He became an indispensable assistant for Korablev as he desired to "make good" on the trust placed in him and to distinguish himself in the eyes of the leadership.

These individuals carried out mass repressive operations throughout 1938 in Vinnitsa. In order to facilitate mass arrests, NKVD investigatory groups were created in March 1938 in a series of districts; elsewhere, the responsibility for mass operations fell to the NKVD District Administrations. From March 22, the number of confessions from detainees began to skyrocket. On April 7, Korablev reported to Uspenskii that 2,500 people had been arrested in the oblast, but that repressions against Poles, Romanians, and other national groups were only beginning. The oblast troika (consisting of Ivan Korablev; the Secretary of the Oblast Committee of the Communist Party, I. Spivak; and the Oblast Procurator, Ia. Ternivskii) met on a daily basis between 19 and 28 April. Korablev requested an increase in the repression quota by three hundred to five hundred people. In response, he received an increased quota of four hundred people in the first category (those who were to be shot).[27]

In April and May 1938, one of the most important mass operations targeted the so-called Polish Military Organization (POV). Groups of Chekists were sent into the districts to implement this campaign. They compiled lists of people to arrest based on information from the district NKVD administrations or information invented by the Chekists themselves. For example, upon his arrival at the Zhmerinka District NKVD Department, Korablev demanded a list of all the Poles living in the district. He made a note on the list to arrest all Poles of middle age. In addition, he issued a directive to the special sections of industrial enterprises and institutions to compile lists of Poles, Germans, and Latvians. The Third Department of the UNKVD then carried out arrests based on these lists. From the outset, the Chekists applied measures of physical and psychological coercion in order to elicit confessions regarding "hostile [*vrazheskoe*] activity." The leadership goaded their subordinates on, saying: "We are not going to joke around with enemies. If two or three kick the bucket, nothing will come of it; none of you will answer for it, I will answer with my own head and my own party card."[28]

Group interrogations featuring inhuman torture and humiliation became a regular practice. The operative group working in Zhmerinka District arrested more than one hundred people from April to May 1938 against whom there was no incriminating evidence whatsoever.[29] A similar practice was utilized at the Vinnitsa UNKVD. Each evening Korablev received a report on the number of "confessions" received. He would take these to the meetings of the troika, which would then confirm the death sentences. Victims were executed immediately in the garage of the UNKVD, where the sounds of bullets and victims' screams were drowned out by the hum of running truck engines. These trucks were then loaded up with corpses, which would be concealed in a park located 383 yards away or at the cemetery on Lesnaia Street, 1.24 miles away. The numerical goal for repression in Vinnitsa Oblast was fulfilled by 11 May 1938. Ivan Korablev sent a report to Uspenskii in which he recounted the results of "investigatory activity."

From 26 March to 10 May, 3,448 people were repressed in the various mass operations. On 26 May, the Politburo extended the nationalities operation until 1 August. On 15 September, a new Politburo decision transferred the investigation of so-called album (*al'bomnye*) cases from the central apparatus of NKVD USSR to the Oblast "special troika."[30] Analysis of surviving reports indicates that in Vinnitsa Oblast between 1937 and 1938 the troika and "high duumvirate [*vyshaia dvoika*]" convicted 19,851 people, of whom 16,806 were shot.[31]

According to Korablev, some Chekists began to sense a change in the political winds in the second half of 1938. One of the first signs of this was the 22 August appointment of L. P. Beria as first deputy to Ezhov. Beria had been the First Secretary of the Central Committee of the Communist Party of Georgia and had taken part in the repression of party cadres in the Caucasus.[32] On 11 September, he received the title of Commissar of State Security of the First Rank, and, on 29 September, the Main Administration of State Security was restored within the NKVD with Beria at the helm.[33] Decrees 00701 and 00702 promulgated on 23 October 1938 by the NKVD of the USSR spoke to the responsibility of cadres to adhere strictly to the rules of investigatory work.[34] The staff of the Vinnitsa UNKVD was familiarized with the decrees at an operational meeting held on 31 October. The Commissar of the Ukrainian republic NKVD, Uspenskii, sensed the looming threat sooner than others. On 14 November, he staged his own suicide.[35]

Three days later, Stalin and Molotov signed a joint decree of the Council of People's Commissars of the USSR and Central Committee of the Communist Party, "Regarding arrests, prosecutorial oversight, and the conduct of investigations" in accordance with which the NKVD and procurator organs were forbidden from conducting operations of mass arrests and the troikas were liquidated. The organs of the NKVD were required to strictly adhere to all rules of the criminal-procedural codices when carrying out investigations.[36] On the same day, Ivan Korablev led a meeting in Vinnitsa on matters of operational work.[37]

On 25 November, Beria acceded to the leadership of the NKVD. On the same day, an operational meeting was held in the Vinnitsa UNKVD at which the 17 November 1938 decree was read and discussed. Korablev announced that at the 19 November meeting of the heads and deputy heads of the NKVD and central committee of the Ukrainian Communist Party, "various chiefs of NKVD [oblast] administrations and their deputies somewhat misapprehended the substance of the decree and spoke nonsense." For example, the leaders from Nikolaev stated that two thousand detainees had been subjected to beatings. In Odessa Oblast, state security staff had beaten fifteen hundred inmates. Noted Korablev, "The Secretary of the Central Committee, comrade Khrushchev, spoke very abruptly on this score, [and] declared that the guilty should be prosecuted for taking such an incorrect approach." Tellingly, in the presence of the Secretary of the Vinnitsa Oblast Party Committee, G. Mishchenko, Korablev did not mention the "nonsense" regarding mass beatings of detainees in Vinnitsa.

At the meeting, Party Secretary Mishchenko stated that he did not wish to speak about violations of the law, but about party oversight: "Apparently your departmental discipline puts itself above party discipline, and this is very bad. . . . To brief secretaries of district party committees regarding active-investigatory work is inadequate, work must be advanced with thorough communication. No one has given district party committee secretaries the right to personally direct NKVD workers and give them orders at the expense of fundamental Chekist work, in the same way that the Chief of the District NKVD Department [cannot] direct the cadres of the district [party] committee." Korablev fully acknowledged the leading role of the Oblast Party Committee: "At present the situation with the hiring in the NKVD is entirely different from before. The hiring, firing, and transfer of Chekist cadres is carried out solely in consultation with the Oblast Party Committee."[38]

On 26 November 1938, NKVD USSR promulgated decree 00762, signed by Beria, "On the course of the implementation of the Council of People's Commissars and Central Committee of the VKP(B) decree of 17 November 1938," which defined the work of agents of state security in accordance with extant legislation and demanded, under the leadership of the party and government, the "achievement of the swift and decisive eradication of all inadequacies and violations in work and the essential improvement of the on-going battle for the complete destruction of all enemies of the people and the purging of our motherland from agents of foreign intelligence services, guaranteeing in this way the further successes of socialist construction."[39] This decree set in motion the purge of the NKVD.

"Each Member of the Party Must Not Forget That the Party Will Demand a Full Reckoning"

In Vinnitsa, Korablev was forced to deal with the NKVD decree of 26 November 1938 (00762). On 1 December 1938, he promulgated a decree within the Vinnitsa UNKVD in which he announced penalties for a series of investigators for having beaten detainees, fabricated interrogation transcripts, and prevented detainees from meeting with procurators. Sergeant of State Security Artem Pavlovich Berkut was jailed for three days for the violations he had countenanced. At that very moment, letters, complaints, and petitions regarding the methods of investigation employed within the UNKVD were flowing to various party and state structures from personnel in the state security organs already freed from concentration camp detention.[40] In December, expert commissions, staffed by personnel new to the central and oblast NKVD apparatuses, began operating. The chiefs of these groups were tasked with auditing the work of the NKVD administrations from the period of mass repressions.

The activity of the organs of state security became a concern for an ever-larger circle of bureaucrats, not to mention the relatives and friends of those victimized by the mass repressions.[41] The activity of the leadership of the Vinnitsa UNKVD was being monitored by the Republic-level procurator's office, the new leadership of the Ukrainian republic NKVD headed by acting NKVD Commissar A. Z. Kobulov, and the Oblast Party Committee. On 26 December, a closed party meeting of the Vinnitsa UNKVD was held under the banner "On the errors and violations in the work of the NKVD admin-istration." Sixty people participated, including the Secretary of the Vinnitsa

Oblast Party Committee, D. Burchenko. The tone of Korablev's comments remained the same: the collective of the administration had conducted major work "toward the decimation of the counterrevolutionary underground of all stripes." However, errors had been committed, which enemies were attempting to exploit. For this reason, 284 members of the NKVD administration had been fired, arrested, or transferred on the basis of incriminating evidence from mid-March to the end of December, and 231 from the oblast police. As such, more than 500 staff were removed, of whom 72 were arrested.[42]

For the first time, Korablev publicly admitted to the beatings of detainees: "There have taken place incidents of the most crude violation of socialist legality, [including the use of] physical methods, employed by certain interrogators toward detainees. . . . Our oblast administration suffers from the same illnesses as other administrations, which is noted in the resolution of the Central Committee of the Communist Party and the Council of People's Commissars of the USSR." Korablev's defense strategy was obvious: violations of the law were typical among security organs and therefore verbal condemnation of illegal measures was sufficient. Among these violations, Korablev noted in particular the methods of Kuras, an NKVD operative in the Kalinovskii District NKVD Administration, who had, by then, been fired. Kuras had exploited teachers, the chairmen and secretaries of village councils, and the head of the special section of the District Executive Committee, forcing them to serve as "witnesses" in uncovering "enemies." These "witnesses" not only wrote contrived witness testimony, but, at the demand of Kuras, also summoned collective farmers and forced them to sign false testimonies.

Korablev spoke out sharply against the fact that, within a week of commencing operations, the investigatory group organized in accordance with the 26 November NKVD decree freed 52 percent of all detainees after examining their incomplete cases. He maintained that those detained were in fact guilty, that the NKVD administration had been wrong to stop arrests, and that the staff was only thinking "how best to avoid trouble."[43]

The Secretary of the Oblast Party Committee, Burchenko, summed up the discussion: "The main reason behind all mistakes in the activity of the organs of the NKVD is the lack of Party spirit [partiinost']. . . . Every member of the Party must not forget that the Party will demand a full reckoning [sprosit za vse]." He stated that the organs of the NKVD would be subordinated to stringent oversight by party organs. The party leader specifically underscored that cases where Communists had slandered honest people had recently increased, and that the former explained their actions on the basis of orders from the

NKVD. But there were also people who denounced everyone around them, and "it is necessary to keep such unmaskers [*razoblachiteli*] at a far distance from the organs of the NKVD." Such a practice had to be stopped immediately. In the end, Korablev was forced to conclude that, "with respect to those mistakes and violations that were countenanced in the work of our administration . . . all of us are guilty."[44]

A few days later, Korablev was removed from his post and B. Shablinskii, Third Secretary of the Dnepropetrovsk Oblast Party Committee, was appointed to serve as the new chief of the UNKVD.[45] On 18 January 1939, Korablev wrote Beria a letter in which he declared that he "worked honorably, as befits a Bolshevik." In a 28 January letter to Stalin, he noted his confusion at his own removal as well as that of just about all NKVD oblast administration chiefs. He wrote that he considered "the policy pursued by comrade Beria toward long-standing Chekist cadres to be a great mistake." It was not they but rather the former People's Commissar of Internal Affairs of the USSR who bore guilt: "In a word, all the guilt belongs to comrade Ezhov and those bastards who occupied leadership roles in the decisive sectors of Chekist work, including Zakovskii [Leningrad NKVD chief], Uspenskii, and the like, who turned out to be enemies of the people. . . . I will die an honest man, an honest Communist and Chekist."[46] On the night of 29 January, Korablev attempted to commit suicide with two shots at point-blank range, but survived.[47] Beria was immediately made aware of the incident and apprised Stalin while the Bureau of the Vinnitsa Oblast Party Committee discussed Korablev's suicide attempt on 3 February as a "shameful anti-Party deed." Korablev was removed from the ranks of the Oblast Party Committee and, after recuperating, left Vinnitsa.[48]

In January 1939, the party commissions organized to review the work of the NKVD administrations began their work. Oblast Party committees examined the personnel files of Communist-Chekists, affirming candidates for further work in the organs of state security. On 14 February 1939, the bureau of the Vinnitsa Oblast Party Committee began confirming candidates for leadership roles within the oblast and district NKVD administrations. Far from all staff were confirmed. Many of them had incriminating evidence against them, which made them subject to dismissal. There was no discussion of violations of the law. The fate of those dismissed is largely unknown. However, one NKVD operative—the deputy head of the Fifth Department, A. Reder, who was fired for concealing his social status as the son of an Austrian citizen and a Jew (rather than a Russian as he wrote in his biography)—became a chief actor in subsequent events in Vinnitsa.[49]

"All of Vinnitsa Is Talking about This Person"

In the course of investigations into violations of socialist legality, as well as the confirmation of candidates for the NKVD, the systematic beatings of detainees and staging of executions became widely known. Victims and their families wrote copious complaints, statements, and letters to a wide variety of Communist Party, state, and NKVD offices at all levels of the regional hierarchy. In Vinnitsa, former Zionists, Bund members, and Red Partisans and their relatives provided documentation for the investigations. All these persons had in the past participated in the revolutionary movement, and Red Partisans had been categorized as participants of armed units fighting for Soviet power during the years of the revolution. Mass operations were conducted against these groups in 1938. On 13 and 14 August and then on 26 August, a special collegium of the Vinnitsa Oblast Court meeting in the prison building sentenced many of these individuals to be shot. In the course of the trial, former Red Partisans refused to acknowledge their guilt and demanded that Chekist investigators be expelled from the room. Defendant K. P. Borisov declared that the "participation of these executioners, agents of Hitler, does not frighten anyone, and the accused will tell the truth." Following the verdict, the victims and their relatives wrote a large number of letters to various organs of the party and state regarding the injustice of their sentences. On 16 November, the Supreme Court of the USSR commuted the death sentences of these people to ten years in concentration camps, though many of these individuals continued to demand a re-examination of their cases.

A significant share of petitions was addressed to the Chief Procurator of the USSR, A. Vyshinskii. Along with his request for a re-examination of his case, Borisov reported that during his interrogation, investigators Antonov and Gunia had conducted a staged execution. On 7 January 1939, F. Ia. Shvarts wrote to Stalin, stating that her husband E. I. Shvarts was arrested, forced to confess to counterrevolutionary activity under torture, and sentenced to death, a sentence later commuted to ten years in a concentration camp. She reported that her husband was beaten by interrogators V. F. Maistruk and F. Reshetnikov (actually Reshetilo) of the Vinnitsa Oblast NKVD Administration and the "trial itself was a violation of the Great Stalin Constitution."

On 8 March 1939, Vinnitsa resident M. G. Bruskin wrote to Vyshinskii from a distant labor camp in the far north, requesting a re-examination of his case. He claimed that the Vinnitsa UNKVD had fabricated his case. He wrote further that, "For all the years of my membership in the Communist

FIG. 1.2 V. F. Maistruk, from November 1937 to May 1939 head of a sector and then department of the Administration of State Security of the Vinnitsa Oblast NKVD. Photo from about 1952, HDA SBU, f. 12, spr. 9179, tom 1, obkladnik. By exclusive permission of the State Archive of the Security Services of Ukraine.

Party I never thought about my personal life, all of my ideals, all of my life was dedicated to the party of Lenin-Stalin and Soviet power.... I ask that you re-examine my case, establish my innocence and return me from this distant camp."[50]

Heightened scrutiny from the Oblast and City Party committees elicited testimony regarding the arrests and convictions of party and state workers. It emerged that Koroblev's co-workers, Prishivtsyn, Reder, and L. N. Shirin, were actively engaged in the falsification of investigatory materials regarding this group and savagely beat them, aiming to elicit confessions of espionage and other hostile activity. In early August 1938, Reder presented a list of between forty and forty-five Communist Party and Komsomol workers to the detained Third Secretary of the Vinnitsa City Komsomol Committee, N. Vasilenko, demanding that he confirm in writing that the individuals were members of a counterrevolutionary youth group.[51] First on the list was the G. Mishchenko, the First Secretary of the Vinnitsa Oblast Committee of the

Communist Party who had been elected only in May. Reder could not have carried out such actions without Korablev and Prishivtsyn's approval.

On 22 June 1939, Reder was arrested and, on 23 June, a closed meeting of the Party Organization of the Vinnitsa UNKVD was held "Regarding violations in the conduct of investigation by the former NKVD administration operative and party member Reder." The party meeting became one of the key moments of the political campaign around the condemnation of violations of the law and the erection of party oversight over the organs of the NKVD in Vinnitsa Oblast. All speakers condemned the violations, particularly the methods of physical coercion employed against detainees. NKVD workers referred to the room where mass beatings and tortures took place as the "laboratory." It was Reder who continuously held a key to this room.

At the meeting it was underscored that Reder and Shirin "specialized" in party workers, staging something akin to a hunt against highly placed members of the party with the aim of showing their treacherous activity. Of course, they also hoped to receive awards and promotions for their efforts. By the end of June 1939, however, the situation had entirely changed. Communist Party members like Saprykin, Fuks, and Mezhbein, who had been arrested under Reder's orders, were released and wrote to the First Secretary of the Oblast Party Committee regarding the illegalities that had taken place. In the Vinnitsa City Party Committee, "Reder was spoken of as an animal." Kostarzhevskii spoke about the purpose of the party meeting: "The crux is that we need to, now, uncover everything that went on under the leadership of Reder. It is a matter of an individual who in the given case has wholly discredited the organs of the NKVD. All of Vinnitsa is talking about this person. This person has no place in our collective." Reder was condemned by everyone in attendance. On 28 July 1939, he hanged himself in his jail cell in Kiev.[52]

The staff of the Vinnitsa UNKVD affirmed its subordination to the Communist Party and the correctness of its line, condemning both the "violations of legality" and the individuals who had dishonored the NKVD. These cadres were now held to be enemies. "Purging itself" of them, the collective was ready to carry on the fight against enemies, but using "more legal methods."

Following the investigations of Reder's case, evidence regarding Prishivtsyn, Shirin, and other Vinnitsa Chekists was sent to Kobulov. On 9 August, the Assistant Division Chief in the Third Department of the Vinnitsa UNKVD, I. G. Vodkin, was arrested for employing illegal methods of interrogation and fabricating investigatory documents. On 19 September, his case was closed, but on 29 November the Military Tribunal of the Kiev Special Military Okrug directed his case to be investigated further.

On 2 February 1940, Zaputriaev was arrested in connection with this matter. The direct participation of Korablev in baseless arrests, illegal methods of interrogation, and the fabrication of investigatory documents was uncovered. On 21 December 1939, materials against Zaputriaev, Korablev, and other former staff were forwarded to NKVD USSR for the purpose of obtaining arrest warrants and bringing the guilty to justice. On 19 April 1940, while the matter was being decided in Moscow, the Military Tribunal in Kiev convicted and sentenced the operative plenipotentiary, Vodkin, to five years' imprisonment and forfeiture of his title as Sergeant of State Security.

Korablev was arrested on 28 May in Moscow and transferred to Kiev on 5 June. His investigation lasted over six months. On 7 February 1941, the new Commissar of the Ukrainian republic NKVD, I. A. Serov, confirmed the indictment against Korablev and Zaputriaev. Korablev, it was said, unquestioningly carried out the orders of the "subsequently unmasked enemy of the people Uspenskii in connection with the treasonous activity of an antisoviet conspiratorial organization existing within the organs of the NKVD." Korablev and Zaputriaev carried out mass groundless arrests. On Korablev's orders, Shirin and Reder put group interrogation into practice in the so-called Laboratory. Regarding the accusations presented, Korablev fully acknowledged his guilt, proclaiming, however, that at that time he did not consider his actions to be criminal. Zaputriaev did not acknowledge his guilt, but did admit to having countenanced "individual mistakes" in 1938. On 16 April 1941, the Ukrainian republic NKVD confirmed the indictments of Korablev, Zaputriaev, and Shirin.[53]

Troika Material

Between 26 April and 6 May 1941, the Military Tribunal of Kiev Military District met in the building of the Vinnitsa Oblast NKVD administration to try Korablev, Zaputriaev, and Shirin. The Tribunal heard the indictment and also witness testimony from former victims, B. Epel'baum, P. Iur'ev (the Secretary of the Vinnitsa Oblast Party Committee), and others. They recounted tortures and humiliation at the hands of Maistruk, Reshetilo, Nadezhdin, Zaputriaev, Shirin, and Reder, among others. At NKVD operational meetings, NKVD operatives who produced the largest number of arrests were labeled "shock-workers" and celebrated. They spoke of the "laboratories" in which mass interrogations and beatings of detainees were conducted. Reder and others beat detainees and forced them to beat each other with a chair leg or rubber hose. They forced detainees to imitate sex acts with the bodies of citizens who had already been shot. This inhumanity, contempt for others, brutality, and collapse of morality among Chekists was reflected in the popular slang term "troika material [*troechnyi material*]." This was what they called prisoners doomed to be shot, people already not considered to be human.

Speaking before the court, Korablev did not acknowledge guilt; Zaputriaev and Shirin did so, but only in part. Korablev declared that the decrees of Ezhov and Uspenskii amounted to one thing: "Lock 'em up, lock 'em up." He interpreted these as orders of the Central Committee of the Communist Party: "I was convinced that I was executing serious party business, and had no hesitations . . . I am of the same mind now, that I am not guilty of conscious disgraces [*bezobraziia*] within the NKVD administration." The former chief denied the gravity of the accusation that thirty people had died in prison. In his view, this was a low number relative to the more than six thousand arrested. This criminal, for whom human life had no value, firmly declared: "I have worked in the organs in Vinnitsa for a long time, but nowhere and never have I been accused of violating socialist legality. I and many others are victims of the criminal activity of the former treasonous leadership." Along with Zaputriaev, Korablev called attention to his working-class background, even though he had born into a peasant family. This was supposed to confirm that they were not class enemies, but "*svoi* [one of their own]," persons loyal to the Communist Party who had countenanced miscalculations on account of inexperience and the conditions created by "treasonous leadership." Zaputriaev also attempted to project the appearance of a terminally ill person, while Shirin deflected blame to others.

The Tribunal sentenced Korablev and Zaputriaev to be shot and opted for a continuation of the case against Shirin. Orders were issued to carry out an investigation of their co-workers who had participated in the "violations."[54] On 24 June, the Military Collegium of the Supreme Court of the USSR examined the appeal (*kassatsionnaia zhaloba*) of Korablev and Zaputriaev, regarding their 6 May 1941 death sentences. The Supreme Court commuted their sentence to ten years of imprisonment with the forfeiture of their titles.[55] On 17 September 1941, the Senior Investigator of the Ukrainian republic NKVD, M. Gubenko, examined the case of Prishivtsyn, Shirin, Danileiko, Maistruk, and Butenko. He found that these individuals had been summoned before the court as witnesses, but in the course of the trial there "arose" mutually contradictory and unproven accusations from witnesses. In Gubenko's view, Prishivtsyn, as Deputy Chief of the Vinnitsa UNKVD, did not beat anyone, did not carry out mass arrests, and concerned himself solely with the conclusion of cases that had already been opened. Furthermore, the final authority regarding arrests was held by the head of the oblast NKVD administration and the Oblast Procurator.[56]

Another individual in this case, Butenko, who since being fired from the NKVD organs became a director of the Timber Agency in Vinnitsa, was accused of the groundless arrest of citizens based only on arrest lists. Subsequent to the decision of the court, however, he was not questioned in connection with the accusations against him, but only as a witness in Korablev's case. The investigator concluded on this basis that the actions of the accused did not lead to serious consequences, that the testimony of witnesses was incorrect or dubious, and that attempting to substantiate them was not possible. Taking all factors into account, the investigator ordered the case closed; the head of the Ukrainian republic NKVD Investigatory Group, Lesnoi, agreed.[57]

V. Maistruk continued his service as the Deputy Chair of the Voroshilovgrad UNKVD. The fate of Danileiko, fired from the NVKD in September 1939, is unknown. Shirin was freed on 17 September 1941 due to the failure to prove his crime. In 1942, he returned to work in the NKVD. From 12 August 1943, he was the head of the Chekist-operational sector of the Administration for Prisoners of War within the NKVD. From 9 May 1943, he was Lieutenant Colonel of State Security.[58] A significant number of employees within the Vinnitsa UNKVD who took part in the mass repressions of 1937 and 1938 were fired from the NKVD during the first half of 1939. That was the full extent of their punishment.

Crime without Punishment

Most of these executioners from the NKVD survived the 1941–1945 war between Germany and the USSR. In August 1942, Korablev was sent from camp imprisonment to the front and was captured in February 1943 before being liberated from a prisoner-of-war camp in May 1945. After 1954, he worked in the postal department of the Kuibyshev Oblast Executive Committee. Maistruk served in the NKVD administrations of Voroshilovgrad, Stalingrad, and Sverdlovsk Oblasts and, following the recapture of Ukraine by Soviet forces, in the Kharkov and Kiev Oblast NKVD administrations. He later fought against Ukrainian nationalists in Ternopol, Drogobych, Lvov, and Zhitomir Oblasts as chief of their oblast NKVD administrations. He received the title of Lieutenant and Honored Worker (*zasluzhennyi rabotnik*) of the NKVD of the USSR and several awards. He retired to Kiev from the security service in 1954, working there as the Chief of the First Department of the Ministry of Higher and Secondary Specialized Education of Ukraine until his death in 1976.[59] Prishivtsyn lived at the Tsiurupa Agricultural Institute in Kherson, where he worked as a mechanic until March 1957.[60]

In 1942, Butenko was serving as the chief of artillery supply for the 142nd Sapper Division on the Southern and Stalingrad Fronts. He was demobilized on account of his health. He then served from April 1943 to April 1950 in the Ministry of Internal Affairs, from which he was eventually furloughed due to a disability. He lived in retirement in Odessa and "took an active role in public work [obshchestvennaia rabota]." Between 1955 and 1957, he was the secretary of the party committee of the housing management [domokhoziaistva] of the Oblast KGB Administration and Administration of Internal Affairs (UVD).[61]

The first stage in the rehabilitation of those individuals who had fallen victim to repression commenced following the death of Stalin. On 14 March 1957, Assistant to the Military Prosecutor of the Transcarpathian Military District, Major of Justice Minkin, having examined the case of the Vinnitsa UNKVD employees Prishivtsyn, Shirin, Danileiko, Maistruk, and Butenko, found that the closing of their cases had not been justified. In his view, the materials of the Korablev case completely incriminated all of these men. He returned their cases to the Ukrainian KGB for further investigation on the basis of criminal article 54-7 (for counterrevolutionary crimes in the Ukrainian penal code). Furthermore, those individuals whose cases had been fabricated by the Vinnitsa UNKVD were rehabilitated in 1956.

During the renewed investigations, Prishivtsyn confirmed that the arrests of party workers in 1938 were sanctioned by the Ukrainian republic NKVD and the orders of Korablev. He did not deny his presence at the interrogation of one P. Iur'ev, but asserted that Iur'ev confessed without torture. He noted in particular the role of Maistruk as the most developed and literate worker, who led the Fourth Department of the Vinnitsa UNKVD after Shirin. For example, because Maistruk sent the case of the former secretary of the Vinnitsa City Party Committee, D. Lun'ko, to the troika before the decree of 17 November 1938, Privshivtsyn claimed that he was allowed in February 1939 to order the examination of the case by a military tribunal.[62]

On 27 March 1957, the Chief of Police for the Savransk District Police Department in Odessa Oblast, F. Reshetilo, presented a formal explanation to the Deputy Chief of the Administration of Internal Affairs (UVD) of the Odessa Oblast Executive Committee, Styrov.[63] Reshetilo was accused of illegal physical coercion against the former head of the personnel section of the Vinnitsa Oblast Executive Committee, P. Bondarenko, and the instructor of the Organizational Department of the Oblast Executive Committee, D. Solonenko, both allegedly recruits of a Right-Trotskyite Organization. Their 1938 arrests were processed by Maistruk without any basis. The case was led by Reshetilo, who was able to elicit their confessions. However, at the 8 September 1938 sitting of the Special Collegium of the Vinnitsa Oblast Court, the defendants renounced their confessions. They were sentenced to be shot in May 1940, but the Supreme Court of the USSR remanded the case for further investigation. On 21 March 1941, the case was closed. The former detainees testified that Reshetilo had beaten them, forcing them to confess.

On 14 August 1957, the Senior Plenipotentiary of the Internal Inspectorate of the Personnel Department of the UVD of the Odessa Oblast Executive Committee, Major Samgin, signed the indictment on the criminal activity of the former employees of the Vinnitsa UNKVD, Reshetilo and Butenko. The phrasing closely followed the formulas of the earlier accusations against them. Samgin proclaimed that Reshetilo and Butenko ought to be brought to the strictest justice on account of their crimes. However, he took into account that Butenko had not subsequently violated the law and took an active role in public life; further, Reshetilo was in the period 1937–1938 a young and inexperienced worker and is "at the present time ill and slated for dismissal [*predstavlen na uvol'nenie*]." On 16 August 1957, Butenko was dismissed from the Ministry of Internal Affairs on account of his health and classified as an invalid of the second group with rights to a pension.[64] On 4 January 1958, the Bureau of the Savransk District Party Committee examined the materials regarding Reshetilo and ultimately decided to limit the scope of its actions to his removal from his post as Chief of the District Police.[65] The Bureau of the Stalin District Party Committee of Odessa did not issue any party reprimand against Butenko.[66]

Meanwhile the Ministry of Internal Affairs of Ukraine prepared a new indictment regarding the case of Butenko, Prishivtsyn, and Reshetilo. It was suggested that Butenko's dismissal be recategorized for cause, as he had discredited his office within the structure of the Ministry of Internal Affairs, and that a petition to this effect should be initiated before the Ministry of Internal Affairs of the USSR. This possibility meant that the accused would be condemned by his former colleagues and would forfeit a portion of his pension. The same fate awaited Reshetilo, except he was allowed to keep his pension. As regarded Prishivtsyn, the reviewers limited themselves to the previously undertaken measures—dismissal from the organs on account of the impossibility of further employment.[67]

On 19 May 1958, the indictment was forwarded to the Ministry of Internal Affairs of the USSR and on 4 July 1958, the Deputy Minister of Internal Affairs of the USSR, K. Cherniaev failed to confirm the recommendations of the Republic-level Ministry. Cherniaev stated that these former security police operatives did much work "for the good of the motherland [*na blago rodiny*]." All charges against the NKVD perpetrators of 1937–1938 were dismissed.[68] Justice was not served.

Over the course of a relatively extended period, the NKVD sentenced hundreds of thousands of people to concentration camps and the death penalty. The Soviet everyday (*povsednevnost'*), at least during the 1930s, became entwined with mass murder; the "normal" became an absolutely anti-human "abnormal." The "purge of the purgers" at the end of the 1930s did not alter this basic fact.

While it is clear that the Great Terror came from above, it was enacted by a chain of command that began with Stalin and Ezhov and continued down the hierarchy to Uspenskii and his oblast NKVD chiefs. It was the latter, however, who specifically directed the course of the annihilation of hundreds of thousands of people. The heads of the oblast NKVD administrations and their subordinates, young and newly promoted to their positions, were to one degree or another loyal to the Communist Party, to Stalin and Ezhov, and ready to fulfill any assignment.

Members of the NKVD felt an acute sense of belonging within a special caste. They had special privileges and worked within a corporate culture all their own. This ésprit de corps reproduced itself over and over again as the Cheka evolved into the GPU/OGPU, then the NKVD, and finally the KGB.[69] Moreover, during the Great Terror, personal connections were extremely important. Uspenskii brought many of "his people" with him when he went to Ukraine. The connections among these Chekists fostered opportunities for these ambitious young men to build their careers. Their extreme cruelty was served by lawlessness, Soviet indoctrination, and a polarized worldview in which the "enemy" was removed from the ranks of human society.

The purge of the purgers had limited results. Notable is the fact that prior to the German-Soviet War, only individual "symbolic figures" who had conducted mass repressions were convicted and punished. They were all accused not only of the violation of socialist legality but also of connection with the previous, treasonous leadership of the NKVD organs. Some cadres were sent to Western Ukraine to fight against the OUN and UPA and were not subjected to punishment.[70] Others were arrested and served time in labor camps; very few were executed. Later, in the course of "destalinization" in the second half of the 1950s, when many of the victims of political repressions were rehabilitated, some NKVD operatives were again subject to investigation. Again, most avoided punishment. In the end, the fact that the Soviet security police served as a primary support for the Communist regime prevented any real coming to terms with the Great Terror.

Notes

1. *Vinnytsia: zlochyn bez kary. Dokumenty, svidchennia, materialy pro bol'shchevyts'ki rozstrily u Vinnytsi v 1937–1938 rokakh*, ed. Ievhen Sverstiuk (Kyiv: Voskresinnia, 1994), 95–97.
2. For an interesting analysis of these reports see John-Paul Himka, "Ethnicity and the Reporting of Mass Murder: Krakivs'ki visti, the NKVD Murders of 1941, and the Vinnytsia Exhumation," in *Shatterzone of Empires: Coexistence and Violence in the German, Habsburg, and Ottoman Borderlands*, ed. Omer Bartov and Eric D. Weitz (Bloomington: Indiana University Press, 2013), 378–98.
3. *Pravda* (12 Aug. 1943), 1.
4. P. M. Kravchenko, "Dokumenty pro areshty svidkiv rozkopok 1943 roku u Vinnyts'komu parku," *Politychni represii na Podilli v XX stolitti: Materialy mizhnarodnoï naukovo-praktychnoï konferentsii (Vinnytsia, 23–24 lystopada 2001 r.)* (Vinnytsia: Veles, 2002), 198.
5. US House of Representatives, Committee on Un-American Activities, "The Crimes of Khrushchev" (Washington, DC: U.S. Government Printing Office, 1959).
6. On the use of these new sources, see *Chervoni zhorna: spohady repressovanykh chleniv ïh rodyn, svidkiv represii*, ed. S. K. Hirenko (Vinnytsia: TOV "Vinnytsia," 1994); A. Malyhin, *Chervona akula: ezhovshchyna na Vinnychchyni: dokumental'no-publitsystychni narysy* (Vinnytsia: TOV "Vinnytsia," 1995); Iu. Shapoval, V. Prystaiko, and V. Zolotar'ov, *ChK-GPU-NKVD v Ukraïni: osoby, fakty, dokumenty* (Kyiv: Abrys, 1997); O. Loshyts'kyi, " 'Laboratoriia': Novi dokumenty i svidchennia pro masovi represii 1937–1938 rokiv na Vinnychchyni," *Z arkhiviv VUChK-GPU-NKVD-KGB*, tom 1–2 (1998), 183–227; O. Loshyts'kyi, "'Laboratoriia-2' Poltava: Dokumental'ni materialy pro masovi represii v Poltavs'kii oblasti u 1937–1938 rr.," *Z arkhiviv VUChK-GPU-NKVD-KGB*, tom 2–4 (2000), 129–78; V. Vasylyev, P. Kravchenko, and R. Podkur, *Politychni represii na Podilli (20–30-ti rr. XX st.)* (Vinnytsia: Logos, 1999); Roman Podkur, "'Dytiachyi GULAG' v konteksti polityky derzhavnoho teroru (1937–1939 rr.)," *Z arkhiviv VUChk-GPU-NKVD-KGB*, tom 1 (2007), 189–204; V. Vasylyev and R. Podkur, *Radians'ki karateli: Spivrobitnyky NKVS—vykonavtski*

"Velykoho teroru" na Podilli (Kyiv: NAN Ukraïny, 2017). These studies are freely available online at www.reabit.org.ua. Further, in the years since Ukrainian independence, five books on Vinnytsia Oblast have been published as part of the state's "Rehabilitated by History [*Reabilitovani istoriieiu*]" project: *Reabilitovani istoriieiu: Vinnyts'ka oblast'* 1–4 (Vinnytsia: DP "DKF," 2006–2012).

7. V. M. Nikol's'kyi, *Represyvna diial'nist' orhaniv derzhavnoï bezpeky SRSR v Ukraïni (kinets' 1920-kh–1950-ti rr.): Istoryko-statystychne doslidzhennia* (Donetsk: DonNU, 2003), 119.

8. Shapoval, Prystaiko, and Zolotar'ov, *ChK-GPU-NKVD v Ukraïni*, 173–74.

9. N. V. Petrov and K. V. Skorkin, eds., *Kto rukovodil NKVD, 1934–1941: Spravochnik* (Moscow: Zven'ia, 1999), 270.

10. V. Litvin, ed. *Politychnyi teror i teroryzm v Ukraïni XIX–XX st.: Istorychni narysy* (Kyiv: Naukova dumka, 2002), 476.

11. V. Zolotar'ov, *Oleksandr Uspens'kyi: osoba, chas, otochennia* (Kharkiv: Folio, 2004), 49.

12. RGASPI [Russian State Archive of Socio-Political History], f. 17, op. 162, d. 22, ll. 113–14. This decision became the basis of NKVD USSR decree 233 signed by Ezhov. See Shapoval, Prystaiko, and Zolotar'ov, *ChK-GPU-NKVD v Ukraïni*, 175–76.

13. RGASPI, f. 17, op. 162, d. 22, l. 127.

14. Taken from the interrogation of A. Volkov on 10 May 1939 in HDA SBU [State Archive of the Security Service of Ukraine], Poltava, spr. 19533, tom 1, ark. 65.

15. The Politburo of the Central Committee of the VKP(B) affirmed Korablev's appointment on 28 February 1938. See: RGASPI, f. 17, op. 3, d. 997, l. 7; and Petrov and Skorkin, eds., *Kto rukovodil NKVD*, 242–43.

16. M. A. Tumshis, *1937. Bol'shaia chistka. NKVD protiv ChK* (Moscow: Iauza Èksmo, 2009), 454–55. Korablev's letter was first published in Ukrainian in Zolotar'ov: *Oleksandr Uspens'kyi*, 102–5.

17. Petrov and Skorkin, eds., *Kto rukovodil NKVD*, 242–43.

18. RGASPI, f. 17, op. 162, d. 22, l. 161.

19. Loshyts'kyi, "'Laboratoriia,'" 215; P. P. Liubchenko—a former "Borot'bist" (i.e., a member of the Ukrainian Party of Socialist Revolutionaries) who served as Chairman of the Council of Ministers of the Ukrainian SSR from 1934 to 1937—committed suicide on 30 August 1937. V. A. Balitskii served as NKVD Ukraine Commissar from July 1934 to May 1937.

20. HDA SBU, f. 12, spr. 31025, ark. 18 zv.; S. Bohunov et al., eds., *Ukraïna v dobu "Velykoho teroru": 1936–1938 roky* (Kyiv: Lybid', 2009), 129.

21. HDA SBU, f. 12, spr. 31025, ark. 17. For a detailed treatment of Prishivtsyn's work at the helm of the Mariupol group see Zolotar'ov, *Oleksandr Uspens'kyi*, 107–8. Prishivtsyn's award citation is published in V. Zolotar'ov and V. P. Stepkin, *ChK-GPU-NKVD v Donbasse: Liudi i dokumenty, 1919–1941* (Donetsk: Aleks, 2010), 430–31.

22. HDA SBU, f. 12, spr. 31025 ark. 4–4 zv.

23. Bohunov et al., eds., *Ukraïna v dobu "Velykho terroru,"* 130.

24. HDA SBU, f. 12, spr. 31025, ark. 2.

25. HDA SBU, f. 5, spr. 66937, tom 1, ark. 105.

26. Zolotar'ov, *Oleksandr Uspens'kyi*, 295.

27. Loshyts'kyi, " 'Laboratoriia,' " 192–93.

28. Malyhin, *Chervona akula*, 25. The cited text is from a pronouncement of the Chief of the Investigatory Department of the Transportation Department of the NKVD of the Ukrainian SSR, Bogdanov, delivered at a gathering of the Zhmerinka active-investigatory group.

29. Loshyts'kyi, " 'Laboratoriia,' " 210.

30. RGASPI, f. 17, op. 162, d. 23, l. 32; d. 24, l. 2. The "album method" was used in the national operations and created on 11 August 1937. Lists of arrested individuals were sent from the provinces to Moscow for confirmation. The "special troika" was an extrajudicial body under the authority of the oblast NKVD administrations established on 17 September 1938 to pass judgment in the national operations following the elimination of the "album method."

31. A. Amons, "Diial'nist' pozasudovykh orhaniv na Vinnychchyni u period masovykh politychnykh represii 1937–1938 rr.," *Reabilitovani istoriïeiu: Vinnyts'ka oblast'*, 2:15–19. The high duumvirate was an extrajudicial body under NKVD USSR and the Procuracy of the USSR created on 11 August 1937 to deal with people arrested in the national operations and listed in the provincial "albums" sent to Moscow for confirmation by the leadership.

32. Petrov and Skorkin, eds., *Kto rukovodil NKVD*, 106–7.

33. Petrov and Skorkin, eds., *Kto rukovodil NKVD*, 106–7.

34. S. V. Mironenko and N. Werth, eds., *Istoriia stalinskogo GULAGa: konets 1920-kh-pervaia polovina 1950-kh godov*, 7 tom (Moscow: Rosspen, 2004–2005) 1:311.

35. Uspenskii spent half a year in hiding in Moscow, Arkhangelsk, Kaluga, and Murom. He was arrested in the city of Miass in Chelyabinsk Oblast in April 1939 and shot in January 1940. See Nikita Khrushchev, *Vremia. Liudi. Vlast': Vospominaniia* (Moscow: Moskovskie Novosti, 1999), 1:172–73; Petrov and Skorkin, eds., *Kto rukovodil NKVD*, 417; William Taubman, *Khrushchev: The Man and His Era* (New York: W. W. Norton, 2003), 123; Zolotar'ov, *Oleksandr Uspenskii*, 206–21.

36. Mironenko and Werth, eds., *Istoriia stalinskogo GULAGa*, 1:305–8.

37. HDA SBU, f. 5, spr. 66937, tom 9, ark. 165.

38. HDA SBU, f. 16, op. 31, spr. 39, ark. 51–52, 55–56, 58–59, 61–62.

39. Mironenko and Werth, eds., *Istoriia stalinskogo GULAGa*, 1:309–12.

40. HDA SBU, f. 5, spr. 66927, tom 5, ark. 219.

41. HDA SBU, f. 5, spr. 66927, tom 5, ark. 27–28.

42. HDA SBU, f. 5, spr. 66927, tom 8, ark. 179.

43. HDA SBU, f. 16, op. 31, spr. 39, ark. 114.

44. HDA SBU, f. 16, op. 31, spr. 39, ark. 188–89, 191–92, 194, 197–98, 202.

45. Petrov and Skorkin, eds., *Kto rukovodil NKVD*, 439.

46. HDA SBU, f. 5, spr. 66927, tom 25, ark. 4, 7–8, 11–13.

47. Loshyts'kyi, "'Laboratoriia,'" 221–22.

48. DAVO [State Archive of Vinnytsia Oblast], f. P-136, op. 1, spr. 367, ark. 23.

49. DAVO, f. P-136, op. 1, spr. 367, ark. 93.

50. HDA SBU, Ukraine, f. 5, spr. 66927, tom 24, ark. 1–3.

51. *Reabilitovani istoriieiu: Vinnyts'ka oblast*, tom 2, 316–17.

52. HDA SBU, f. 5, spr. 66937, tom 5, spr. 201, 203–4, 207–8, 224–25, 231, 234–35, 243–45, 252, 256.

53. HDA SBU, f. 5, spr. 66937, tom 1, ark. 58; tom 4, ark. 300–7; tom 5, ark. 103, 105, 109, 245.

54. These included former NKVD operatives F. Maistruk, G. P. Danileiko, A. Ia. Prishivtsyn, N. S. Butenko, D'iakov, and Babinko.

55. HDA SBU, f. 5, spr. 66937, tom 8, ark. 257.

56. HDA SBU, f. 12, spr. 207, ark. 36.

57. HDA SBU, f. 12, spr. 207, ark. 35–38.

58. Zolotar'ov and Stepkin, *ChK-GPU-NKVD v Donbasse*, 344–45.

59. Petrov and Skorkin, eds., *Kto rukovodil NKVD 1941–1954*. On V. Maistruk, see Roman Podkur, "'Nasha partiia ie derzhavnoiu partiieiu, partiia, shcho keruie derzhavoiu . . .': vykonavets' rishen' Kompartiï polkovnyk derzhbezpeky V. Maistruk," *Z arkhiviv VUChK-GPU-NKVD-KGB*, tom 1 (2018), 5–71.

60. HDA SBU, f. 12, spr. 207, ark. 53–54.

61. HDA SBU, f. 12, spr. 207, ark. 47–54.

62. HDA SBU, f. 12 spr. 207, ark. 162–64.

63. HDA SBU, f. 12, spr. 207, ark. 47–54.

64. HDA SBU, f. 12, spr. 207, ark. 47–54.

65. HDA SBU, f. 12, spr. 207, ark. 47–54.

66. HDA SBU, f. 12, spr. 207, ark. 471.

67. HDA SBU, f. 12, spr. 207, ark. 503–4.

68. HDA SBU, f. 12, spr. 207, ark. 510.

69. A. G. Tepliakov, *Mashina terrora: OGPU-NKVD Sibiri v 1929–1949 gg.* (Moscow: Novyi Khronograf, 2008), 600.

70. OUN was the Organization of Ukrainian Nationalists, and UPA was the Ukrainian Insurgent Army.

"The Party Makes Mistakes, the NKVD—Never"

THE NKVD IN ODESSA

Andrei Savin and Aleksei Tepliakov
Translated by Simon Belokowsky

IN THE LATE autumn of 1938, the new People's Commissar of Internal Affairs of the USSR, Lavrentii Beria, began a far-reaching purge of the NKVD for "violations of socialist legality." In 1939, 7,372 people were dismissed from the NKVD, which amounted to nearly a quarter (22.9%) of all operative workers. Among these, 973 were arrested. If those who were arrested in the last months of 1938 (also under the auspices of Beria's purge) are included, the arrest figures grow to 1,364 people.[1] Those destined for the defendant's bench were mainly leaders of the state security organs—the chiefs of krai and oblast administrations, operative departments, and sections.[2] Russian historian Nikita Petrov has characterized this purge as the "first complete cadre revolution in the organs of state security aimed at the radical remaking of its personnel."[3]

This chapter focuses on the purge of Chekist cadres immediately after the cessation of the NKVD mass operations, with an emphasis on the role that Beria's purge played within the interrelationships among the Communist Party, the state security police, and state authorities and society as a whole. It is based on materials from the personnel and criminal case files of Odessa Oblast UNKVD workers arrested over the course of 1939 to 1941 as well as the documents of the judicial proceedings against them.

Andrei Savin and Aleksei Tepliakov, *"The Party Makes Mistakes, the NKVD—Never"* In: *Laboratories of Terror.*
Edited by: Lynne Viola and Marc Junge, Oxford University Press. © Oxford University Press 2023.
DOI: 10.1093/oso/9780197647547.003.0003

Odessa and Odessa Oblast: Regional Specifics in the Context of Mass Repression

Regional distinctions in the conduct of mass operations by the NKVD over 1937 and 1938 were based on both underlying geographical and administrative factors particular to Soviet regions and the presence of various social and ethnic groups subject to punitive action by the organs of the security police. Repression was more intense in industrial regions than in agricultural ones, as well as in border areas and in cities with important military-industrial factories. The intensity of repression also depended upon the presence of so-called special contingents (exiles in this case) and non-Russian ethnic groups, who supposedly played the role of a potential "fifth column." When these factors were combined, arrests skyrocketed, as was the case in the city of Odessa and Odessa Oblast.[4]

The total number of victims convicted in 1937 and 1938 in the course of NKVD operation 00447 in Odessa Oblast was 13,054 people, of whom 7,044 were sentenced to death.[5] In 1938, the mass operations were extended; while operation 00447 was gradually reined in, the so-called national operations expanded dramatically. Altogether, Odessa Chekists arrested 7,192 people between 1 January and 1 August 1938. The total number of those sent to the camps and executed in Odessa Oblast in both operation 00447 and the national operations comprised no fewer than 20,000 people.

As was the case throughout the Soviet Union, the primary victims of the NKVD in Odessa Oblast were ordinary people. Nonetheless, the number of victims among Communists was also high. In a report presented to NKVD USSR on 7 January 1938, the head of the Odessa Oblast UNKVD, N. N. Fedorov, wrote that 562 members of the "right-Trotskyist underground" within the Communist Party had been arrested from June to December 1937, including the secretary of the Oblast Party Committee, E. I. Veger.[6] The assault on the Odessa Party organization continued in 1938. From 1 January to 1 August, the Odessa Oblast UNKVD arrested 213 Trotskyites and rightists, 27 participants of a supposed military fascist conspiracy, 44 Mensheviks, 15 members of the Bund, 96 Socialist Revolutionaries (SRs), 29 anarchists, and 119 Zionists.[7] The vast majority of these 543 persons were Communist Party members at the time of their arrest. Those who survived and were released from prison in 1939 subsequently played an important role in the campaign for the "restoration" of "socialist legality."

The Odessa Oblast UNKVD during the Great Terror

Experienced, long-serving workers predominated in the Odessa Oblast UNKVD leadership. At the outset of the Great Terror, the Odessa UNKVD was composed largely of those installed by the long-tenured head of the OGPU-NKVD in Ukraine, V. A. Balitskii. During the Great Terror, the Odessa Oblast UNKVD was managed by an entire procession of experienced Chekists who replaced one another in rapid succession. This personnel turnover was connected with the mass purges taking place within the administrative apparatus of the Ukrainian republic NKVD following the arrests, after roughly equal intervals, of the Republic's Commissars of Internal Affairs, V. A. Balitskii in July 1937 and I. M. Leplevskii in April 1938, and the flight of A. I. Uspenskii in November 1938.[8] In the eighteen months beginning in summer 1937, the following people served as chiefs of the Odessa Oblast UNKVD: A. B. Rozanov, G. A. Grishin-Klivgant (acting), N. N. Fedorov, D. D. Grechukhin, P. P. Kiselev, and S. I. Gaponov (acting).

From July 1937 to February 1938, the Odessa Oblast UNKVD was headed by the former Chief of the Border Detachment in Leningrad Oblast, Lieutenant, then Colonel, N. N Fedorov. Fedorov turned out to be such an energetic perpetrator of terror that, upon the arrival of Uspenskii, he was transferred from Odessa to lead the Kiev UNKVD and was soon engaged by Ezhov to work in the central apparatus of the NKVD, where, on 20 November 1938, he was arrested and in February 1940 executed.[9] The experienced Chekist D. D. Grechukhin, a former colleague of Uspenskii's in Siberia, replaced Fedorov in Odessa when the latter went to Kiev. By accelerating the terror, Grechukhin earned the favor of Uspenskii. In May 1938, he was promoted to deputy chair of the Ukrainian republic NKVD. P. P. Kiselev, a typical *vydizhenets* of the time and the former head of the Department of Operative Technology at the republic NKVD, took his place. From 28 May 1938, he headed the Odessa UNKVD and proved himself among the more productive perpetrators of terror. On 15 November 1938, immediately after Uspenskii's flight, Kiselev was arrested and, shortly thereafter, executed. From November 1938 to January 1939, S. I. Gaponov headed the UNKVD. Among all the leaders of the Odessa Oblast UNKVD during the Great Terror, only Gaponov would avoid execution and live to see freedom.

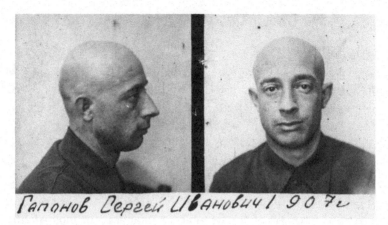

Гапонов Сергей Ивановичꞏ / 9 0 7ꞏ

FIG. 2.1 S. I. Gaponov, from November 1938 to January 1939 head of the Odessa Oblast NKVD. Prison photo from 1941, HDA SBU, f. 5, spr. 67987, tom 5, ark. 5. By exclusive permission of the State Archive of the Security Services of Ukraine.

The Campaign to Restore "Socialist Legality" in Odessa Oblast

A key question in understanding the Beria purge is why certain NKVD workers were chosen for punishment in the campaign against "violations of socialist legality." Some had drawn the negative attention of leaders and procurators by violating direct orders from Moscow—for example, substantially exceeding arrest quotas or continuing to mete out death sentences sanctioned by troikas even after this was categorically prohibited by the center. Others distinguished themselves among their peers in "applying measures of physical influence" (torture) to the point of killing those under investigation. Yet the main share of convicted NKVD workers found themselves under prosecution as a result of complaints from victims who survived and were freed after the 17 November 1938 directive halting the mass operations.

Very few of these survivor-witnesses were the victims of the mass operations. Victims of the "kulak" and "national" operations and their relatives knew little about the investigations pertaining to their cases and the indictments promulgated against them. If those who avoided execution and were sent to the camps dared to complain, their complaints, as a rule, went unanswered. Moreover, Chief Procurator of the USSR Andrei Vyshinskii decreed on 17 April 1938 that procurators should reassess convictions in the mass operations only "in exceptional cases." As such, the typical response to petitioners was that decisions were final and cases were not subject to re-examination.[10]

Consequently, there remained only one small group of victims of the Great Terror who wielded sufficient status, connections, and clout to protest their convictions. As a rule, they had spent some months in detention and were well versed in the nuances of investigation. The mass releases at the end of 1938 and in 1939 allowed them to seek justice against the Chekists who had tormented them. They were primarily members of the Communist Party representing the Soviet political elite. It was precisely their complaints and their quest for rehabilitation in the party that dictated the circle of Chekists subject to prosecution in Beria's purge of the NKVD. While these Chekists certainly employed the notorious "measures of physical influence," the practice of torture was not the main criterion for selecting NKVD "scapegoats" since the entire state security apparatus had practiced torture in some measure during the Great Terror.

According to the internal statistics of the NKVD, as of 17 November 1938, the organs of the Ukrainian republic NKVD had open cases against 15,143 detained suspects. Additionally, in accordance with the 26 November 1938 NKVD USSR Decree 00762 regulating the course of the implementation of the 17 November 1938 directive of the Council of People's Commissars and the Central Committee of the Communist Party, cases for another 10,808 persons that had been transferred for sentencing to the troikas and Special Council (*Osoboe soveshchanie*) of the NKVD USSR were returned for further investigation. Thus, the Chekists were faced with the need to close out the investigations of nearly 26,000 people.[11] At the end of the 1938–1939 period, nearly 20 percent and even up to 30 percent of these victims in Ukraine were released, spared by the 17 November 1938 resolution. A significant portion of those freed were former members of the Communist Party.

We were able to examine the materials of three criminal case files for eight members of the Odessa Oblast UNKVD convicted of "violating socialist legality." These cases included two chiefs of the Secret Political Department (SPO) of the Oblast UNKVD—V. F. Kaliuzhnyi and Gaponov—as well as six of their subordinates (D. B. Kordun, E. A. Abramovich, Ia. I. Berenzon, N. M. Tiagin, V. A. Mashkovskii, and A. E. Gnesin). Individual cases were opened against Kaliuzhnyi and Tiagin, while Kordun, Abramovich, Berenzon, Mashkovskii, and Gnesin were classified as defendants under the Gaponov case. Aside from the case files, we were also able to examine the personnel files of Mashkovskii and Gnesin. These eight people were far from the only members of the Odessa Oblast UNKVD convicted and/or expelled from the NKVD in the course of Beria's purge, but their cases are a representative source base for the study of the campaign to discipline the NKVD, given

FIG. 2.2 V. F. Kaliuzhnyi, in 1938 chief of the Secret Political Department of
the Odessa Oblast NKVD. Prison photo from 1939, HDA SBU, f. 5, spr. 38580,
tom 1, ark. 22a. By exclusive permission of the State Archive of the Security
Services of Ukraine.

that the SPO was one of the most important operative departments in the
state security organs.

Of those Chekists who participated in the repression of party members
and found themselves in the defendant's chair, four out of these eight Odessa
Chekists (Kordun, Abramovich, Berenzon, and Gnesin) were workers from
the First Section of the SPO. Their duties included the operative "servicing" of
individuals connected with the Communist Party. Seeming exceptions were
Junior Lieutenant Mashkovskii, assistant to the chief of the Sixth ("Church
[*tserkovnyi*]") Section of the SPO, and Tiagin, the chief of the Second Section
of the SPO, whose section was tasked primarily with the fight against SRs,
Mensheviks, anarchists, members of the Bund, and Zionists.

Mashkovskii and Tiagin: Random Selections or a Conscious Targeting of Scapegoats?

Why, then, did Mashkovskii and Tiagin find themselves in the company of
their colleagues from the First ("Party") Section of the SPO? Mashkovskii
"managed the section on clergy" (*otdelenie po tserkovnikam*). From 1 January
1938, he independently led investigations into 138 people; by October this

figure had reached 180, all of whom were convicted.[12] Tiagin, a worker in the security organs from 1923, was by 1937 "leading work on fighting the German counterrevolution and managing the work of peripheral organs along this line of investigation." Under the direct leadership of Tiagin, 545 people were arrested, all of whom were convicted by the troika, and 374 of them were sentenced to death.[13] In 1938, serving as the chief of the Second Section of SPO, Tiagin, it was said, "personally uncovered underground counterrevolutionary committees of Zionist spies, Menshevik terrorist spies, and Dashnak terrorist spies." Seventy-one "Zionists" were convicted, 21 "Mensheviks," and 34 "Dashnaks." Aside from this, an "anarchist organization was uncovered and liquidated" per Tiagin's efforts, consisting of 13 persons, all of whom were convicted.[14]

Had Mashkovskii and Tiagin's activity over 1937 and 1938 been limited solely to clergy, sectarians, German counterrevolutionaries, Dashnaks, and anarchists, then it is likely that they would have escaped Beria's purge and continued their careers in the organs of state security. To their misfortune, those they had persecuted included former Communists who would be released in 1939.

Mashkovskii was drawn into interrogations in the so-called KPK case in which highly placed Communists—members of the Party Control Commission (KPK) of the Central Committee of the Odessa Oblast Communist Party—were arrested and convicted. The reasons Tiagin ended up in the defendant's chair are less straightforward. Tiagin was arrested on 19 April 1939 on the basis of accusations that he had exposed NKVD methods and fabricated cases. Aside from this, Tiagin personally conducted and completed an investigation into a supposed "counterrevolutionary Trotskyist-terrorist group of seven people existing within the oblast UNKVD." This label cloaked repression targeted specifically at Jewish Chekists, overrepresented at that time in the Ukrainian NKVD.[15]

Nevertheless, Tiagin did engage with members of the Communist Party and state in repressive campaigns. In 1938, there was a shift in the epicenter of repression in Ukraine away from punitive actions targeting kulaks and criminals and toward "other antisoviet elements" including members of antisoviet political parties, mainly moribund (e.g., SRs, Mensheviks, anarchists, Zionists, and the Bund). The arrests of members of these groups in June and July 1938 merged with the waves of repression against Odessa Communists. Some of those prosecuted in these fabricated cases were freed in 1939. They proceeded to bring accusations against Odessa Oblast UNKVD workers, including Tiagin.[16] Thus, Mashkovskii and Tiagin found themselves under judicial scrutiny as former representatives of the Soviet and Communist Party elite leveled charges of violations of socialist legality against them.

Chekists under Fire: The KPK Case

The KPK case would play a large role in the fate of the Odessa Chekists. State security workers began to fabricate this case after the late January 1938 visit to the oblast UNKVD of G. I. Samarin, the Secretary of the oblast KPK (Party Control Commission). He demanded a report from UNKVD party organizer and chief of the SPO, V. F. Kaliuzhnyi.[17] Since the end of 1937, according to Samarin, the oblast KPK had been receiving "signals" regarding crude violations of "revolutionary legality" by Chekists.

The reaction of Chekists against this potential threat was lightning fast and deadly. On 4 February 1938, Berenzon began a covert case (labeled "Untouchables") against Samarin, after which Kaliuzhnyi received permission from the Chief of the UNKVD, Fedorov, to arrest Samarin and a series of KPK plenipotentiaries. Aside from Samarin, D. M. Kanfer-Berkovich, G. A. Aleksandrov, A. M. Agranskii, V. F. Sorokovik, A. A. Ivanov, and F. F. Vasiurenko were also arrested as part of this case. The arrests of the KPK workers were conducted over the month of February 1938, subsequent to which "no KPK worker was even permitted into the Obl[ast] UNKVD, motivated by the notion that there was a preponderance of enemies of the people in the KPK."[18] After a lengthy investigation, all these individuals were convicted by the Military Collegium of the Supreme Court of the USSR as members of a Trotskyite group. Samarin was sentenced to be shot on 23 September 1938; the same fate awaited Aleksandrov, Agranskii, Kanfer-Berkovich, and Sorokovik on 10 October 1938. Ivanov and Vasiurenko were sentenced to fifteen years in the camps.

Had the KPK case been limited to the arrest and conviction of these individuals, it is likely that the Chekists would not have had to subsequently answer for their actions in court. On 29 May 1938, however, one more KPK investigator was arrested, S. Ia. Shpak. Shpak withstood a fourteen-month-long investigation. He was released from prison in September 1939 and began immediately to attack the "gang of enemies, which, using 'Gestapo' tactics, fabricates 'phony' counterrevolutionary organizations and turns faithful Communists into 'enemies.'"[19]

Shpak became a true nightmare for the Chekists and a revelation for the investigation into the former Chief of the SPO of the Odessa Oblast UNKVD that was at that moment already underway. A capable witness, Shpak had the ability during his time in detention to communicate with nearly all of the arrested party functionaries. Following his release from prison, he used his party connections to seek if not the conviction then at least the ouster and expulsion from the party of the more odious UNKVD workers. His sharp criticism was limited to the "rotten" falsifiers in the NKVD and did not touch on the broader system of power. He raised no doubts as to the necessity of repression in general against enemies of Soviet power.

Shpak was far from alone. By November 1938, the First Section of the SPO of the Odessa Oblast UNKVD had several fabricated cases in process against a series of Odessa party functionaries in which investigations had not yet been completed. The accused in these cases were ultimately released at the end of the 1938–1939 period and came forward with allegations against the NKVD. The cases involved workers from the Financial Department of the oblast government administration including its former chief, I. F. Senkevich;[20] the workers of the newspapers *Black Sea Commune* and *Bolshevik Banner* including the former head of the *Black Sea Commune* Department of Culture, M. S. Eidel'man;[21] the former head of the Kolkhoz Organizational Sector (*orgkolkhoznyi sector*) of the Odessa Oblast Land Department, M. B. Barger;[22] the former Chair of the Odessa City Council and Deputy of the Supreme Soviet of the USSR, I. F. Iakubits;[23] the former instructor of the Odessa Oblast Committee of the Ukrainian Communist Party, A. A. Kitsenko; the former deputy head of Odessa Oblast Welfare (Sobes), Ia. D. Brant;[24] the director of the pedagogical institute, A. O. Lunenok;[25] and many other Communists of middling and higher ranks within the oblast. In their letters, statements, and testimony, these Communists delivered to investigators a mass of detailed accounts regarding the "violation of socialist legality" by NKVD workers.

The victims under investigation in Odessa were subjected to practically the entire arsenal of investigatory methods used during the mass operations: hours-long "standings" (*vystoiki*) and "sittings" (*vysidki*), "conveyor-belt" (*konveiernye*) interrogations, beatings, and vulgar insults (*maternye rugani*). Interrogators spat in their faces, screamed in their ears, put out cigarettes on them, deprived them of food and water, threatened their relatives, staged mock executions, and used the false testimony of "pro forma witnesses" (*shtatnye sviditeli*), including those gathered from secret agents and informers.

Even more important, these newly freed party members' testimonies portrayed UNKVD workers as having lost all perspective on their proper place (*o svoëm real'nom meste*) in the hierarchy of Communist power, convinced of their infallibility and imagining themselves as standing above the formal trappings of legality and the party itself. They charged these workers with seeking to discredit and "crush" the party by putting themselves—without any oversight—above the ruling system. The former suspect N. A. Mosalev testified regarding the investigator Berenzon: "At my references to the decision of the February-March Plenum of the Central Committee of the CPSU, Berenzon responded, 'wipe your ass with it [*podotris*].' "[26] Investigator Abramovich, in answer to detainee Teplitskii's request for a meeting with the procurator, gestured to his genitals, stating, "here is your procurator."[27] Barger was repeatedly told by his investigator, "Why are you sitting like a putz, this ain't the Oblast Committee for you," "the NKVD is not a charity."[28] Meanwhile, Senkevich declared that when Abramovich spoke of the party he never pronounced the word "secretary" (*sekretar'*) as anything other than "shitretery" (*srakatar'*).[29]

This "verbal" (*slovesnyi*) arsenal reflected a perception by Chekists of a new stasis having come together as a result of the Great Terror and, likewise, their new place in the system of power. Consequently, the Chekists reacted negatively to efforts by the party to re-establish the traditional order. One of the "honest" workers of the Odessa Oblast UNKVD, operative plenipoten-tiary P. S. Kononchuk, colorfully described in his 17 October 1939 statement the reaction of one worker from the SPO's First Section to the measures taken by the Odessa Oblast Communist Party Committee toward strengthening oversight over "the organs":

> Once, in [N. I.] Burkin's office, Berenzon declared in regard to the Oblast Committee and KPK that "They've trained all sorts of shit to come here and demand files." . . . Displeased at discussions held with him in the personnel department during his appointment and confir-mation as chief of the district department of the NKVD . . . Berenzon stated, "What are they, my mother, to talk to me like that? . . . You're beating detainees . . . who gave them the right, they know me, I have served through two Oblast Committees, it is not correct to speak to me like that."[30]

The disruption in the balance of power between the NKVD and the Communist Party was also manifested in such a sensitive issue as the collec-tion of compromising materials against party functionaries for the purpose of recruiting future secret agents. Irrespective of the 26 December 1938 decree of the NKVD USSR "On the prohibition of the recruitment [of secret agents] from several categories of workers in party, soviet, economic, professional, and public organizations," Odessa Chekists continued to investigate members of the party-state elite. P. S. Kononchuk stated in his handwritten testimony of 20 December 1939 that "Abramovich and Berenzon spoke out in displeasure against the decree of the People's Commissar forbidding the placing of covert operatives in party organizations."[31] However, it was not only rank-and-file NKVD workers who had no plans of renouncing their usual methods of work. Gaponov confessed in February 1940 that he had evidence regarding the moral corruption (*moral'no-bytovoe razlozhenie*) of the new Chief of the UNKVD, A. I. Starovoit, during his time as instructor of the Oblast Party Committee and Secretary of the Andre-Ivanovsk District Party Committee.[32]

Newly released representatives of the party-state elite played a major role in the judicial proceedings against Chekists. It is practically impossible to imagine repressed priests or "nationalists" convicted by troikas—whose fate did not worry Communists—in their place as witnesses. Such a weighty role for freed party members in Beria's purge of the NKVD organs was no accident. While casting no doubt on the main goals of the mass operations, these party members were able to sound the alarm to the center regarding the thoroughly disturbed balance in the hierarchy of power and the necessity of a campaign to establish discipline at all levels of the organs of state security. It was precisely these individuals who personified the "restored" Soviet order and triumph of legality.

Defense Tactics of Free Chekists

During the campaign to restore socialist legality, NKVD personnel developed and put into practice four main defensive tactics. The first tactic was to elicit as many confessions as possible from among suspects and those whose cases had been returned for further investigation. Second, Chekists could attempt to tarnish and discredit those who had already been released in order to minimize the damage of potential accusations. The third tactic sought to block the efforts of the procurators. The final tactic was to become a leader in the campaign to restore order, facilitating the release of victims of repression and likewise exposing the more odious individuals among their colleagues. Odessa Chekists employed all these tactics to varying degrees.

As prisoners became increasingly aware of the "shifting winds" at the summit of Soviet political power in November 1938, those under investigation began to renounce their confessions en masse, stating to procurators and courts that they had confessed and named their "accomplices" while under psychological and physical torture by the NKVD. These accusations led many

Chekists to move as many cases forward as quickly as possible, hoping to prove that they were in the right. As a result, it is plausible that the pressures against suspects, physical ones included, not only did not diminish after 17 November 1938, but may even have increased.

There is a massive amount of evidence supporting this supposition within the criminal case files. The director of the Lunacharsky Sovkhoz (State Farm), Suslov, reported in his 27 November 1939 statement to the Secretary of the Odessa Oblast Party Committee, A. G. Kolybanov, that on 16 January 1939 the deputy chief of the UNKVD, Gaponov, "categorically" demanded from him confirmation of the interrogation transcripts he had signed in 1938. After Suslov's refusal, Gaponov personally beat the suspect to the point of unconsciousness. Thirty minutes after being awakened with cold water, he was beaten by section chief Abramovich and then by both Abramovich and Berenzon.[33] Three days earlier, on 13 January 1939, Gaponov had cruelly beaten the former chief of the Oblast Financial Department I. F. Senkevich.[34] Senkevich, for his part, testified on 27 April 1940 that "approximately until May 1939 within the walls of the [NKVD] Oblast Administration [one could hear] constant screaming [of those being beaten] everywhere."[35]

Yet as the waves of the released grew, the workers of the SPO invented yet another defensive mechanism. Konochuk described it as follows: "Berenzon and Abramovich, upon the release of a suspect from detention . . . [and] in order to avert the writing of complaints or statements against them [would say]: 'as far as how you were dealt with, there were orders for it from the Central Committee.'"[36] A sense of impunity, a maniacal confidence in their infallibility, a feeling of corporate solidarity, and a fear of potential punishment resulted in NKVD workers' acting in concert to block any outside attempts to denigrate them.

Further, it is important to note that the NKVD was suspicious of procurators, regarding them as weak representatives of the "formal" trappings of legality. It was dangerous for procurators to oppose Chekists even in the context of the campaign to restore socialist legality. For example, the assistant military procurator of the 434th Military Procuracy, regimental commissioner Ia. T. Novikov, who led the questioning of suspects of the Odessa Oblast UNKVD in late 1938 and early 1939, played a role in the release of Shpak. Novikov had participated in Shpak's interrogation.[37] The latter, upon realizing that a procurator was before him, gave him a statement of complaint against illegal methods of investigation. Novikov was receptive and heard out this complaint.[38] In order to neutralize the officious procurator, the SPO workers went so far as deciding, in May 1939, to open a dossier on him, which signified a covert investigation of the procurator with the prospect of arrest.[39] In court, in 1943, however, Gaponov stubbornly denied that his subordinates had done this.

The aggressive defensive tactics to which these state security workers resorted at the end of the 1938–1939 period resulted from the severe imbalance caused by the transfer of power from the party-state to the organs of the NKVD in the course of the Great Terror. At the same time, the suspicious and malicious attitude toward procurators was largely a direct consequence of NKVD workers' having lost their fear of and respect for the party.

Defense Tactics of Chekists under Investigation and Prosecution

The campaign to restore socialist legality unfolded with the arrest and conviction of only two of the eight subjects of this chapter. On 19 April 1939, Kaliuzhnyi was arrested. By that time, he had become acting chief of the Ninth Department of the Ukrainian republic NKVD. He was charged with conducting groundless arrests, fabricating nonexistent counterrevolutionary organizations, and providing his own targets quotas for arrests to subordinates. The Military Tribunal for Kiev Military District Troops, held from 23 to 26 December 1940 in the building of the Odessa Oblast UNKVD, sentenced Kaliuzhnyi to death, though his sentence was later commuted to ten years in the camps.[40] Tiagin, as Kaliuzhnyi's closest confidant, was arrested on the same day as Kaliuzhnyi on charges of exposing NKVD methods, fabricating counterrevolutionary organizations, and falsifying investigatory materials. On 25 August 1939, he was convicted by the Military Tribunal for Odessa NKVD Troops under statute 206-17 (a) of the criminal code of Ukraine and sentenced to seven years' confinement in the camps without forfeiture of his rights.[41]

For the remaining six "perpetrators of excesses" (*peregibshchiki*), the situation was at first not entirely bad. They were all forced out of the Odessa UNKVD, but they remained free; moreover, most continued their service. Gnesin successfully passed through two special reviews in August 1938 and February 1939. Only on 4 April 1940 was he dismissed from the NKVD, by a resolution of the Bureau of the Odessa Oblast Party Committee citing his "use of perverse methods of conducting investigations against subsequently rehabilitated detainees and falsification of cases under investigation."[42] By a 17 December 1940 decision of the Bureau of the Odessa Oblast Party

Committee, Gnesin was likewise expelled from candidacy for party membership. The main role in Gnesin's dismissal from the NKVD was played by an Odessa Oblast Party member, Laiok, who, in Gnesin's phrasing, spent a whole year essentially "hunting" him after receiving complaints from party members.[43]

Gaponov was dismissed from the NKVD by a 19 April 1939 order of the Deputy People's Commissar of Internal Affairs of Ukraine, A. Z. Kobulov.[44] Following his dismissal, Gaponov worked as the chief of a telephone station in Odessa. Remaining in Odessa proved to be a tactical error on his part. On 24 July 1940, the Bureau of the Stalin District Party Committee expelled him from the Communist Party; meanwhile, the leading figure in the complaints against him was, again, Shpak.[45]

While Gaponov was expelled from the party, Abramovich, having been sent to serve in the Gulag system in the Far East, was conversely accepted into the party in 1940. In the second half of 1939 and the beginning of 1940, he had already risen to work as a section chief in the Third Department of the Amur Labor Camp for the Far Eastern Krai. From May 1940, he worked as the chief of the Second Section of the State Security Administration (UGB) of the Jewish Autonomous Oblast UNKVD. Kordun remained in the Odessa Oblast UNKVD until November 1938, after which, in December, he was appointed to the position of a sector chief of the Iagrin labor camp; from 1 March 1940 to January 1941, he worked as the chief of a brick factory for NKVD construction project No. 203 located in the Archangelsk Oblast city of Molotov (Severodvinsk). Berenzon was dismissed from the NKVD in July 1939, but the following year became the political director of the 15th Auto-Transport Battalion based at the time in Stanislav (Ivano Frankivsk). Mashkovskii was relieved of his duties on 2 July 1939 on account of "the impossibility of further employment in the organs of the NKVD," possibly because he was Polish.

In the summer of 1940, there was a sharp turn in the fate of the former workers of the SPO in the Odessa Oblast UNKVD. Per a 7 June 1940 resolution from the assistant military procurator, Barinov, of the Kiev Special NKVD Military District, the case regarding Gaponov and his subordinates was split off from the Kaliuzhnyi case.[46]

The new investigation developed slowly, however. In December 1940, Deputy People's Commissar of Internal Affairs of the USSR I. A. Serov agreed with the opinion of NKVD investigators that Gaponov did not have any part in the KPK case and thus it was sufficient to leave the matter with his dismissal from the NKVD.[47] Yet the implacability of the procurators overcame the opinion of Beria's deputy. Consequently, Gaponov was arrested on 16 January 1941 in Taganrog; Gnesin on 25 January 1941 in Odessa; Kordun on 28 January 1941 in Molotovsk; Abramovich on 5 February 1941 in Birobidzhan; and Berenzon on 3 March 1941 in Stanislav. Mashkovskii was also arrested at some point in early 1941. The looming war added its own correctives in the subsequent unfolding of events. All the suspects were convoyed to Siberia, to Prison No. 3 in Tomsk where, with the exception of Gaponov, they remained until March 1943, at which point they were transferred to Prison No. 1 in Novosibirsk in anticipation of their trial, which would be held in April 1943.

The materials of the judicial inquests regarding Kaliuzhnyi and Tiagin are less reflective of the campaign for the restoration of "socialist legality" than those against Gaponov and his "Gaponovites." First, Kaliuzhnyi was considered during the proceedings to be a protégé of Grechukhin and Uspenskii who, for their part, had given testimony against him as having participated in a conspiracy against the NKVD, as opposed to the accusation of "violations of socialist legality" that more often featured in the Beria purge. Second, in these cases "internal" NKVD documents figured more prominently than witness testimony from Communists.

Finding themselves under investigation and then prosecution, the Odessa Chekists employed three defensive tactics. The first was the denial of personal culpability, ascribing all guilt to superiors, peers, and also (relatively rarely) local party organs. This was a natural response, as these Chekists found themselves in a situation where they were faced with the task of answering for having executed official orders coming directly from Moscow and Kiev. Thus, Kaliuzhnyi, for example, was accused of "establishing target quotas for the arrest of citizens." Repression quotas, a key element of the mass operations, mutated unexpectedly into the personal criminal initiatives of individual provincial NKVD leaders.

In transferring guilt onto higher leadership, the suspects all sketched a largely accurate picture of the harsh pressures exerted on practically all levels of the state security apparatus during the mass operations. Here, the youngest and least experienced had a certain kind of advantage before the court. Gnesin, who at age twenty-one had been mobilized into the security organs in March 1938 by a decision of the Odessa Oblast Committee of the Komsomol, described in a petition to Khrushchev the course of his "socialization" in the ranks of the NKVD. He said that he had not learned anything but vulgarity and beatings.[48]

The Chekists preferred not to speak about the role of the leadership of the Communist Party so as to not put themselves in danger. However, they occasionally "slipped up [*progovarivalis'*]," demonstrating that they understood perfectly who sanctioned and oversaw mass repressions. Gaponov, for example, stated at the beginning of 1940, "Was it not the [Party] Oblast Committee personified in its secretary, Teleshev, that held the city in the grip of fear and horror; was it not he who slandered Chernits, Shpak, and Berger, who sanctioned the arrests of Communists including in the KPK and 'Black Earth Commune' [cases], who but him?"[49]

The second defensive tactic used by these Chekists involved contesting the accusations against them by denying and minimizing the crimes they had committed. One part of this strategy was the effort to discredit witnesses among released suspects; another part was to represent themselves as champions of the fight against "fraud [*lipachi*]" in their own ranks. Thus, Gnesin admitted that he conducted "lengthy interrogations of detainees [for up to] 15 to 20 hours" and acknowledged "insulting and using vulgarities against detainees," but no more. Supposedly, he beat detainees only once, as part of a group, having received orders from above. In his 14 December 1940 statement to military procurator P. V. Lekhov, Gaponov also acknowledged two beatings, but claimed they had the sanction of higher authorities.[50] Abramovich had allegedly written to Stalin regarding the disgraces transpiring in the administration, but Gaponov claimed the mantle of superiority in the restoration of socialist legality. He assured investigators in February 1940 that immediately after the directive of 17 November 1938, he informed the Secretary of the Odessa Oblast Party Committee and the Politburo of the Communist Party of Ukraine about the state of affairs and "transpiring disgraces" on the second day after the arrest of Kiselev and "canceled the decision of two or three troikas, returning the cases for further investigation."[51] Gaponov also said he "personally and immediately undertook an investigation of the Third Department's group case against 100 Red Partisans and proved their detention to be groundless . . . [thus exposing] the destructive practices of Tiagin, Makievskii, Aizman, Rybakov, and Raev and flagging several of them for prosecution."[52] Despite the supposedly robust activity toward the freeing of innocent detainees that the Chekists undertook in 1939, they had no doubt as to the rectitude and necessity of the mass operations as whole. The Chekists readily acknowledged "insignificant" violations of the law, which, they claimed, served a worthy purpose in the fight against enemies of the people. They rejected all other accusations unequivocally.

The third defense tactic employed by the Chekists was an attempt to demonstrate to investigators and jurists that they were and remained faithful Stalinists. They insisted on their loyal service in the Cheka and their allegiance to the party. Such pronouncements were made, as a rule, at a high emotional register. On 22 April 1941, Abramovich wrote: "I ask for Stalinist truth. Forgive me my beloved motherland! Forgive me Komsomol, my teacher. Forgive me my beloved party, which took me into its ranks two years ago. An innocent Communist is going to his death—a thirty-two-year-old worker, a caster. Long live Communism! Long live the Great Stalin! I ask [you] to remember that I deserve punishment, but not execution."[53]

The defensive tactics of these NKVD operatives under investigation and prosecution are a testament to the fact that Chekists who found themselves among the "perpetrators of excesses" ultimately counted on the authorities to not severely punish them for undue cruelty to "enemies of the people." And on the whole, this is indeed what happened. Nevertheless, firm measures for disciplining NKVD personnel proved necessary as there turned out to be too many individuals among their ranks partial to "excesses" and unwilling to give up the new position Chekists had taken in the hierarchy of power as a result of the Great Terror.

Gaponov: Executioner and Victim of the Great Terror

Sergei Ivanovich Gaponov was a "chemically pure" type of Chekist, demonstrative of NKVD leaders during the Great Terror. Gaponov was born on 9 August 1908 in the city of Enakievo in Bakhmut Uezd of Ekaterinoslav Gubernia. He was raised in a family of professional revolutionaries. After partially finishing a secondary school, Gaponov studied to be a turner in a factory school in Dnepropetrovsk and, in 1926, began working as a metal turner at the Spartak factory while simultaneously studying in the Vocational Department (*rabfak*) of a metallurgical institute. Around the same time, he graduated from an evening party school of the second level, which signified his ambitions. In 1928 and 1929, Gaponov worked as a metal turner at the Saturn Plant in Dnepropetrovsk.[54]

The beginnings of Gaponov's collaboration with the organs of state security are connected with his study at the "Young Metalworker [*Iunyi metallist*]" School of Factory Apprenticeship (*FZU*) where there existed a circle of young Trotskyites. Local Chekists recruited him first to uncover "several dozen Trotskyites conducting substantive Trotskyite work in Dnepropetrovsk, Kharkov, and Moscow," and by April 1928, he was already working directly with the County (*okrug*) Department of the State Political Administration

(GPU) as a valuable informer.[55] At the command of his Chekist overseers, Gaponov allowed himself to be expelled from the Komsomol and Party candidacy and, moreover, was subsequently arrested in the course of the final obliteration of Dnepropetrovsk Trotskyites. Almost immediately thereafter, he was hired officially by the Dnepropetrovsk County Department of the GPU and reinstated into the party.

The twenty-year-old Gaponov began openly serving as a Chekist in May 1929 in the capacity of a supplementary archivist (*sverkhshtatnyi arkhivarius*) in the Dnepropetrovsk County Department of the OGPU. Beginning in August, he engaged in operative activities and from 1 January 1930 he was appointed an apprentice and supplementary aide to a plenipotentiary in the OGPU Information Department. Gaponov did not complete any formal training, but instead learned the Chekist craft through the example of his senior comrades. According to a personal review (*kharakteristika*) drafted in January 1933, Gaponov "servicedstet [*obsluzhival*] former functionaries of the Ukrainian Communist Party and city educators. Gaponov soon made his mark in the Cheka. He was sent to Orekhov District to execute the exceedingly harsh orders of Stalin and the Ukrainian leadership to break the resistance among the lower ranks of party and soviet officials to the impossibly high grain-requisitioning quotas. Gaponov naturally uncovered "organized sabotage" on the part of district leaders.[56] Gaponov spent the first six years of his official (*glasnaia*) Chekist career in the Dnepropetrovsk County Department, and later in the Oblast Department of the OGPU-NKVD where he transitioned from an archivist to a plenipotentiary of the Secret Political Department.

Gaponov's career took off in 1937 when young operative workers began to be massively promoted into leadership work. On 25 May, Gaponov was appointed acting assistant to the Chief of the Third Section of the SPO of the Vinnitsa Oblast UNKVD, where he proved himself an effective investigator who personally elicited the confessions of more than ten detainees.[57] On 1 October 1937, he was promoted to Kamenets-Podolsky Oblast, where he worked as a section chief and deputy chief of the UNKVD SPO. Here he managed to "uncover" an organization of the Ukrainian Communist Party consisting of seventy-five people who subsequently were sentenced to be shot.[58]

At the end of March 1938, Gaponov was sent back to Kiev where he became the Deputy Chief of the First Section of the SPO of the Ukrainian republic NKVD and, from 4 April, acting chief of the Sixth Section of the SPO, making him a visible figure at the republic level. Because of this, on 13 July, he was appointed the chief of the SPO of the UNKVD of one of the most significant oblasts in Ukraine, Odessa.[59] It was here that he reached the height of his career when he was named the head of the Odessa UNKVD.

Gaponov inherited a difficult situation from his predecessors—not only a mass of incomplete cases but also a horrific torture chamber known as the "TsAD" (*Tsentral'nyi arestnyi dom*, or Central Detention Building).[60] Gaponov's time as chief turned out to be short-lived. On 15 January 1939, the new leadership of the Ukrainian republic NKVD promoted former district Party committee secretary A. I. Starovoit to lead the UNKVD.[61] Gaponov remained as his deputy and on 7 March 1939 moved back to serving as an SPO chief. In this role, he would work on the most politically sensitive cases.

Despite his significant operative experience, Gaponov quickly came to be perceived as an undesirable element in the NKVD system. His close relatives, including his wife, had been labeled unreliable. His colleagues would underscore this in deciding Gaponov's fate.[62] Following a 19 April 1939 order from Deputy People's Commissar of the Ukrainian republic NKVD A. Z. Kobulov, Gaponov was dismissed and transferred to work in the NKVD oblast signal service (*sistema oblastnoi sviazi*).

The harsh posture taken by party authorities in examining his personnel file played a negative role in deciding Gaponov's fate. As an individual unwilling to acknowledge his complicity in the liquidation of "faithful Communists," he was expelled from the party on 24 July 1940 for violations of legality and for not being forthright in discussing his "mistakes."[63] On 16 January 1941, Gaponov was arrested under statute 206 of the Criminal Code and detained for over a year. At the beginning of July 1941, the Military Tribunal for Kiev Military District NKVD Troops held a preliminary sitting devoted to the case, but due to the war, it was put on hold and Gaponov was sent to a prison in Tomsk.[64] There, he was able to exploit the appointment to head of the Novosibirsk Oblast UNKVD of L. A. Malinin, a former leader of the Odessa UNKVD who had brought with him an entire assemblage of Odessa Chekists. At Gaponov's requests, the former Odessa Chekists in Novosibirsk gave him positive references.[65]

Gaponov was freed on 14 March 1942 at the initiative of the Novosibirsk Oblast UNKVD. Immediately after his release, he began to petition for reinstatement in operative work. By 19 March, a resolution from Malinin had already appeared in response to Gaponov's appeals, stating, "It is necessary to collect all materials and come to a decision on the matter of rehabilitation." That same day, Gaponov was hired to work in the Administration of Reform Labor Camps and Colonies (UITLK) of the Novosibirsk Oblast NKVD, where he was charged with organizing the search for escaped inmates. Seven of his old Odessa colleagues promised Moscow that Gaponov was a responsible and faithful Chekist.[66]

Nevertheless, the military procurators in Novosibirsk were not ready to come to terms with the suspension of the case against Gaponov. On 17 December 1942, they ordered that he be detained once more. The Military Tribunal of Western Siberian District NKVD Troops in Tomsk could not, however, begin examining the case of Gaponov, Kordun, Abramovich, Berenzon, Mashkovskii, and Gnesin on 25 January 1943 as scheduled because Gaponov was, from autumn 1942, deployed as an active agent of the UNKVD. Berenzon was transferred from Tomsk to Reform Labor Colony (ITK) No. 6 and was likewise not delivered for the session. The case was briefly paused, although the procurators soon succeeded in bringing Gaponov and Berenzon into court. The indictment against them underscored their use of "medieval" and "inquisitorial" torture. Gaponov and his accomplices denied the testimony of witnesses and stressed their loyalty to the NKVD and Soviet power.[67] During the war years, judges generally sent convicted Chekists to the front, and so it was in this case. Having received lengthy sentences on 26 April 1943, the defendants were immediately amnestied and sent into active military duty. Gaponov was the last to go. At the end of 1943, Novosibirsk Oblast UNKGB leadership requested permission to keep Gaponov at their disposal. Soon finding himself in the Red Army as a Quartermaster (Intendant) of the Second Rank (Lieutenant Colonel), Gaponov avoided the front lines and lived to see victory. After the war, he quietly returned to Kiev and, as an accomplished Communist and veteran, served into old age in economic work.[68]

Over the course of his entire Chekist career, Gaponov demonstrated behavior typical of workers in the organs of state security. Perceiving his role as a warrior of the "party's leading armed detachment" operating at the front lines of the battle against the class enemy—and, simultaneously, as a vulnerable, expendable cog of the great punitive machine—contributed to the characteristic deformations of Gaponov's professional identity. These included above all the absence of hesitation regarding the infallibility of "the organs" (i.e., the NKVD), cruelty, careerism, and confidence that his victims should have no rights even after release and rehabilitation.

Gaponov's profile is typical for his generation of NKVD workers, by whose hands Stalin carried out the Great Terror. His socialization coincided with the years of the civil war. He had grown up and come into adulthood in the Soviet secret police, which shaped him in its own image. As a result, he became not only an obedient executor of criminal orders "from above," but also made his own active contributions to mass repression. He was the archetypal Chekist leader of the Great Terror—a quick rise through the ranks, an abrupt fall from the height of power, and, ultimately, survival in the postwar Soviet Union.

Rehabilitated Chekists

The Soviet regime generally displayed a permissive attitude toward the crimes committed by those considered *svoi* (their "own"), serving in the fight against "enemies of the people." Chekists were traditionally seen as paragons of political loyalty, and for this reason punishment was usually lenient. The quintessential nonjudicial punishment of Chekists at this time was transfer to work in the Gulag and, later, mobilization to the front or to work in the newly annexed western part of Ukraine.[69]

The war presented Chekists who had escaped execution in the years 1939–1941 with significantly greater possibilities for rehabilitation than the camp system. The mass amnesty for former state security workers conducted over 1941 and 1942 came as a kind of idiosyncratic response to the unprecedented purge of "the organs" at the end of the 1930s. Already from the very first days of the war, the Military Collegium of the Supreme Court of the USSR began to alter Chekists' sentences, even those subject to execution, to orders to the front. Convicted NKVD workers were freed according to decrees of the Presidium of the Supreme Court of the USSR adopted on Beria's initiative. The releases apparently proceeded in two waves: at the end of 1941 and the end of 1942. In December 1941, Beria appealed to Stalin about the lack of cadres at the front, asking him to free 1,610 NKVD workers serving sentences largely for violating legality.[70] Over the autumn of 1942, another large group of former Chekists was released from prison or the camps; others were released individually in the years leading up to 1945. Over the entirety of the war years, nearly two thousand Chekists were amnestied. After release, many of them were sent into reconnaissance-sabotage squads and special divisions as well as penal companies. A significant share ended up in combat units and did not engage in Chekist work. However, hundreds of amnestied former NKVD workers managed to restart their Chekist careers by working in special investigatory units during the war. They sought to rehabilitate themselves once and for all in the eyes of the state, employing their usual practice of fabricating large-scale cases and beating testimony out of detainees. For their part, the leadership of the NKVD-NKGB demanded the same uncovering of "counterrevolutionary organizations" and mercilessness toward "enemies of the people" as before. In response to these orders, the classic methods of Stalin's security services were used at the front: the use of provocations (*provokatsii*), informers, lies, extortion, and torture.[71] During the war years, the NKGB organs alone uncovered nearly five thousand "antisoviet counterrevolutionary organizations."[72] At the same time, it cannot be denied that a share of amnestied Chekists contributed to military successes at the front lines through sabotage-reconnaissance activity.

The fate of Gaponov and the "Gaponovites" was in many ways typical of amnestied NKVD workers. The Novosibirsk Oblast UNKVD put Gaponov to work "as an agent for investigating people inclined to antisoviet moods." For a certain time, the Novosibirsk Chekists were even able to sabotage the decision of superiors in Moscow who decreed on 21 January 1944 that, "taking into account the crimes committed by Gaponov," he was to be transferred to the jurisdiction of the Novosibirsk Oblast Military Committee to be sent to the front.[73] Still, Gaponov was only sent to the Oblast Military Committee two months later, on 25 March 1944, citing "operational necessity."[74] Judging by the information available from Gaponov's case file, he did not participate in fighting. On 23 May 1944, Quartermaster of the Second Rank Gaponov entered into the service of the commandant of the city of Rostov.[75]

Mashkovksii returned to the Chekist path. Following his release, he participated in battle on the Western and Third Belarusian Fronts and suffered two concussions. By the spring of 1944, he was already working as the secretary of the frontline NKVD Prisoner of War Transfer (*priemno-peresylochnyi*) Camp No. 24, where he served as an interrogator. According to his 26 April 1945 commendation for the medal "for battle deeds [*Za boevye zaslugi*], Mashkovskii "uncovered crimes committed by those performing their military service at the camp."[76]

Gnesin received the same award in August 1946. From August 1943 until September 1945, he had served as a sniper in the First Artillery Company of the 386th Artillery Regiment of the 60th Artillery Division of Internal NKVD Troops. He arrived at the front in May 1943 as a part of the 219th Artillery Guard Regiment of the 71st Artillery Guard Division, participated in battle on the Third Ukrainian Front, was lightly wounded, suffered shell shock, and after his convalescence was sent to serve in the 386th Artillery Regiment of Internal NKVD Troops.

Less fortuitous was the military fate of Abramovich. He was deployed at the front from 13 June 1943 to 22 September 1945, serving as a private in the 262nd Infantry Division of the 43rd Army on the First Baltic Front. Abramovich suffered a serious head wound in fighting on the night of 18 September 1943; however, prior to this, he managed to rescue two wounded soldiers from the field. Upon his demobilization, Abramovich was classified an Invalid of the Fatherland War of the Second Rank and on 6 November 1947 was honored with the Order of the Red Star.

The subsequent fates of Kordun and Berenzon are currently unknown.

Restoring the Balance between the NKVD and the Communist Party

The question of the relationship between the Communist Party and the NKVD is among the most controversial matters in the study of the mass operations. The Odessa materials testify to the fact that the disturbance of the balance between the party and the NKVD that occurred at the highest levels was not only as the result of the appointment of NKVD leaders to high posts in the party and state.[77] Indeed, one of the most significant results of the Great Terror was the imbalance "below," where NKVD workers of the middle and even lowest ranks of state security came to perceive themselves as more important than the party organizations. In this, they followed Ezhov, who already in mid-1937 bragged: "I am the People's Commissar of Internal Affairs; I am the Secretary of the Central Committee; I am the chair of Party Control. If anyone tries to complain about me, where will you go? To the NKVD? I have my own people here. . . . To the Central Committee? I will receive a report immediately. And in Party Control, I'm the Chair after all, how could any matter be decided without me. You see how it turns out, you can't cast a stone without hitting Ezhov [*kuda ne kin', vse Ezhov*]. . . . Internal and external affairs are in my hands now. . . . The [NKVD] chiefs on the local level presently have immense power; in many places they are now the leading figures [*pervye liudi*]."[78] During the Great Terror, the NKVD became an organization that effectively terrorized the local party committees, became the main power base, and took charge of selections of cadres for party and state offices. In November 1938, the center pulled back the NKVD's punitive and cadre-building duties. It was necessary to visibly demonstrate to local NKVD actors the extent to which the acceptable bounds of their behavior had been narrowed, particularly with respect to the party organizations.

This is not meant to suggest that Chekists ever left the purview of the higher party leadership altogether. The operations of the Great Terror were tightly controlled by the center. Nevertheless, the Chekists' freedom of action was vast (to the point of the arbitrary inflation of quotas for executions, as in the Turkmen SSR).[79] The course of the terror at the local level took on its own particular dynamics, particularly considering the unrelenting demands and pressure from Moscow. Testimony about "accomplices"—the naming of names—was beaten out of suspects. That fed a chain reaction of arrests. This was especially widespread with respect to members of the party-state elite.[80] For their part, the party committees undertook the ideological and propagandistic facilitation of the Great Terror. Siberia and the Ukrainian, Belarusian, Georgian, and Azerbaijani republics each had leaders like N. S. Khrushchev, P. K. Ponomarenko, L. P. Beria, M. J. Baghirov, I. I. Alekseev, L. N. Gusev, and A. S. Shcherbakov who actively organized repression. Despite the role of these party leaders, following November 1938, all of them participated in the punishment of the NKVD "perpetrators of excesses."

That the highest party leaders perceived a serious danger in this developing imbalance is evidenced by the 1 December 1938 resolution of the Politburo of the Central Committee of the Communist Party, "On the Order of Sanctioning Arrests," and the NKVD USSR decree, "On the prohibition of the recruitment [of secret agents] from several categories of workers of Party, Soviet, economic, professional, and public [obshchestvennye] organizations" affirmed by the Politburo of the Central Committee on 26 December 1938.[81] Both documents sought to protect party members from the threat from the state security organs. Regardless, until the very end of the Stalin period, the party-state elite would remain a target of the operative work of the NKGB-MGB organs, subject to surveillance, recruitment, provocation, and selective repression.[82]

The story of Beria's Purge serves as a highly visible confirmation that the main victim of the Great Terror was the ordinary population of the USSR. In regulating the situation and disciplining the NKVD, authorities did not seek to re-establish justice with respect to ordinary citizens. Even the conviction of NKVD cadres, never mind their expulsion from the organs of state security, remained an internal administrative affair and did not lead to the re-examination and cancellation of sentences in the vast majority of the cases that had been led by convicted Chekists. The campaign to "restore" socialist legality had only a marginal effect on the great bulk of its victims. The Soviet people stood merely as a peripheral beneficiary of the Stalin-Beria campaign to discipline the NKVD.

Notes

1. Nikita Petrow, "Die Kaderpolitik des NKWD 1936–1939," in *Stalinscher Terror 1934–1941: Eine Forschungsbilanz*, ed. Wladislaw Hedeler (Berlin: W. Hedeler, 2002), 31. See also the introduction to this book for a discussion of the statistics.

2. To best comprehend the scale of Beria's purge, it is worth comparing it with Ezhov's purge of "Iagoda-ites" (*Igodintsy*). From October 1936 until the middle of August of 1938, 2,273 NKVD SSSR staff were arrested. See N. V. Petrov and K. V. Skorkin, eds., *Kto rukovodil NKVD, 1934–1941: Spravochnik* (Moscow: Zven'ia, 1999), 501; and Petrow, "Die Kaderpolitik," 29.

3. Petrow, "Die Kaderpolitik," 31.

4. For more detail, see A. I. Savin, "Etnizatsiia stalinizma? 'Natsional'nye' i 'kulatskaia' operatsii NKVD: sravnitel'nyi aspekt," *Rossiia. XXI vek*, tom 3 (2012), 40–61.

5. See Marc Iunge et al., eds., *"Cherez trupy vraga na blago naroda": "Kulatskaia operatsiia" v Ukrainskoi SSR 1937–1941 gg.*, tom 1 (Moscow: Rosspen, 2010), 385.

6. N. Cherushev, *Udar po svoim: Krasnaia Armiia, 1938–1941 gg.* (Moscow: Veche, 2003), 403–4.

7. Iunge et al., eds., *"Cherez trupy vraga,"* tom 2, 148.

8. Vadym Zolotar'ov, *Oleksandr Uspens'kyi: osoba, chas, otochennia* (Kharkiv: Folio, 2004), 165–67.

9. Vadym Zolotar'ov and Olha Bazhan, "Mykla Fedorov: odes'kyi tramplin v kar'ieri," *Iugo-Zapad. Odessika. Istoriko-kraevedcheskii nauch. al'manakh*, tom 4 (Odessa: Optimum, 2007), 202–19; Zolotar'ov, *Oleksandr Uspens'kyi*, 67; and M. A. Tumshis and Vadim Zolotar'ov, eds., *Evrei v NKVD SSSR, 1936–1938 gg.: Opyt biograficheskogo spravochnika* (Samara, 2012), 297.

10. Iunge et al., eds., *"Cherez trupy vraga,"* tom 2, 41–42.

11. State Archive of the Security Service of Ukraine (HDA SBU), f. 16, op. 31, spr. 49, 93–96.

12. HDA SBU, f. 16, op. 31, spr. 49, ark. 93–96.

13. Arkhiv USBU po Odesskoi oblasti (Archive of the Security Service Administration of Ukraine for Odessa Oblast), ASD (arkhivo-sledstvennoe delo) na 38299 (N. M. Tiagin), ark. 356–58.

14. Arkhiv USBU po Odesskoi oblasti, ASD na 38299 (N. M. Tiagin), ark. 356–58. (Dashniaks were an Armenian nationalist and socialist political party.)

15. Iu. Shapoval and V. Zolotar'ov, "Evrei v rukovodstve organov GPI-NKVD USSR v 1920–1930-kh gg.," *Z arkhiviv VUChK-GPU-NKVD-KGB*, tom 1 (2010), 53–93; Arkhiv USBU po Odesskoi oblasti, ACD na 38580 (V. F. Kaliuzhnyi), tom 1, ark. 287–88.

16. Arkhiv USBU po Odesskoi oblasti, ASD na 38580 (V. F. Kaliuzhnyi), tom 2, ark. 38–45.

17. Arkhiv USBU po Odesskoi oblasti, ASD na 03424 (S. I. Gaponov et al.), tom 2, ark. 138.

18. Arkhiv USBU po Odesskoi oblasti, ASD na 38580 (V. F. Kaliuzhnyi), tom 3, ark. 244 zv.

19. Arkhiv USBU po Odesskoi oblasti, ASD na 38580 (V. F. Kaliuzhnyi), tom 3, ark. 244 zv.

20. Senkevich was expelled from the party on 21 June 1938, arrested on 2 July 1938, and released on 4 June 1939.

21. Eidelman was arrested on 8 August 1938; he was released from prison in July 1939.

22. Barger was in prison from 6 July 1938 to 4 November 1939.

23. Iakubits was arrested in the headquarters of the Odessa Oblast Committee of the Communist Party on 15 June 1938.

24. Brant was arrested on 16 July 1938 and released on 14 January 1939.

25. Lunenok was arrested on 10 June 1938.

26. Arkhiv USBU po Odesskoi oblasti, ASD na 03424 (S. I. Gaponov et al.), tom 2, ark. 30.

27. Arkhiv USBU po Odesskoi oblasti, ASD na 03424 (S. I. Gaponov et al.), tom 1, ark. 39–42.

28. Arkhiv USBU po Odesskoi oblasti, ASD na 03424 (S. I. Gaponov et al.), tom 1, ark. 86.

29. Arkhiv USBU po Odesskoi oblasti, ASD na 03424 (S. I. Gaponov et al.), tom 1, ark. 96–106.

30. Arkhiv USBU po Odesskoi oblasti, ASD na 03424 (S. I. Gaponov et al.), tom 1, ark. 123–123 zv.

31. Arkhiv USBU po Odesskoi oblasti, ASD na 03424 (S. I. Gaponov et al.), tom 1, ark. 148.

32. Arkhiv USBU po Odesskoi oblasti, ASD na 03424 (S. I. Gaponov et al.), tom 4, ark. 1–10.

33. Arkhiv USBU po Odesskoi oblasti, ASD na 03424 (S. I. Gaponov et al.), tom 1, ark. 15–16.

34. Arkhiv USBU po Odesskoi oblasti, ASD na 03424 (S. I. Gaponov et al.), tom 1, ark. 47–51.

35. Arkhiv USBU po Odesskoi oblasti, ASD na 03424 (S. I. Gaponov et al.), tom 1, ark. 115.

36. Arkhiv USBU po Odesskoi oblasti, ASD na 03424 (S. I. Gaponov et al.), tom 1, ark. 137–38.

37. Shpak was released from prison on 14 September 1939.

38. Arkhiv USBU po Odesskoi oblasti, ASD na 03424 (S. I. Gaponov et al.), tom 1, ark. 52–53.

39. Arkhiv USBU po Odesskoi oblasti, ASD na 38580 (V. F. Kaliuzhnyi), tom 3, ark. 31.

40. Arkhiv USBU po Odesskoi oblasti, ASD na 38580 (V. F. Kaliuzhnyi), tom 3, ark. 276–77, 285.

41. Arkhiv USBU po Odesskoi oblasti, ASD na 38299 (N. M. Tiagin), ark. 373.

42. Arkhiv USBU po Odesskoi oblasti, os. spr. no. 34 na A. E. Gnesina, ark. 35–38 zv.

43. Arkhiv USBU po Odesskoi oblasti, os. spr. no. 34 na A. E. Gnesina, ark. 35–38 zv.

44. Arkhiv USBU po Odesskoi oblasti, ASD na 03424 (S. I. Gaponov et al.), tom 3, ark. 22–23.

45. Arkhiv USBU po Odesskoi oblasti, ASD na 03424 (S. I. Gaponov et al.), tom 3, ark. 24–28.

46. Arkhiv USBU po Odesskoi oblasti, ASD na 03424 (S. I. Gaponov et al.), tom, ark. 1.

47. Arkhiv USBU po Odesskoi oblasti, ASD na 03424 (S. I. Gaponov et al.), tom 5, ark. 21.

48. Arkhiv USBU po Odesskoi oblasti, ASD na 38580 (V. F. Kaliuzhnyi), tom 2, ark. 278.

49. Arkhiv USBU po Odesskoi oblasti, ASD na 03424 (S. I. Gaponov et al.), tom 4, ark. 1–10.

50. Arkhiv USBU po Odesskoi oblasti, ASD na 03424 (S. I. Gaponov et al.), tom 2, ark. 244–47.

51. Arkhiv USBU po Odesskoi oblasti, ASD na 03424 (S. I. Gaponov et al.), tom 4, ark. 1–10.

52. Arkhiv USBU po Odesskoi oblasti, ASD na 03424 (S. I. Gaponov et al.), tom 4, ark. 1–10.

53. Arkhiv USBU po Odesskoi oblasti, ASD na 03424 (S. I. Gaponov et al.), tom 4, ark. 370.

54. Arkhiv USBU po Odesskoi oblasti, os. spr. S. I. Gaponova, tom 2, ark. 8 zv, 67 zv.

55. Arkhiv USBU po Odesskoi oblasti, os. spr. S. I. Gaponova, tom 2, ark. 94.

56. Arkhiv USBU po Odesskoi oblasti, os. spr. S. I. Gaponova, tom 2, ark. 105, 106, 133.

57. Arkhiv USBU po Odesskoi oblasti, os. spr. S. I. Gaponova, tom 2, ark. 46.

58. HDA SBU, f. 468, op. 5, spr. 4, ark. 72.

59. Arkhiv USBU po Odesskoi oblasti, os. spr. S. I. Gaponova, tom 2, ark. 53.

60. Arkhiv USBU po Odesskoi oblasti, ASD na 38580 (V. F. Kaliuzhnyi), tom 3, ark. 264.

61. Petrov and Skorkin, eds., *Kto rukovodil NKVD*, 393–94.

62. Arkhiv USBU po Odesskoi oblasti, os. spr. S. I. Gaponova, tom 2, ark. 224.

63. Arkhiv USBU po Odesskoi oblasti, os. spr. S. I. Gaponova, tom 2, ark. 162.

64. Arkhiv USBU po Odesskoi oblasti, os. spr. S. I. Gaponova, tom 2, ark. 159; Arkhiv USBU po Odesskoi oblasti, ASD na 03424 (S. I. Gaponov), tom 3, ark. 201–10. Article 193-17 was the equivalent article in the Russian penal code for the Ukrainian article 206.

65. Arkhiv USBU po Odesskoi oblasti, ASD na 03424 (S. I. Gaponov), tom 5, attached envelope.

66. Arkhiv USBU po Odesskoi oblasti, os. spr. S. I. Gaponova, tom 2, ark. 325, 331–38.

67. Arkhiv USBU po Odesskoi oblasti, ASD na 03424 (S. I. Gaponov et al.), tom 4, ark. 572, 578, 585–86 zv.

68. Arkhiv USBU po Odesskoi oblasti, ASD na 03424 (S. I. Gaponov et al.), tom 2, ark. 595–601.

69. A. G. Tepliakov, *Mashina terrora: OGPU-NKVD Sibiri v 1929–1941 gg.* (Moscow: Novyi khronograf, 2008), 97, 499.

70. V. N. Khaustov, V. P. Naumov, and N. S. Plotnikova, eds., *Lubianka: Stalin i NKVD-NKGB-GUKR "Smersh" 1939–mart 1946* (Moscow: Materik, 2006), 563.

71. A. G. Tepliakov, "Amnistirovannye chekisty 1930-kh v period Velikoi Otechestvennoi voiny," *Klio* 67, no. 7 (2012): 75–76.

72. Khaustov, Naumov, and Plotnikova, eds., *Lubianka. Stalin I NKVD-NKGB-GUKR "Smersh"*, 575.

73. Arkhiv USBU po Odesskoi oblasti, ASD na 03424 (S. I. Gaponov et al.), tom 5, ark. 215.

74. Arkhiv USBU po Odesskoi oblasti, ASD na 03424 (S. I. Gaponov et al.), tom 5, ark. 244.

75. Arkhiv USBU po Odesskoi oblasti, ASD na 03424 (S. I. Gaponov et al.), tom 5, ark. 246.

76. Here and below are materials from the website "Pamiat' naroda": http://www.pamyat-naroda.ru.

77. Ezhov's *vydvizhentsy* became members of the Council of People's Commissars of the USSR (M. D. Berman became People's Commissar of Transportation, L. N. Bel'skii beame Deputy People's Commissar of Transportation, and S. N. Mironov and V. G. Dekanozov became statutory representatives [*polpred*] and deputies of the People's Commissariat of Foreign Affairs), while K. N. Valukhin, G. G. Teleshev, and others became secretaries of oblast party committees.

78. TsA FSB RF (Central Archive of the Federal Security Bureau of the Russian Federation), ASD na 975047 (S. F. Redens), tom 1 (Redens' confession of 14 May 1939).

79. Oleg Hlevnjuk, "Les mecanismes de la 'Grande Terreur' des années 1937–1938 au Turkménistan," *Cahiers du monde russe* 39, nos. 1–2 (1998): 197–208.

80. Tepliakov, *Mashina terrora*, 454–59.

81. V. N. Khaustov, V. P. Naumov, and N. S. Plotnikova, eds., *Lubianka: Stalin i glavnoe upravlenie gosbezopasnosti NKVD, 1937–1938* (Moscow: Materik, 2004), 624–25, 631–32.

82. N. G. Smirnov, *Rapava, Bagirov i drugie: antistalinskie protsessy 1950-kh gg.* (Moscow: AIRO-XXI, 2014); A. G. Tepliakov, "Shovinizm i natsionalizm v organakh VChK-MGB-MVD SSSR (1918–1953 gg.)," *Sovetskie natsii i natsional'naia politika v 1920–1950-e gody: materialy VI mezhdunarodnoi nauchnoi konferentsii. Kiev, 10–12 oktiabria 2013 g.* (Moscow: Rosspen, 2014), 649–57.

3

"A Sacrificial Offering"

KARAMYSHEV AND THE NIKOLAEV NKVD

Marc Junge
Translated by Aaron Hale-Dorrell and Caroline Cormier

IN APRIL AND May 1939, three intelligence agents working under the codenames "Gerd," "Dobrovolskii," and "Ivanov" reported a dangerous plot among a group of inmates released from pretrial detention. This information arrived at the Secret Political Department of the Nikolaev UNKVD. The main function of the Secret Political Department was to fight against political opponents including Trotskyites, Right Oppositionists, religious believers, and nationalists. The matter described by the agents was so explosive that the head of the Nikolaev UNKVD, I. T. Iurchenko, personally informed the Ukrainian republic NKVD in Kiev. He made this decision because the conspiracy had the potential to impact national defense since it involved individuals who occupied high posts in Shipbuilding Plant No. 200 in Nikolaev, which employed 9,000 workers. The leaders of the conspiracy in the shipyard had been arrested as a Trotskyite group by the Nikolaev UNKVD more than six months earlier on charges of sabotage for having caused a major fire in the shipyard that had nearly destroyed the entire plant.[1]

In the summer of 1939, it was surprisingly not the supposedly highly dangerous Trotskyite conspiracy that was singled out. Rather, the handlers from the Nikolaev UKNVD Secret Political Department, namely those who had ordered agents "Gerd," "Dobrovolskii," and "Ivanov" to write the reports, were arrested instead. On 23 March 1941, they were tried for "abuse of power" and, more specifically, for "violating socialist legality" by the Military Tribunal for the NKVD Troops of the Kiev Military District. One was condemned

Marc Junge, *"A Sacrificial Offering"* In: *Laboratories of Terror.* Edited by: Lynne Viola and Marc Junge,
Oxford University Press. © Oxford University Press 2023. DOI: 10.1093/oso/9780197647547.003.0004

to death, another to ten years, and the last to eight years. Petr Vasil'evich Karamyshev, who had been the head of the Nikolaev UNKVD until he was dismissed in January 1939, was also sentenced to death. A central allegation in the indictment against these officers of the Secret Political Department was that they had forced their agents to provide false information about a group of alleged Trotskyite conspirators to save their own skins. Moreover, even before the indictment, they had used "unlawful measures" (i.e., torture) in interrogating prisoners and had also falsified files, evidence, and interrogation records. Similar cases were common throughout Ukraine and were also found across the Soviet Union following the 17 November directive of the Central Executive Committee and the All-Union Council of People's Commissars, scaling back the Great Terror. Virtually everywhere, between 1938 and 1943, Chekists were convicted of violating socialist legality.

How did it happen that those arrested were not the members of the would-be "counter-revolutionary Trotskyite sabotage organization" accused of planning a major act of sabotage in a war-industry enterprise, but the NKVD personnel who only a few months previously had been masters of others' fates? Did the accusations of crude violations of "socialist legality," outlined in the important 17 November 1938 directive, correspond to reality? Had they discredited Soviet power in what was essentially a correct and essential campaign? Or should the NKVD personnel be viewed primarily as scapegoats who were necessary to shield the party and the government from responsibility for the mass terror that had been carried out on a scale spanning the whole Soviet Union but which was halted by an order from Moscow in November 1938? Or, perhaps the main goal in the repression of the Chekists was the neutralization of the patronage network of the disgraced former All-Union People's Commissar of Internal Affairs Nikolai Ezhov by his successor, Lavrentii Beria?

The Fire

The fire at the enormous shipbuilding plant, which was located on the edge of the city of Nikolaev on the banks of the Southern Bug River, began on 2 August 1938, at approximately 7 P.M. The center of the conflagration was located in the heart of the wharf, in the production shop. The fire spread rapidly for several reasons, including that "within the site, inasmuch as eyewitnesses could tell, shavings, containers of acid, other waste materials, etc. were strewn about." The fire brigade could not cope with the fire and the plant was threatened with total destruction.[2] As a result, two people died and thirty were injured. The fire's material damage was calculated at 2.6 million rubles.[3]

The embers of the fire had not yet burned out when the Nikolaev UNKVD leadership arrived at the scene. The head of the UNKVD, Karamyshev, later reported with pride that "through enormous efforts we were able to liquidate the fire and save the plant, with the aid of the local communists as well as military formations and units summoned by us."[4]

Setting up their operation in the office of the plant director, the Chekists quickly initiated interrogations and a search for the guilty. Late in the evening, Karamyshev was already taking part in an emergency session of the Organizational Bureau (Orgburo) of the Nikolaev Oblast Party Committee, where he intended to secure the party leadership's support for taking action via the UNKVD. The evaluation of the fire presented at the Orgburo session stated, "The bureau of the oblast party committee considers . . . that the fire was an act of sabotage by enemies, carried out as a result of the loss of class vigilance and a criminal lack of discipline by the management and party committee of the plant."[5]

From the beginning, Karamyshev was convinced that this was not an ordinary fire caused by carelessness, but an act of sabotage, a certainty he maintained to the end. He ordered the gathering of all compromising evidence against the plant's personnel and the detention of suspicious individuals.[6] After the Chekists decided who was to play the role of the main suspect, the UNKVD leadership sent a telegram to the leadership in Moscow to inform them what had happened.[7]

The investigation into the case was assigned to the Secret Political Department, that is, to the Fourth Department of the Nikolaev UNKVD (reclassified as the Second Department at the end of 1938),[8] which was then the sector "serving" the defense industry enterprises. This sector was headed by P. S. Voloshin.[9]

In the end, eleven of the arrested workers at the plant were brought to trial. On the initiative of the head of the UNKVD Secret Political Department, Iakov Luk'ianovich Trushkin, eight of the main suspects in the apparent arson attack on the wharf were transferred into the hands of a military tribunal, while three more secondary suspects were sent by the investigators for trial in the Special (*Osobaia*) Troika.[10] The trial of the main suspects was delayed, but the Special Troika sentenced all three accused to death on 26 October 1938, two months after the incident. The sentences were swiftly implemented.[11]

Within a few days of the fire, the Nikolaev UNKVD again entered into a state of frantic activity. First, Konstantin Efremov,[12] who was, like Voloshin, a onetime head of the defense sector of the Secret Political Department, went around with the inspectors to verify the fire safety measures of the two large shipbuilding plants: No. 200, "Communard," and No. 198, "André Marty."[13] The inspection uncovered a catastrophic fire safety situation. Inside Plant No. 200, alongside the railroad tracks were located petroleum storage tanks, which at any moment could go up in flames from the sparks of steam locomotives passing by. Inside Plant No. 198, wood was stored everywhere. Nonetheless, Efremov was able to report that "all of this was resolved only because of UNKVD intervention." He also reported on the results of his inspection to a session of the Nikolaev Oblast Party Committee.[14]

Karamyshev soon became involved in the investigation. After carefully studying the case files in detail, he reported to the oblast party committee. On the basis of Karamyshev's report, the committee adopted a resolution, "On the purging of the plants," and authorized additional arrests, which were later carried out by UNKVD personnel.[15]

The state security organs had had the shipbuilding plants in their sights even before the fire. According to Efremov, Karamyshev visited the wharves in person many times and he succeeded, with the aid of the arrested engineers, who were not listed by name here, "to take measures" for improving the organization of the labor process.[16] Karamyshev himself reported a whole host of problems. Year after year, the André Marty Shipbuilding Plant had not fulfilled its plan, while fires and accidents occurred regularly. The plant, according to Karamyshev, had deteriorated to such a degree that NKVD personnel were stationed there permanently. Moreover, if it had not been for the UNKVD, supported by the Oblast Party Committee, the fire would have completely destroyed the enterprise's docks.[17]

In his final analysis, Karamyshev considered the arrests, along with the UNKVD efforts to oversee the situation in the factories, to be a major success: "As a result of our measures, carried out by the troika, we initiated and achieved the situation that the defense plants began not only to fulfill, but even to overfulfill, state orders and plans for finished products."[18] The UNKVD chief saw another key to success in the Chekists' operational initiatives. In particular, Karamyshev wrote, "As a result of our operational measures, the replacement of the enemy management . . . and also the more energetic involvement of the party organizations, the plants quickly began to move on from the breakdowns."[19]

The NKVD had become not only a political police force targeting ideological opponents of the regime, but also an organization responsible for solving economic problems by way of punitive methods. During the years

FIG. 3.1 P. V. Karamyshev, from March 1938 to January 1939 head of the Nikolaev Oblast NKVD. Photo from 1938, HDA SBU, f. 12, spr. 31017, tom 1 (convert). By exclusive permission of the State Archive of the Security Services of Ukraine.

of the Great Terror, this oversight function of the state security organs was strengthened. The Chekists were tasked with exercising oversight for key sectors of the economy, including solving organizational problems. The main task of the state security organs in the economic sphere was to stabilize the work of the most important industrial enterprises and support the functioning of the collective farm system.

Interference from Above

The Nikolaev UNKVD did not function in a vacuum. The Chekists justified their energetic measures in the struggle with the supposed Trotskyite sabotage organization by referring to, among other things, orders and directives from above, in the first instance from Moscow. In addition, highly placed state security officers from Moscow and Kiev visited Nikolaev on inspection tours. They were especially interested in the state of the shipbuilding plants and issued concomitant orders.

On 17 June 1938, all NKVD administrations received a coded telegram from the Deputy All-Union People's Commissar for Internal Affairs, Mikhail Frinovskii, which confirmed that "notwithstanding the liquidation of the main nests of enemies (the Right-Trotskyite, espionage-sabotage, and other counterrevolutionary formations) at a host of the most important defense plants that play a decisive role in the technological armament of the Red Army, during the first five months of 1938 these factories have systematically failed to fulfill government orders."[20] As an example, the telegram named— alongside a whole host of other enterprises of military significance producing aviation motors, artillery, and explosives—the André Marty Shipbuilding Plant, No. 198, which fulfilled only 58 percent of its orders under the plan for delivering ships to the Soviet fleet.[21] In Frinovskii's unambiguous appraisal, "Such criminally disgraceful work by defense plants in supplying the Red Army [was to be] unacceptable henceforward."

The overall explanation given by Frinovskii for the deplorable state of affairs came down to "contamination, beginning with the suspicious and ending with the clearly antisoviet elements, representing a fertile ground for all manner of enemy formations." As far as the NKVD administrations were concerned, Frinovskii pinpointed the following: first, the absence of "a serious, systematic struggle with the consequences of wrecking [or sabo- tage]," which was caused by previously liquidated Trotskyite groups; second, unsatisfactory organization of the struggle with the remains of not-yet fully destroyed "enemy formations," primarily with "lower-level sabotage organiza- tions"; third, a lack of "measures for the struggle for a total purge" of enemy elements from enterprises; and, finally, insufficient "operational enterprise- level measures directed at rendering practical aid to the plants in fulfilling production plans."[22] In the wake of this criticism, the deputy people's com- missar required remedying all indicated shortcomings before the end of July 1938, that is, within six weeks, with reports to him on work completed every fifteen days.

During the investigation and their trial, the former personnel of the Nikolaev UNKVD, including Karamyshev, Trushkin (the head of the Secret Political Department), and his deputy, Mikhail Vasil'evich Garbuzov, referred to this telegram from Frinovskii as justification for the arrests that they had carried out in July 1938 at the shipbuilding plants. Trushkin spe- cifically referenced the third point of Frinovskii's demands.[23] That point read: "In all investigations and agent dossiers, again review all unmasked but not-yet repressed enemies so as to implement their arrest in the next few days."[24]

It was the implementation of this demand that led to the arrest of L. P. Fomin, who since 1933 had held the post of head of the hull-fabrication shop, which had burned down in the fire. Trushkin declared to the investigators, "On the basis of this telegram from Frinovskii and at the suggestion of Karamyshev, a report on Fomin was drawn up."[25]

After this, Karamyshev got the approval of the first secretary of the Nikolaev Oblast Party Committee, P. I. Starygin, and of I. F. Tevosian, the first deputy to the All-Union People's Commissar of Defense Industry, who was then on an inspection tour in Nikolaev. In his own turn, Garbuzov declared to the investigation that the visit by Tevosian led to numerous arrests among the engineers. Garbuzov's testimony about the direct involvement of Tevosian in the "case of the engineers" was confirmed by Trushkin. The signature of the deputy people's commissar is present on the reports related to a host of shipbuilding plant personnel included in the case. These personnel were arrested, however, even before the major fire.[26]

On 16 July 1938, a month after the Frinovskii telegram, Nikolaev was visited by Ukrainian republic People's Commissar of Internal Affairs Aleksandr Uspenskii. He took part in an operational meeting attended by the entire operational staff of the UNKVD apparatus, as well as their counterparts at the town and district levels. The meeting was prepared by a brigade led by the head of the Third Department of the Ukrainian republic NKVD in cooperation with the local UNKVD, which was sent specially to Nikolaev three days before Uspenskii's arrival. In his report on the conduct of the meeting, Uspenskii noted that Chekists had uncovered subversive actions by Japanese, English, and German intelligence in the harbor and on the wharves and, moreover, that in plant No. 200 subversion was supposedly carried out through the plant's director, Shcherbina, who was immediately arrested. According to the NKVD agents, Shcherbina also was a member of the right-Trotskyite organization, among whose members Uspenskii named Starodubtsev, the former chief witness in the case of the fire on the wharves. Uspenskii was especially disturbed that the wharf was undefended against attack by enemy submarines.[27]

The interest of the higher NKVD organs in the situation at the Nikolaev shipbuilding plants heated up still further due to the fire that occurred two weeks later. The orders from Frinovskii clearly had arrived too late, and the visits by Uspenskii and Tevosian did not achieve the desired results. As a result, the republic NKVD took direct part in the "discovery" of the roles of Trotskyite sabotage groups in the arson on the wharf. An aircraft was quickly dispatched from Kiev to Nikolaev carrying a brigade from the Seventh

Department of the Ukrainian republic NKVD, which was responsible for the state of affairs at defense industry enterprises. The brigade was headed by the director of the department, A. M. Zlobinskii. He came with NKVD personnel well proven in the task of "operational service" to Soviet industrial enterprises; many of them would go on to future careers connected to this area of NKVD activity.[28] They included A. G. Nazarenko, head of the First Special Department (Accounting-Registration) of the Ukrainian republic NKVD; Z. A. Novak, operational plenipotentiary of the Tenth Section of the Third Department (Counterintelligence) of the republic NKVD since April 1938; and the operational plenipotentiaries of the Third Department of the republic NKVD P. K. Pugach and A. E. Rudnyi. Even Moscow got involved in investigating the fire, requiring an increase in the pace of the investigation. According to the testimony of Trushkin, a telegram from the center containing an order to this effect was sent through procuracy channels.[29]

It is perfectly obvious that even before the fire at the shipbuilding plant, the Nikolaev UNKVD was under significant pressure from above, as a result of which NKVD personnel attempted to remedy their own personal oversights in liquidating "the Trotskyite sabotage group," as if this would result in a substantive increase in the productivity of the wharves. In operational terms, they carried out all orders from their superiors in Kiev and Moscow. Yet they could not prevent the fire at plant No. 200, which would result in an upsurge of arrests.

Release

Something quite unusual happened next. At the beginning of April 1939, the arrested members of the "Trotskyite sabotage organization," who had been responsible for setting fire to Shipbuilding Plant No. 200, according to the UNKVD leadership and its republic-level superiors, were released. The ensuing commission of inquiry came to the conclusion that "the fire could have occurred not only as the result of an act of sabotage, but also could have happened completely accidentally."[30]

Most of those released returned to their jobs. The so-called head of the saboteurs, Fomin, was released on 8 April 1939 and again became head of the plant's hull-fabrication shop. G. P. Afanas'ev, who according to the investigation was to realize Fomin's criminal designs, became an engineering technician in addition to his previous post as head of a subsection of the shop. However, he died in early 1940 due to the injuries he had suffered during his interrogation.[31] The former head of the shop, D. A. Bondar', had to settle for the position of technician. Afanas'ev and Bondar' both were released on the same day as Fomin. Two days later, on 10 April 1939, Gavrilov was released and assigned to work in the oblast land administration.[32] On 9 April 1939, Gladkov was set free and resumed working as an aide to the head of the shop. After his release, T. I. Chikalov resumed his job as a foreman.[33] One of the few "conspirators" who was not from the plant itself, M. F. Chulkov received his former position as an instructor at the Nikolaev Shipbuilding Institute. A. I. Bazilevich, S. S. Melamud, and V. I. Nosov also were cleared of charges.[34]

Even the former second secretary of the Nikolaev Oblast Party Committee, D. Kh. Derevianchenko, who had been "unmasked" as a Trotskyite and large-scale bribe-taker, was set free.[35] Also liberated at the same time was D. F. Kobtsev, who from May to July 1938 had been the second secretary of the Nikolaev City Party Committee and had been arrested on 24 July 1938 on charges of Trotskyism and bribe-taking. After his release, he occupied a post as senior engineer in the André Marty Shipbuilding Plant No. 198.[36] In contrast to Chulkov, Gavrilov, and Gladkov, neither Derevianchenko nor Kobtsev was listed among the direct participants in the sabotage organization. Instead, the NKVD organs had charged them with participation in the unmasked Trotskyite conspiracy, which encompassed the entire Nikolaev Oblast.

The former detainees received financial compensation, likely commensurate with their lost wages, as well as free trips to a health spa. They were also reinstated into the party.[37] A UNKVD employee, Konstantin Afanas'evich Voronin, was required to repay Kobtsev 900 rubles, which had been confiscated during his arrest and not properly recorded. Additionally, Kobtsev received from the UNKVD Financial Department 1,000 rubles that had been officially confiscated from him.[38]

Help came too late for those supposed participants in the "Trotskyite sabotage organization" who had been sentenced by the Special Tribunal, which was used by NKVD personnel as an extrajudicial court for sentencing the rank-and-file personnel of so-called counterrevolutionary organizations. A. A. Barsukov, N. V. Chernokhatov, and S. V. Matskovskii were sentenced to death by the troika in September 1938 and shot at midnight on 4 November 1938.[39] Only in 1941 did the Military Tribunal for NKVD Troops of the Kiev Military District overturn their death sentences, which at least gave their relatives the possibility of petitioning for compensation.[40] The executed men were rehabilitated in 1957.[41]

The First Trial

Notwithstanding the efforts of the new UNKVD chief to make his subordinates look good, at the beginning of August 1939 Trushkin and Karamyshev were arrested.[42] In mid-May 1940, Karamyshev, Trushkin, Garbuzov, and Voronin were indicted. The authors of the charges preferred to utilize the "old" testimony given by the agent "Gerd" in October 1939, which contained considerably more evidence incriminating the Chekists. Similarly, all other charges in the indictment, which were earlier noted in the directive for their arrest, were bolstered by a sufficient mass of eyewitness testimony from both UNKVD colleagues and their victims, documents from numerous face-to-face confrontations with witnesses, and certain other items of incriminating evidence. A month later, the Military Collegium of the USSR Supreme Court in Moscow sanctioned the indictment and ordered the Military Tribunal for the NKVD Troops of the Ukrainian Military District to organize and hold a trial.

The actual trial, held six months later, took place over a week, from 27 December 1940 to 4 January 1941. The trial occurred behind closed doors in the UNKVD building in Nikolaev and was presided over by Military Jurist, First Rank, Gur'ev. The other members of the judicial panel were the lay judges, Chepikov and Lyskov, and the court recorder was Technician-Quartermaster, First Rank, Miliakov. Neither the procurator nor defense counsel was admitted to the trial. The indictment cited criminal abuses of office under Article 206-17 Part B of the Ukrainian republic criminal code, that is, serious misconduct for which the death penalty was stipulated.

The tribunal called forty-four witnesses, of whom six could not appear in court. These witnesses were current or former Nikolaev UNKVD personnel and released detainees who had been victims of the NKVD's methods. Among the latter, however, a careful preliminary selection had been carried out: only those who had worked before their arrest in the enterprises and shipbuilding plants of Nikolaev both before their arrest and, in the main, after their release were called. The witnesses from among those collective farmers whose cases had also been a subject of the investigation were not called. In response to a petition by Karamyshev, the court had an additional five witnesses give testimony, all of whom were NKVD personnel.[43]

The accused were (relatively) young men who, except for Trushkin, had recently joined the NKVD and the party but had quickly achieved career success. Thus, at the time of the court trial, Karamyshev was thirty-five years old. Born in 1905, he was a native of Ekaterinburg, Russian by nationality, and possessed an incomplete high school education. At thirty-three, Karamyshev had become a captain of state security and head of the Nikolaev UNKVD, a post he held from April to December 1938, even though at that time he had served only ten years in the organs, beginning in 1928. In 1928, he had also entered the Communist Party, with his party membership preceded by a six-year stint in the Komsomol. He had one daughter.[44]

Iakov Trushkin was born in 1904 in the city of Kerch'. He had become a party member at fifteen years old and, in 1921 at seventeen, had begun working in various posts in the security organs. However, his career took off only during the years of the Great Terror. From 1 June 1938 through 30 July 1939, Trushkin temporarily filled the post of head of the Fourth (later the Second) Department of the Nikolaev UNKVD, earning the rank of Senior Lieutenant. Of Russian nationality, Trushkin had no previous convictions and no disciplinary measures against him. He was married and had two children.

Mikhail Garbuzov, a Russian, was born in 1909 in Deriugino, a railway junction in Kursk province. At the time of the trial, he was thirty-one years old and the youngest of the accused. Before serving in the state security organs, Garbuzov had worked for three and a half years in industry and had not served in the Red Army. He became a party member in 1931 and, from 1932 through 1940, he worked in the security organs. From 15 August 1938 through 10 March 1940, he—at the age of twenty-nine—filled the post of the deputy director of the Secret Political Department of the Nikolaev UNKVD, earning the rank of sergeant. During his time working in the NKVD organs, he had been disciplined once and given ten days' detention—which he did not serve—with the sanction subsequently rescinded. He was married and had a dependent child.

Konstantin Voronin was thirty-four years old. He was born in 1906 in Odessa and was a Ukrainian by ethnicity. Before joining the state security organs, he had worked for six years in industry as an engine mechanic. From 1928 through April 1929, he served in the OGPU security troops, from which he was transferred into the OGPU-NKVD. He served there from April 1929 until 1 March 1940. From October 1937 through 17 August 1938, he served as the head of one of the sections of the Secret Political Department of the Nikolaev UNKVD. He held the rank of sergeant and had no previous convictions.

Except for Karamyshev, who grew up in a peasant family, the accused came from working-class backgrounds and had only a primary education. None had previous convictions and, to the contrary, had often been commended for their work. Trushkin had several commendations and citations. In 1938,

Garbuzov had been awarded a badge, "Esteemed Agent of the VChK-GPU." Voronin "several times had been given bonuses for good work in the NKVD organs," and Karamyshev had even been awarded the Order of Lenin in 1937.[45]

The men had a multipronged defense strategy. First of all, Karamyshev did not for a second allow for doubts about the necessity and correctness of those actions carried out by the oblast UNKVD under his leadership. He continually highlighted its major achievements, as well as the difficulties overcome by the Chekists in solving enormous economic and organizational problems, especially at the shipbuilding plants. Moreover, he claimed, they acted under conditions of constant internal and external threat. Karamyshev declared to the court:

> English, German, Japanese, and Polish intelligence—especially Polish—were actively engaged here. . . . It was difficult to get oriented. In 1938, these same large plants, especially the shipbuilding ones, were infested with class-alien elements. This *was* the home turf of Trotsky. . . . We had a huge amount of work here to destroy the enemies, yet all the same their intelligence networks functioned such that no sooner had we managed to set up a machine at the André Marty plant than [news of] it was already published in the foreign press.[46]

All the accused emphasized that they had a sufficient amount of revelatory testimony from their agents as well as the testimony of witnesses to proceed against their victims. Moreover, they repeatedly argued that they had worked in direct contact with, and even with the active participation of, party organizations and the procuracy, especially in instances relating to individuals of high political or administrative status.[47]

All four of the NKVD operatives claimed that the material in the agent dossier of "Retivye," which was opened in August 1939, was incontrovertible proof of the actual participation of their victims in the antisoviet counter-revolutionary Trotskyite group, which, in turn, fully justified in hindsight the subjects' arrest in the summer of 1938. More than once they underscored that they made use of this agent dossier with the active support of the acting director of the Nikolaev UNKVD, I. T. Iurchenko. They characterized the witnesses in the case (from among shipbuilding plant workers, primarily those who had been arrested) as unreliable witnesses. They argued that some had a suspect past and some had been expelled earlier from the party and were thus embittered by their arrest and detention.

The accused considered the damaging testimony of the majority of their former colleagues as a desire to settle "personal scores" with them, inasmuch as both Karamyshev and Trushkin had more than once punished them because they had, through their unwarranted actions, broken the law. According to Karamyshev, these witnesses were not credible and acted exclusively "in the interest of their careers and personal gain."[48]

Of all the Chekists on trial, Karamyshev especially distinguished himself in demonstrating, both in the course of the preliminary investigation and in court, his impeccable devotion to party and state. Consequently, he disputed all accusations against himself and underscored that both in the past and the present he had done everything to oppose violations of socialist legality. His first action in the post of Nikolaev UNKVD boss in April 1938 had been to liquidate "a special chamber for beating detainees" that had been established by his predecessor, I. B. Fisher.[49]

During the trial, Karamyshev tried to use to his advantage the conclusions of two commissions that, under orders from the Ukrainian republic NKVD and led by N. D. Gorlinskii, had inspected the activities of the Nikolaev UNKVD, including the UNKVD troika at the end of September 1938 and again in January 1939. Moreover, in January 1939, Gorlinskii was already acting in the role of Deputy People's Commissar of Internal Affairs of the Ukrainian republic. According to Karamyshev's statement, the Gorlinskii commission characterized him, in his role as UNKVD boss, as "one of the best in the oblast cities of Ukraine" and said it had "no complaints" about him.[50] The Secret Political Department under Trushkin's leadership similarly received exclusively good marks.[51] All mistakes in the work of the UNKVD noted by the commission—and in this Karamyshev was supported by Trushkin—were acknowledged and corrected by the Chekists. According to Trushkin, this was above all about improving the work of the agent network, which was required by the 17 November 1938 directive of the All-Union Council of People's Commissars and the Central Committee of the Communist Party.[52]

According to Karamyshev's individual testimony, after the September 1938 inspection and, subsequently, after 17 November 1938, he worked tirelessly to carry out a whole host of disciplinary inquiries into the UNKVD personnel, determining the "abnormalities" in their work or their violations of socialist legality. Some of these Chekists were even arrested and sentenced to long terms of imprisonment in the camps. As one of the clearest examples of disciplinary action, Karamyshev noted his actions toward the former boss of the Vladimirov district NKVD, Z. D. Livshits. In addition, Karamyshev also mentioned other heads of district NKVD administrations, in particular

Gavrilenko and Darov, whom he turned over to be put on trial.[53] This was also true of I. G. Belov, whom Karamyshev detained for twenty days for having carried out arbitrary detentions.[54] In addition to Belov, he also punished Lavrinenko, A. I. Mishustin, Martynenko, L. I. Vinnitskii, and Iu. M. Poberezhnyi.[55] In the cases of these NKVD personnel, Karamyshev implemented disciplinary measures, transferred them to other posts, and, as an exception, dismissed them from the organs.[56] "If there existed specific instances on the part of personnel—unlawful investigation methods—then I imposed disciplinary measures on these personnel, ordered the commandant to go around the offices and required Goncharov, the aide to the head of the administration, to observe compliance," Karamyshev announced in court.[57]

Karamyshev's line of argumentation was based on a strategy he had worked out even before the investigation. It boiled down to portraying the investigation as tendentious, while at the same time portraying the Chekists in the best light. Karamyshev made repeated assertions about the narrow-minded, "unprincipled, and inflammatory approach to the case" and about the selection of witnesses. He told the court: "The evidence on the work of the troika included in the protocol of the commission drawn up by investigator Burdan conceals the essence of the case and falsifies the state of things."[58] Further, he argued: "The investigation's comments on the All-Union NKVD Directive No. 00606 are arbitrary and based on a tendentious selection of evidence."[59]

Karamyshev was actively supported by Trushkin, who repeatedly complained during the preliminary investigation and in court about the pressure put on him, about falsification of witness testimony, and even about being beaten.[60] Trushkin did not perceive the large number of released former detainees as a sign that the members of his department had been mistaken. For him, the wave of releases was only a sign that the authorities had swung from one extreme to the other. In turn, Karamyshev expressed dissatisfaction that the investigation and the court had not referenced his high-level political positions and honors, concealing his "self-sacrificing execution of important government tasks." Karamyshev considered all of this, whatever it was, as "not the objective, party-minded way."[61]

Fully in keeping with the spirit of the 17 November 1938 directive, Karamyshev explained to himself and to the tribunal the dishonest nature of the preliminary investigation and the overblown accusations formulated by the investigators about the pervasiveness in the NKVD organs of "enemies of the people" who continued to carry out their evil deeds. In Ukraine, such "enemies of the people" were the protégés of former Ukrainian republic People's

Commissar of Internal Affairs Uspenskii and included the investigators who had carried out the preliminary inquiry into Karamyshev's case. The suggestion of links to Uspenskii was a serious accusation. Karamyshev declared, "All of these Tverdokhlebtsy, all this lot from Kaluga are proxies of Uspenskii, who have knocked off a good half of the NKVD cadres, and they did the same to me, while giving false information to the bosses."[62]

By sorting out the good from the bad NKVD operatives, Karamyshev opened up for himself and the others accused the possibility of, first, putting themselves on the right side and, second, explaining all the mistakes and excesses in the actions of the state security organs. Thus, in relation to themselves, Karamyshev, Trushkin, Garbuzov, and Voronin acknowledged only the existence of "certain shortcomings," but in no instance the commission of crimes.[63] If these mistakes and excesses had nonetheless existed, then this was, according to Karamyshev, also the fault of "enemies" who had wormed their way into the organs and whose hostile activities had made these mistakes unavoidable. "One must keep in mind that at that time," he stated, "there were in the NKVD organs a large number of enemies who along with the correct leadership acted according to a hostile line, and, as a result, there were many mistakes not only here, but also in other locales."[64] Further, he asked, rhetorically, "What could I do in these actual situations? It is known that the subjective will of specific personnel here was without effect. But nonetheless I did everything I could to eliminate the possibility of these mistakes and to correct those mistakes made."[65]

To rehabilitate himself as much as possible, Karamyshev disputed every article in the indictment. Responding to the charge that he had created within the UNKVD a general climate making possible the application of physical force, that is, torture, he initially referred to authorization from the Moscow bosses to apply measures of physical force toward specific "enemy elements."[66] In addition, he claimed that he gave his subordinates sanction to apply these measures only five times, and each time he had a substantive basis for this, for example, when Derevianchenko assaulted an investigator.[67] As far as incidents of applying "unlawful methods of investigation" without his sanction were concerned, Karamyshev accounted for this oversight by noting he was overburdened with work and had not been informed about the beatings by his deputy or other subordinates. Specifically, Karamyshev testified:

> My frequent absences were exploited in the departments and [Karamyshev's former deputy A. F.] Poiasov possibly knew more about unlawful methods of investigation, but he did not tell me. If we also

add to this my duties as a deputy [in the soviet] and duties as a member
of the oblast party committee, then I was often absent.[68]

The former UNKVD boss also rejected the accusations of unjustified
arrests, referring in the more important instances to direct orders from Moscow
or Kiev. Karamyshev altogether denied any violation of the instructions of
Directive No. 00606. The investigation, however, possessed documentary at-
testation to the fact that Karamyshev acted in violation of the directive and a
supplementary circular, No. 189, according to which only individuals arrested
prior to 1 August 1938 were subject to trial by the so-called national troikas.
Furthermore, the national troika was a punitive body designated exclusively
for extrajudicial sentencing of members of national diasporas, but in Nikolaev
Oblast it was used to sentence a significant number of Russians, Ukrainians,
and Jews, as well as members of other nationalities. The restrictions by which
these troikas were banned from sentencing highly qualified specialists were
likewise not observed.

In his own defense, Karamyshev confirmed that these violations had
occurred in exceptional cases, but often with approval from Kiev or Moscow.
According to him, Uspenskii had given approval for up to 30 percent of
troika victims to consist of representatives of "non-profiled" nationalities.[69]
In instances where the troika sentenced Russians, Ukrainians, or Jews, at issue
were border violations or individuals included in group cases. These groups
supposedly could not in any instance be divided, "due to state interests."[70] In
sum, Karamyshev underscored, "I considered and still consider that the troika
acted completely correctly and in the interests of state security."[71]

It was very important for Karamyshev and Trushkin to distance themselves from "enemy of the people" Uspenskii. In their testimony, the former
people's commissar figured exclusively as a proponent of radical measures,
while these Chekists strove to "dilute" his orders, and therefore always felt
that they were under the sword of Damocles. Moreover, Karamyshev did not
miss the opportunity to put forth his own former deputy, Poiasov, as an individual in Uspenskii's confidence:

From Uspenskii came a directive to arrest 1,000 individuals, which
I did not fulfill. He hated me and called Poiasov in for a conference,
but not me. . . . The issue of punishing via the troika was put to us in
strong terms, because the directive indicated that the troika might im-
pose sentences either to VMN [the death penalty] or 10 years imprisonment, and only in a few instances to 8 years, but we in no way took

the responsibility for it. For this, Uspenskii called me up and said over the phone: "You must stop playing the liberal, get your hard tack ready for boarding." [The reference here is to arrest, sentencing, and transport to a camp.][72]

According to Karamyshev, under his leadership the Nikolaev UNKVD on the whole "worked through" some five or six times fewer cases than other regions of Ukraine, which attested to the fact that "we approached the arrests more carefully, and only according to the evidence we had."[73]

Still another article in the indictment stated that Karamyshev had treated his subordinates poorly and likewise had neglected party work. In response to this, he argued: "Despite the fact that I had a reward fund of 12,000 rubles, I expended 18,000 rubles monthly. This speaks to the fact that I listened alertly to the needs of personnel and never heard any reproach from them."[74] The party organization never had any issues with him, as even "in the very heat of an operation I proposed setting aside a special day for political instruction."[75] In his "last words" before the court, Karamyshev offered his final defense:

> Over the course of ten years I worked in reality doing low-level operational work, working day by day, night by night, for years never using time off to get out into nature . . . and never lost the revolutionary outlook . . . because I never lost my pure motives: the interests of the party and the state. I had no personal interests, there were none and there could have been none! . . . I am not a criminal and never engaged in criminal activity; quite the opposite, I have for my entire conscious life struggled against criminals and enemies, defending the positions of the party and soviet power. . . . For what other reason could I have been elected a deputy of the Supreme Soviet and awarded the highest of honors: the Order of Lenin . . . for selfless execution of government assignments? I am a sacrificial offering, and the party does not need such a sacrifice, and therefore I ask that you acquit me.[76]

Karamyshev's strategy turned out to be successful. On 4 January 1941, the Military Tribunal acquitted him. Garbuzov was also released. His two-year camp sentence was replaced by a three-year suspended sentence and, moreover, the court noted that Garbuzov represented no danger to society. His "partner in crime," Voronin, was sentenced to three years' imprisonment. Garbuzov and Voronin were sentenced under criminal code Article 206-17 Part A, for official misconduct, even though they had been initially charged with crimes punished under the more serious Part B of that article. Trushkin received the harshest punishment of all, but even he was able to get off relatively lightly. Under Article 206-17 Part B, he was sentenced to the death penalty—to be shot—but in light of his continuous service in the state security organs and the Red Army from an early age, as well as the fact that he did not commit his crimes out of venal self-interest, the tribunal granted Trushkin a pardon, substituting eight years' imprisonment for his death sentence.[77]

The Second Trial

The not-guilty verdict in the case of Karamyshev was, in his words, "sympathetically received by the majority of the Chekist collective." Karamyshev himself was called to return "to the life of that collective," to which he was "organically connected and [with whom] he had actively fought in the front ranks of the class struggle, defending the positions of the party and soviet power."[78]

The shock was therefore all the greater when, on 9 January 1941, five days after Karamyshev's release, he was re-arrested. In his letter to M. A. Burmistenko, a secretary of the Central Committee of the Communist Party of Ukraine and chair of the Ukrainian republic Supreme Soviet, Karamyshev wrote, "this is beyond my endurance," but, as before, he believed in the "triumph of Bolshevik truth."[79]

What Karamyshev could not have known was that the chief justice of the Military Tribunal for the NKVD Troops of the Kiev Special Military District, Gur'ev, had on 4 January 1941, the day the not-guilty verdict was issued, already officially handed down his own "special opinion." Although he did not criticize the not-guilty verdict in Karamyshev's case, Gur'ev nonetheless characterized the verdicts reached in the cases of Trushkin and Voronin as exceedingly "light."[80] The "special opinion" of Gur'ev, and the corresponding protest that followed, was almost certainly sent to the All-Union People's Commissar of Justice and clearly became the main reason for the second arrest of Karamyshev and Garbuzov.

The formal decision to hold a new trial was adopted only in the course of the appeal process, on 4 March 1941, two months after the completion of the first trial. This decision was adopted at the highest levels in Moscow, by the Military Collegium of the All-Union Supreme Court. The most important innovation compared to the first court proceeding was that both lay judges who were responsible for the unsatisfactory verdict were purposely replaced by two NKVD workers, Svirskii and Voedilo. Moreover, the presiding judge was also replaced. In place of Gur'ev, the tribunal was headed by Military Jurist Feld'man. Along with the quick second arrest of Karamyshev, this was another sign that the 4 January 1941 verdict had provoked dissatisfaction in Moscow. Gur'ev's "special opinion" did not help the situation.[81]

The second court proceeding was quickly organized. It took place from 18 to 23 March 1941, again in the oblast UNKVD building in Nikolaev.[82] On the whole, the second trial did not differ from the first. In addition to the witnesses already known, only a few new ones were called, such as Poiasov, the former Nikolaev UNKVD deputy chief. Neither the new witnesses nor the witnesses testifying a second time, however, gave the proceeding any new quality. As before, the witnesses not only sharply criticized and accused the NKVD personnel on trial, but also boundlessly praised them. As they say, however, the devil is in the details. Only during the second examination did a strengthening of a tendency already present in the first trial, but not fully developed due to the "incorrect" composition of the tribunal, become notable: the court strove to condemn the accused Chekists for arbitrariness and an inclination to excesses. As a result, even more stress was placed on the NKVD's obligations to oversee investigations, examples given of irresponsible treatment of their subjects of investigation, and attention paid to their testimony and incriminating evidence. The core of the accusations of abuses of office were portrayed as negligence toward official obligations, neglect of work with agent networks, making changes to interrogation protocols and other investigatory documentation, their incompleteness and selective nature, violation of directives and orders, unauthorized actions, and the application of "physical force measures." These were precisely the criticisms of the 17 November 1938 directive.

The former UNKVD boss, Karamyshev, was the only one of the four accused who noticed these new features in the trial, which did not immediately reveal themselves, but were not to be discounted due to the new composition of the court. In contrast to Karamyshev, Trushkin practically did not defend himself. Clearly, he understood that his final hour had arrived. He not only refused to make a closing statement, but even made an escape attempt during the trial. He was captured in the vestibule of the UNKVD building.[83]

In the second trial, the verdict handed down to Karamyshev was not acquittal; instead, he was sentenced to be shot. The same fate was applied to Trushkin. The punishment of Voronin was made significantly more severe, increased from three years in a camp to ten. Garbuzov, who had previously received a suspended sentence, was sentenced to eight years in a camp.[84] No appeal was permitted. Trushkin and Karamyshev were shot, presumably in May 1941, after first the Military Collegium of the All-Union Supreme Court and then the Presidium of the All-Union Supreme Court had overruled all objections.[85]

The height of the campaign to restore socialist legality in Nikolaev occurred in the fall of 1939. At the time, a special commission comprising personnel from the office of the special plenipotentiary of the Ukrainian republic NKVD and the special plenipotentiary from the all-union NKVD surveyed the terrain to select which cases to pursue. This was not an easy task, inasmuch as those Chekists "chosen with hindsight," especially personnel of the UNKVD apparat, had earlier received the full support of the bosses. The would-be accused also fully supported each other in opposing the arrests and trial that threatened them. In the course of this very real struggle, the Chekists sometimes expressed thoughts they could not state openly in their defense: their personal criticism of the actions of the political leadership of the country appeared at times in agent reports and in statements made by now-released individuals previously under investigation. In these statements, the central leadership was depicted as naïve and indecisive. These statements similarly sounded oblique warnings of the dangerous consequences of the campaign to punish violators of "socialist legality." Further, it was noted that it was the

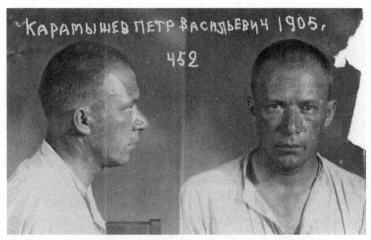

FIG. 3.2 P. V. Karamyshev's prison photo from 1939, HDA SBU, f. 5, spr. 67990, tom 1, ark. 9 (convert). By exclusive permission of the State Archive of the Security Services of Ukraine.

party and state that had prepared the ground for the mass repressions. Yet these passages should not be interpreted as a criticism of the system itself: the Chekists only alluded to the possibility of lighter and more consistent treatment of those who had spared no strength in carrying out the directives of the party and state. The authorities neither responded to these warnings and appeals, nor paid attention to the attempt to discredit the former victims who had been under attack by the Chekists. This appeal to the authorities went unheeded, moreover, because the NKVD personnel formulated it in the familiar but out-of-date style of the struggle with Trotskyism. The situation had fundamentally changed, as a result of which the military tribunals had stopped reacting to accusations of Trotskyism.

The high degree of activity and organization employed in self-defense by the Chekists in the first trial—for example, in the acquittal of Karamyshev—to a significant degree resulted from cooperation between the accused Chekists and the leadership of the Nikolaev UNKVD. This chance conjuncture, however, had fatal consequences for the Chekists, because subsequently the courts began to punish this kind of cooperation. It is more than likely that both the new judge heading the tribunal and the lay judges were aware of Moscow's undivided attention. Consequently, they demonstrated particular zeal, considering themselves obligated to hand down especially harsh sentences. Keeping in mind Karamyshev's not-guilty verdict in the first trial, there is some basis to speak of a strong corporate culture among Chekists. At the same time, the most important protector of the accused, the UNKVD boss Iurchenko, had been mobilized to work in the organs from the ranks of the party and fell into disgrace because of his attempts to protect his former colleagues.[86]

For all convicted Chekists in Nikolaev, the preliminary investigation and review was a profound event and, most of all, psychologically unbearable. Without exception, they were loyal Stalinists and, in their own eyes, had stood up for the goals of the state and party with all their strength. During the investigation and the trials, they intended to demonstrate political and moral loyalty to the regime. They could not, did not want to, and were required not to question their system, unlike the Nazi perpetrators tried at Nuremberg. The Chekists rightly claimed victimhood because of the sudden change in policy by the political and administrative leadership. These NKVD personnel had the perfectly valid sense that they were being scapegoated for the mass persecutions during the Great Terror. They had done what had been asked of them, even though they had made what they called "little mistakes," but they considered the mistakes neither uncorrectable nor punishable. Under these conditions, showing remorse for the crimes committed was impossible.

The sentencing of the Nikolaev Chekists to death or to long prison sentences between 1938 and 1943 showed some similarities to the Great Terror. Yet the purge of the purgers was not a process of random selection, as was the case with the mass persecutions associated with the Great Terror, but instead took the shape of a Soviet Union–wide campaign to punish the violation of socialist legality. A direct similarity to the Great Terror's mass persecution is the secret conduct of the trials, even if they can be described as semi-public due to the significant participation of NKVD colleagues as victims and witnesses. In Nikolaev and in other regions of the Soviet Union, the trials were closed to the public. The exceptions were in Siberia and Moldavia, where commentary on two trials was published in the newspapers.[87] Chekists were acquitted only in exceptional cases in a few regions of Ukraine. In common with the Great Terror, the accused had no defense counsel. Once again, the exceptions prove the rule. For example, in Zaporozh'e, the Chekists had defense attorneys. Unlike in the extrajudicial proceedings used in the Great Terror, the accused could defend themselves while on trial, an element similar to the rural show trials but distinct from the mass operations.[88]

Nonetheless, in Soviet circumstances, the trials of the Nikolaev Chekists appeared to be completely normal judicial proceedings, while the "courts" of troikas and the Military Collegium of the All-Union Supreme Court were not. This can be explained precisely in the falling away of fictive "political" articles in the indictments. Moreover, methods of investigation now substantively differed from those used by the Chekists themselves during the Great Terror. Only in exceptional instances were the accused tortured and mistreated. The psychological pressure on them was much less. The investigators were less likely to use manipulation, exaggeration, or falsification. The court trials took much longer, often several days. Consequently, the presupposition that criminals among the Nikolaev UNKVD personnel fell victim between 1939 and 1941 of the very same punitive system that they had previously served in appears to be a crude oversimplification. The situation between 1939 and 1941 was much more favorable for the observation of the legal requirements and the laws.[89] The state and party leadership once again decided to open the path to legality and law. In this way, there was no question of the believability or unbelievability of the proofs, as in the acceptance of proof of guilt of the Trotskyite sabotage organization put forth by the Nikolaev UNKVD.

The most striking difference from the Great Terror is the substantive content of the campaign. The focus on punishing violations of socialist legality can be considered unique in the history of the Soviet Union, even though similar attempts to widely combat violations of socialist legality had already been made in in the early 1930s in the wake of collectivization and rapid industrialization.[90] Even in the very course of the Great Terror there were investigations of violations of socialist legality, but they fizzled out, and at most only led to dismissal and transfers of personnel.[91] In Ukraine and Moldavia, similar trials occurred in all regions.[92] In Ukraine, the sentencing of Chekists followed the disciplinary measures defined in Article 206-17 Parts A and B of the republic criminal code. Chekists were convicted for abuses of office. This was the main accusation made against them by the Soviet state beginning in the autumn of 1938, when it replaced accusations of a political nature—as a rule, of Trotskyism—that virtually always were earlier used to convict Chekists and other members of the party-state elite.

The political articles of the criminal code, including the infamous Article 58—in Ukraine it was Article 54—with their many sub-sections, faded into the background. Between 1936 and 1938, the ritualized accusations of Trotskyite (or Bukharinist or Zinovievite) deviation were driven to the point of absurdity, emptied of meaning. It was replaced—and not only in the cases of the Chekists—with a more rational punitive practice for which the main reference point was the interests of Soviet governance.

Uniquely, the Soviet Union convicted "its own" perpetrators without a change of regime. The perpetrators were therefore forced to realize that they were now being investigated and even charged by a state that had previously ordered, or at least suggested and tolerated, what they had done, something that is significantly different from the Nuremberg Trials. Their sense of powerlessness was compounded by the fact that, as individual perpetrators, each had participated in his own way in a project that they accepted, supported, and believed in.

Notes

1. "Spravka vremenno ispolniaiushchego obiazannosti nachal'nika 7-go otdela UGB UNKVD po Nikolaevskoi oblasti D. B. Davidenko o kolichestve rabochikh na oboronnykh zavodakh No. 198 i No. 200. 19.01.1939," in *"Cherez trupy vraga na blago naroda": "Kulatskaia" operatsiia v Ukrainskoi SSR, 1937–1938 gg.,* ed. Marc Iunge et al. (Moscow: Rosspen, 2010), 2:585–86.

2. "Protokol doprosa obviniaemogo P. V. Karamysheva, 19.10.1939," State Archive of the Security Services of Ukraine (Haluzevyi derzhavnyi arkhiv Sluzhby bezpeky Ukrainy, hereafter HDA SBU), f. 5, spr. 67990, tom 1, ark. 165.

3. "Akt ekspertnoi komissii inzhenerov fabriki No. 200 g. Nikolaeva. 28.08.1938," State Archive of Nikolaev Oblast (Derzhavnii arkhiv Mikolaïvs'koï oblasti,

hereafter, DAMO), f. 5859, op. 2, spr. 5747, ark. 330–31. In comparison with the very low living standard in the Soviet Union, this was a huge sum. In 1939, lower-level NKVD staff earned between 500 and 800 hundred rubles a month.

4. HDA SBU, f. 5, spr. 67990, tom 1, ark. 165.

5. "Protokol No. 31 zasedaniia orgbiuro TsK KP(b) Ukrainy po Nikolaevskoi oblasti 'O pozhare na zavode No. 200,' 02.08.1938," DAMO, f. 7, op. 1, spr. 20, ark. 130–31.

6. "Protokol zakrytogo sudebnogo zasedaniia Voennogo tribunala voisk NKVD Kievskogo okruga po obvineniiu P. V. Karamysheva, Ia. L. Trushkina, M. V. Garbuzova, K. A. Voronina 27.12.1940–04.01.1941," HDA SBU, f. 5, spr. 67990, tom 1, ark. 112, 121, 129, 229.

7. "Protokol zakrytogo sudebnogo zasedaniia Voennogo tribunala voisk NKVD Kievskogo okruga po obvineniiu P. V. Karamysheva, Ia. L. Trushkina, M. V. Garbuzova, K. A. Voronina, 18–23.03.1941," HDA SBU, f. 5, spr. 67990, tom 13, ark. 424.

8. In the majority of documents used, of which the largest number date to 1939 and afterward, this is about the Second, rather than the Fourth, Department of the Nikolaev UNKVD. At the end of 1938, the NKVD structure was changed, during which the Fourth (Secret Political) Department was reorganized into the Second.

9. The creation of an independent Seventh Department to oversee shipbuilding occurred only at the end of 1939. HDA SBU, f. 5, spr. 67990, tom 13, ark. 111–236.

10. HDA SBU, f. 5, spr. 67990, tom 13, ark. 226 and 424. On the trials of these three individuals by the osobaia troika, see "Prigovor," HDA SBU, f. 5, spr. 67990, tom 13, ark. 484–88. The "special troikas" were established by Directive No. 00606, and replaced the dvoika used earlier in the National Operations. See "Prikaz No. 00606 Narodnogo komissara vnutrennykh del SSSR 'Ob obrazovanii Osobykh troek dlia rassmotreniia del na arrestovannykh v poriadke prikazov NKVD SSSR No. 00485 i drugikh,' 17.09.1938," in Bol'shevistskii poriadok v Gruzii, tom 2, Dokumenty o Bol'shom terrore v Gruzii, ed. Marc Junge and Bernd Bonvech (Moscow: AIRO XXI, 2015), 165–67. See also V. N. Khaustov, V. P. Naumov, and N. S. Plotnikova, eds., Lubianka. Stalin i glavnoe upravlenie gosbezopasnosti NKVD, 1937–1938 (Moscow: Materik, 2004), 549.

11. HDA SBU, f. 5, spr. 67990, tom 13, ark. 484–88.

12. In 1940, Konstantin Ivanovich Efremov worked as assistant to the director of the André Marty Plant for cadres.

13. The former was one of the oldest shipbuilding enterprises of the Russian Empire. The battleship Potemkin had been built there. In 1920, it was organized under the name "Tremsud" (Trust for Oceangoing Shipbuilding) by combining three plants, "Russud," "Remsud," and "Temvod." In 1931, the plant was renamed in honor of the sixty-one workers from the "Russud" shipbuilding plant who had been shot by Denikin's White forces on the night of 20 November 1919. André Marty (1886–1956) was a French communist activist, a member of the French National Assembly from 1924 to 1955 (with interruptions), Secretary of the Comintern from 1935 to

1943, and a Comintern political commissar leading the International Brigades in Spain from 1936 to 1938.

14. "Protokol sudebnogo zasedaniia," HDA SBU, f. 5, spr. 67990, tom 13, ark. 111–226 ob.

15. HDA SBU, f. 5, spr. 67990, tom 13, ark. 174.

16. HDA SBU, f. 5, spr. 67990, tom 13, ark. 174.

17. HDA SBU, f. 5, spr. 67990, tom 13, ark. 227.

18. HDA SBU, f. 5, spr. 67990, tom 13, ark. 263.

19. "Protokol doprosa obviniaemogo P. V. Karamysheva, 19.10.1939," HDA SBU, f. 5, spr. 67990, tom 13, ark. 165.

20. *Reabilitovani istoriieiu: Mikolaivs'ka oblast'* (Nikolaev: Svitohliad, 2008), 4:261–63.

21. *Reabilitovani istoriieiu,* 4:261–63.

22. *Reabilitovani istoriieiu,* 4:262.

23. "Protokol sudebnogo zasedaniia," HDA SBU, f. 5, spr. 67990, tom 13, ark. 405–58; and "Protokol sudebnogo zasedaniia," HDA SBU, f. 5, spr. 67990, tom 3, ark. 133–41, 274–87.

24. "Telegramma zamestitelia narodnogo komissara vnutrennikh del SSSR M. P. Frinovskogo nachal'niku UKNVD Nikolaevskoi oblasti P. V. Karamyshevu, 17.06.1938," HDA SBU, f. 9, spr. 672, ark. 187–94.

25. "Protokol doprosa obviniaemogo Ia. L. Trushkina, 05.10.1939," HDA SBU, f. 5, spr. 67990, tom 3, ark. 274–87.

26. "Dopolnitel'noe pokazanie M. V. Garbuzova, 12.09.1939," HDA SBU, f. 5, spr. 67990, tom 3, ark. 147–49.

27. "Raport Narodnogo komissara vnutrennikh del Ukrainy A. I. Uspenskogo ob operativnoi zasedanii ot 16 iiuliia 1938 g. so vsem sostavom apparata UKNVD i gorraiotdelenii Nikolaevskoi oblasti, 16.07.1938," HDA SBU, f. 16, spr. 300, ark. 42–49.

28. "Protokol doprosa obviniamogo Karamysheva, 03.10.1939," HDA SBU, f. 5, spr. 67990, tom 1, ark. 131–34; and "Protokol sudebnogo zasedaniia," HDA SBU, f. 5, spr. 67990, tom 13, ark. 111–226 zv.

29. "Protokol zudebnogo zasedania," HDA SBU, f. 5, spr. 67990, tom 13, ark. 405–58.

30. HDA SBU, f. 5, spr. 67990, tom 13, ark. 451.

31. *Reabilitovani istoriieiu: Mikolaivs'ka oblast'* (Nikolaev: Ilion, 2005), 1:269–270.

32. "Protokol sudebnogo zasedania," HDA SBU, f. 5, spr. 67990, tom 13, ark. 405–24.

33. "Protokol sudebnogo zasedania," HDA SBU, f. 5, spr. 67990, tom 13, ark. 111–226, 405–58.

34. "Obvinitel'noe zakliuchenie starshego sledovatelia sledstvennoi chasti UGB NKVD USSR N. A. Burdana po delu P. V. Karamyshev, Ia. L. Trushkina, M. V. Garbuzova, K. A. Voronina, 11.05.1940," HDA SBU, f. 5, spr. 67990, tom 13, ark. 347–58.

35. *Reabilitovani istoriieiu: Mikolaivs'ka oblast',* 1:266.

36. Kobtsev was freed on 2 April 1939. "Protokol sudebnogo zasedaniia," HDA SBU, f. 5, spr. 67990, tom 13, ark. 111–226 zv.

37. "Svodka agenta 'Gerd' 2-mu otdelu UNKVD Nikolaevskoi oblasti, 12.05.1939," HDA SBU, f. 5, spr. 67990, tom 9, ark. 132–33; and "Dokladnaia zapiska nach. UNKVD po Nikolaevskoi oblasti I. T. Iurchenko zam. Narkoma vnutrennikh del. USSR A. Z. Kobulovu, 22.07.1939," HDA SBU, f. 5, spr. 67990, tom 9, ark. 147–52.

38. HDA SBU, f. 5, spr. 67990, tom 13, ark. 201.

39. "Vypis'ki iz akta rastrela," DAMO, f. 5859, op. 2, spr. 5747, ark. 354, 356, 358.

40. "Protokol sudebnogo zasedaniia," HDA SBU, f. 5, spr. 67990, tom 13, ark. 485–86 zv.

41. *Reabilitovani istoriieiu: Mikolaivs'ka oblast'*, 1:458.

42. "Dokladnaia zapiska," HDA SBU, f. 5, spr. 67990, tom 9, ark. 147–52.

43. "Protokol sudebnogo zasedaniia," HDA SBU, f. 5, spr. 67990, tom 13, ark. 111–11 zv.

44. "Petr Karamyshev: Nashi deputaty Verkhovnogo Soveta USSR" [Our Deputies to the Supreme Soviet of the Ukrainian Republic], *Iuzhnaia pravda* 116 (30 May 1938). The author thanks Maria Panova and Irina Bukhareva for searching for and reviewing the newspaper *Iuzhnaia pravda*.

45. "Protokol sudebnogo zasedaniia," HDA SBU, f. 5, spr. 67990, tom 13, ark. 112–13 zv.

46. "Protokol sudebnogo zasedaniia," HDA SBU, f. 5, spr. 67990, tom 13, ark. 262.

47. "Protokol sudebnogo zasedaniia," HDA SBU, f. 5, spr. 67990, tom 13, ark. 114–115 zv, 232, 242.

48. HDA SBU, f. 5, spr. 67990, tom 13, ark. 114–15 zv, 232, 242.

49. "Protokol doprosa Karamysheva, 15.08.1939," HDA SBU, f. 5, spr. 67990, tom 1, ark. 91–94.

50. The commission headed by Gorlinskii worked in Nikolaev on 17 and 21 September 1938, and later over the course of several months beginning in January 1939. HDA SBU, f. 5, spr. 67990, tom 13, ark. 115, 173, 232. In September 1938, Gorlinskii was still serving as the operational plenipotentiary of the Fourth Department, Main State Security Administration, Ukrainian republic NKVD. If this is true, then one can suppose that in September 1938 he headed a commission dispatched directly on the orders of Moscow, whereas the January 1939 commission was formed by an order that assigned to it personnel of the Ukrainian republic NKVD apparat, inasmuch as in December 1938, Gorlinskii was appointed deputy people's commissar of internal affairs for Ukraine.

51. HDA SBU, f. 5, spr. 67990, tom 13, ark. 245.

52. "Protokol sudebnogo zasedaniia," HDA SBU, f. 5, spr. 67990, tom 13, ark. 113–15, 232.

53. "Prigovor," HDA SBU, f. 5, spr. 67990, tom 13, ark. 305–10.

54. "Protokol sudebnogo zasedaniia," HDA SBU, f. 5, spr. 67990, tom 13, ark. 111–226 zv. Ivan Grigor'evich Belov (b. 1897) had been a member of the Communist Party since 1925, having served in the VChK-OGPU-NKVD since 1919. In 1938, he was

head of the Novo-Troitsk district NKVD, and in 1940 occupied the post of head of the Golo-Pristan district NKVD in Nikolaev Oblast.

55. Lavrinko was dismissed for "abnormalities" during investigations. Mishustin was likewise dismissed from the NKVD for "abnormalities" during investigations, but Karamyshev explained this only during the second trial. "Protokol sudebnogo zasedaniia," HDA SBU, f. 5, spr. 67990, tom 13, ark. 405–58. Martynenko was the secretary of the Elanetsk District NKVD. The issue of turning Martynenko over to the courts was considered because he had concealed cases of "abuses" of socialist legality. Lazar' Il'ich Vinnitskii (b. 1915) was in 1940 a senior operational plenipotentiary of the Drohobych UNKVD in the Ukrainian republic. In 1938, Vinnitskii worked first in the Third Department of the Nikolaev UNKVD, and then was transferred to the Second, subordinate to Trushkin.

56. "Protokol sudebnogo zasedaniia," HDA SBU, f. 5, spr. 67990, tom 13, ark. 112–13 zv, 232.

57. "Protokol sudebnogo zasedaniia," HDA SBU, f. 5, spr. 67990, tom 13, ark. 232. In 1940, Grigorii L'vovich Goncharov worked as an aid to the head of the State Bank Administration for armored car security, but before that had worked as head of the Skadovsk district NKVD and aide to the head of the Nikolaev UNKVD.

58. HDA SBU, f. 5, spr. 67990, tom 13, ark. 233.

59. HDA SBU, f. 5, spr. 67990, tom 13, ark. 263..

60. "Zaiavleniia obviniaemykh Ia. M. Vasiutinskomu," HDA SBU, f. 5, spr. 67990, tom 13, ark. 14–19 zv, 46–49 zv, and "Protokol sudebnogo zasedaniia," HDA SBU, f. 5, spr. 67990, tom 13, ark. 254.

61. HDA SBU, f. 5, spr. 67990, tom 13, ark. 46–49.

62. HDA SBU, f. 5, spr. 67990, tom 13, ark. 233. As special plenipotentiary of the Ukrainian republic NKVD, A. M. Tverdokhlebenko worked on cases of violations of socialist legality by UNKVD personnel. Uspenskii had worked in Kaluga as head of the Orenburg UNKVD prior to coming to Ukraine. He brought with him many NKVD workers from his patronage network, hence the reference to Kaluga.

63. HDA SBU, f. 5, spr. 67990, tom 13, ark. 245, 261, 262, 265.

64. HDA SBU, f. 5, spr. 67990, tom 13, ark. 262.

65. "Zaiavlenie P. V. Karamyshev L. P. Beriiu, 27.11.1939," HDA SBU, f. 5, spr. 67990, tom 1, ark. 186–86 zv.

66. No document sanctioning the use of torture has yet been found.

67. HDA SBU, f. 5, spr. 67990, tom 13, ark. 232.

68. HDA SBU, f. 5, spr. 67990, tom 13, ark. 262.

69. HDA SBU, f. 5, spr. 67990, tom 1, ark. 277–81.

70. HDA SBU, f. 5, spr. 67990, tom 1, ark. 100–4, 142–45, and HDA SBU, f. 5, spr. 67990, tom 13, ark. 263.

71. HDA SBU, f. 5, spr. 67990, tom 13, ark. 263.

72. HDA SBU, f. 5, spr. 67990, tom 13, ark. 231.

73. HDA SBU, f. 5, spr. 67990, tom 13, ark. 232.

74. HDA SBU, f. 5, spr. 67990, tom 13, ark. 264.

75. HDA SBU, f. 5, spr. 67990, tom 13, ark. 113.

76. "Zaiavlenie P. V. Karamyshev L. P. Beriiu, 18.08.1939," HDA SBU, f. 5, spr. 67990, tom 1, ark. 98–99 zv.; "Zaiavleniia obviniaemykh Ia. M. Vasiutinskomu," HDA SBU, f. 5, spr. 67990, tom 13, ark. 46–49 zv; "Protokol sudebnogo zasedaniia," HDA SBU, f. 5, spr. 67990, tom 1, ark. 98–99 zv; and "Protokol sudebnogo zasedaniia," HDA SBU, f. 5, spr. 67990, tom 13, ark. 264.

77. "Prigovor," HDA SBU, f. 5, spr. 67990, tom 13, ark. 305–10.

78. "Zaiavlenie P. V. Karamysheva sekretariu TsK KP(b)U i predsedateliu Verkhovnogo Soveta USSR O. M. Burmistenku, 15.01.1941," HDA SBU, f. 5, spr. 67990, tom 13, ark. 510.

79. SBU, f. 5, spr. 67990, tom 13, ark. 510.

80. "Osoboe mnenie predsedatel'shchego Voennogo tribunala voisk NKVD Kievskogo okruga Gur'eva po delu Ia. Trushkina i drugikh [January 5, 1941]," HDA SBU, f. 5, spr. 67990, tom 13, ark. 304a (envelope).

81. "Opredelenie Voennoi kollegii Verkhovnogo suda Soiuza SSR, 04.03.1941," HDA SBU, f. 5, spr. 67990, tom 13, ark. 369–69 zv.

82. "Protokol sudebnogo zasedaniia," HDA SBU, f. 5, spr. 67990, tom 13, ark. 405–58.

83. HDA SBU, f. 5, spr. 67990, tom 13, ark. 405–58.

84. "Prigovor," HDA SBU, f. 5, spr. 67990, tom 13, ark. 484–88.

85. Serhii Kokin and Jeffrey Rossman, "Prestuplenie i nakazanie. Dokumenty iz arkhivnykh ugolovnykh del na sotrudnikov NKVD USSR, osuzhdennykh za 'narusheniia sotsialisticheskoi zakonnosti' vo vremia Bol'shogo terrora," in *Ekho bol'shogo terrora: Dokumenty iz arkhivnykh ugolovykh del na sotrudnikov organov NKVD Ukraina, osuzhdennykh za narusheniia sotsialisticheskoi zakonnosti (oktiabr' 1938 g.–iiun' 1943 g.),* ed. Marc Junge, Lynne Viola, and Jeffrey Rossman, tom 2, book 2 (Moscow: Probel 2000, 2019), 7–124; also see "Opredelenie Voennoi kollegii Verkhovnogo suda SSSR po delu P. V. Karamysheva i drugikh sotrudnikov NKVD, 30.04.1941," 509–10.

86. "Protokol operativnogo soveshchaniia nachal'stviuiushchego sostava UNKVD Nikolaevskoi oblasti, 05.04.1940," HDA SBU, f. 16, spr. 421, ark. 108–19.

87. See Andrei Savin, Aleksei Tepliakov, and Mark Iunge, eds., "Protsesy nad chekistami v zerkale regional'noi pressy," in *Ekho bol'shogo terrora: Chekisty Stalina v tiskakh "sotsialisticheskoi zakonnosti." Ego-dokumenty 1938–1941 gg.,* ed. Marc Junge, Lynne Viola, and Jeffrey Rossman, tom 3 (Moscow: Probel, 2018), 481–514.

88. At the major show trials (in Moscow), the defendants had defense counsel.

89. The exceptions to this rule were the territory of Moldavia and the Baltic countries occupied by the Soviet Union after the war. See David Shearer, *Policing Stalin's Socialism: Repression and Social Order in the Soviet Union, 1924–1953* (New Haven, CT: Yale University Press, 2009), 405–36.

90. Aleksei G. Tepliakov, "Chekisty Kryma v nachale 1920-kh gg.," *Voprosy istorii* 11 (2015): 139–45. The Party's action against the excesses of the secret police in relation

to the violation of socialist legality between 1918 and 1921 is considered a special case because of the conditions of civil war.

91. In January 1938, Vyshinskii, Stalin, and Molotov referred to the "unjustified arrests of secretaries of the Communist Party district committees and the illegal methods of investigation used by the NKVD of the Tatar ASSR." See "A. Vyshinskii, I. V. Stalinu i V. M. Molotovu o materialakh o neobosnovannykh arestakh sotrudnikami NKVD Tatarskoi ASSR," *Voprosy istorii* 1 (2017): 103. On 27 March 1938, an article, "Dikii proizvol" (Wild Arbitrariness), appeared in the newspaper *Krasnoiarskii rabochii* and reported on the leader of the district police division known as Grigor'ev, who arrested young people as hooligans even though he was not authorized to do so. On 8 May 1938, the same newspaper reported that all the facts had been proven and that Naidenov, the leader of the militia in Krasnoiarsk territory, had given the order to free Grigor'ev and to hand him over to the military tribunal because of his actions in violation of socialist law. Additionally, all employees of the district and city police had been warned that they would be made accountable if they violated socialist laws: "Dikii proizvol," *Krasnoiarskii rabochii* (27 March 1938), 3, and *Krasnoiarskii rabochii* (8 May 1938), 4.

92. See the trial documents published in Marc Junge, Lynne Viola, and Jeffrey Rossman, eds., *Ekho bol'shogo terrora*, tom 2, books 1 and 2 (Moscow: Probel 2000, 2018–2019).

4

"Enemies Within"

PERTSOV AND THE NKVD IN KHARKOV AND ODESSA

Vadym Zolotar'ov
Translated by Simon Belokowsky

NKVD INVESTIGATORS DAVID Pertsov, Ivan Kriukov, Iakov Sereda, and Aleksei Kopaev were imprisoned for "violations of socialist legality" against their own (former) NKVD colleagues. The "annihilation of honest Chekist cadres" was of course attributed to many investigators of the NKVD, but as a rule this charge was accompanied by other accusations—conspiracy, espionage, sabotage. The logic of the accusations made against Pertsov and his colleagues suggested that they acted strictly within the bounds of "socialist legality" with respect to ordinary Soviet citizens and were only particularly zealous in interrogating their own colleagues. Was this the case in reality? Were the indictments and convictions justified?

David Aronovich Pertsov was born into the family of a Jewish shoemaker in the town of Aleksandriia (an uezd or county seat of the former Kherson Gubernia) on 30 May 1909.[1] He had two brothers, Savelii and Ruvim (Robert), who, in the mid-1930s, served in the Dnepropetrovsk Oblast UNKVD, as well as a sister, Ol'ga, married to the NKVD agent Isaak Shapiro.[2] Pertsov began his working career on 15 February 1925 in the city of Ekaterinoslav at the Ukrainian Meatpacking and Slaughterhouse where he spent four years, moving up from the positions of butcher's apprentice and butcher's assistant to butcher. Not only did the difficult work of slaughter and meat-carving temper the young Pertsov physically, it also engrained within him a certain cruelty and habituated him to a bloody environment. Alongside his work, Pertsov simultaneously studied at a trade school where he received

Vadym Zolotar'ov, *"Enemies Within"* In: *Laboratories of Terror*. Edited by: Lynne Viola and Marc Junge,
Oxford University Press. © Oxford University Press 2023. DOI: 10.1093/oso/9780197647547.003.0005

a general education completed in 1928. In March 1929, he found a job at the Dnepropetrovsk Okrug Audit Commission (*revizionnaia komissiia*) where, over the course of nine months, he worked as an inspector, senior inspector, and deputy commercial agent.[3] The Audit Commission worked in close coordination with the security police staff. The Chekists there took a liking to the jaunty young man and offered him a job.

From 15 December 1929, Pertsov began his service as an auxiliary plenipotentiary of the Information Department of the Dnepropetrovsk Okrug GPU, where he gained his first experience in intelligence-gathering.[4] On 15 September 1930, he was appointed assistant plenipotentiary of the Secret Department of the Zaporozhe City GPU, before being transferred on 20 November to the role of plenipotentiary in the Zaporozhe GPU Special Department, where he immediately joined the investigation of the "Spring" case.[5] In 1931, he became assistant plenipotentiary of the Zaporozhe GPU Secret Political Department and was a participant in the falsification of a case against a local cell of the so-called Laboring Peasants' Party, in connection with which twelve people were convicted.[6] During the course of that investigation, the Chekists liberally applied measures of psychological and physical coercion: beatings, forced standing for long periods, the dangling of a high-powered electric lamp in front of victims' eyes for days on end, and nonstop, days-long interrogations.[7]

On 1 March 1932, Pertsov was appointed operative plenipotentiary of the Special Department of the 23rd Zaporozhe Aviation Brigade; on August 23 he was transferred to Kharkov to the position of plenipotentiary of the Second Section of the Special Department of the Ukrainian republic GPU and the Ukrainian Military Okrug.[8] Pertsov's move to the capital of Soviet Ukraine was connected with a change in the leadership of the Special Department of the Ukrainian republic GPU, taken up in June 1932 by Goma Leoniuk who had earlier hired Pertsov to work in the organs of the GPU and knew all about his "successes" in Dnepropetrovsk and Zaporozhe. On 17 August 1933, Pertsov was appointed plenipotentiary of the Third Section of the Foreign Department of the Ukrainian republic GPU and, on 1 December, assistant chief of the Third Section of the Foreign Department of the Ukrainian republic NKVD.[9] On 9 January 1936, he was promoted to the rank of Junior Lieutenant of State Security.[10]

Following the disbanding of the Foreign Department of the Ukrainian republic NKVD in early 1938, Pertsov was appointed assistant to the chief of the Fourth (Central European) Section of the Third (Counterespionage) Department of the Ukrainian republic NKVD. From the very start, the counterespionage operatives were confronted not only with new strategic goals (over the first quarter of 1937 they opened 556 cases against 1,257 citizens, 1,187 of whom were arrested), but also with bureaucratic reshufflings (*chekharda*). In just the first seven months of its operation, the leadership of the department turned over four times.[11]

On 2 August 1937, Pertsov, together with the new chief of the Third Department, Vladimir Styrne, interrogated a member of the Central Committee of the Communist Party of Ukraine, who served as the director of the party press. They were able to elicit the following testimony: "I became so entwined with Ukrainian nationalists that when Kost'-Kotko and Ialovoi suggested to me, a Jewish man, to enter into a Ukrainian nationalist organization I interpreted this as my being put forth as 'savior' of the Ukrainian people. This appealed to my ambitions. Without hesitation, I agreed to participate in the organization."[12] The interrogation of a member of the Ukrainian Central Committee was a testament to the trust placed in Pertsov by the new People's Commissar of Internal Affairs in Ukraine, Izrail' Leplevskii.

FIG. 4.1 D. A. Pertsov, from April 1938 deputy and then head of the Kharkov Oblast NKVD. Photo from 1938, HDA SBU, f. 12, spr. 31602, chastina 5, ark. 5 (convert). By exclusive permission of the State Archive of the Security Services of Ukraine.

On 8 August 1937, Pertsov was appointed assistant to the chief of the Fourth (Secret-Political) Department of the Ukrainian republic NKVD.[13] As the position of deputy chief of the department was vacant, Pertsov in effect assumed the second highest position in the department under the chief of this branch, Matvei Gerzon, his former colleague from Dnepropetrovsk. Gerzon would later indicate that "our selection of new cadres for managing positions was undertaken on the principle of . . . personal loyalty" to Leplevskii.[14]

Personal loyalty meant obtaining results at any cost. The manner in which Pertsov achieved this was later recalled by the personnel clerk of the Council of People's Commissars of Ukraine, Dmitrii Konovalov, from whom evidence was demanded about an underground Ukrainian nationalist organization allegedly led by his late superior, Afanasii Liubchenko. Late one night, Konovalov was brought to a specially outfitted room on the premises of the Personnel Department where Pertsov, together with his underlings, awaited him. According to Konovalov, "they all pounced on me like animals, knocked me to the ground, took to twisting my arms, pulled my fatigues over my head and, having torn off my pants and drawers, splayed me out on a specially purposed table on which they beat me with rulers and bottles until I began to lose consciousness. Following this torture, they threw me into a corner and took to pouring the liquid from a spittoon into my mouth, washing away the blood that I was choking on. Failing to get any information out of me, I was carried on a stretcher to the NKVD internal prison and thrown onto a bare cement floor."[15] The investigators took turns with Konovalov, pinned a fascist swastika to his sleeve, and pressured him to give the testimony demanded by Pertsov.[16]

Leplevskii took a liking to Pertsov's shock work in annihilating "rightists, Trotskyites, [and] Ukrainian nationalists." On 17 November 1937, Pertsov was awarded an early military promotion to Senior Lieutenant of State Security.[17] On 19 December 1937, another significant event occurred in the life of Pertsov: he was awarded the Order of the Red Star "for his exemplary and selfless execution of government assignments."[18]

On 27 January 1938, Aleksandr Uspenskii became the new head of the Ukrainian republic NKVD and immediately implemented a number of personnel changes in the Commissariat including the appointment of the chief of the Fourth Department of the NKVD, Aron Khatanever, as Acting Deputy Commissar of the Ukrainian republic NKVD for Personnel Coordination (*sovmestitel'stvo*).[19] By virtue of Khatanever's transfer, the bulk of the work involved in the management of the Fourth Department fell upon Pertsov's shoulders. Soon enough, Pertsov was considered the Acting Deputy Chief of the Fourth Department of the State Security Directorate of the Ukrainian republic NKVD.[20]

A new direction in the work of the Secret Political Departments of the various arms of the NKVD was the fight against the "antisoviet Zionist underground." As of 22 February 1938, 437 "active participants of a Zionist organization" had been arrested in Ukraine and, by the beginning of March, subordinates of Khatanever and Pertsov had "liquidated" 15 local Zionist committees and detained 607 people.[21] In pursuit of the necessary results, the chief of the Fourth Department of the Ukrainian republic NKVD and his deputy engaged in the falsification of interrogations, about which NKVD operative Lazar' Shirin later testified: "Khatanever, Pertsov . . . on their own volition inserted facts to which the accused did not speak."[22]

One of the major directions of Uspenskii's work was yet another purge of the Ukrainian NKVD, conducted on the direct orders of Ezhov.[23] Already by the end of February 1938, the contingent of staff arrested among the ranks of the Ukrainian NKVD amounted to 79 people: 11 in the central apparatus and 68 among the oblasts.[24] Between 15 February and 5 April, 554 people were dismissed from the Ukrainian republic NKVD, 154 of whom were arrested.[25] As of 1 April, 105 people from the staff of the Worker-Peasant Police Directorate of the Ukrainian republic NKVD were under arrest and 700 had been fired.[26] On 3 March 1938, Uspenskii reported to Moscow that there were 203 arrests among the command-political staff (*komandno-politicheskii sostav*) of the Internal and Border Guard Directorate of NKVD in Ukraine.[27]

Traditionally, investigations of NKVD staff were placed in the domain of a special plenipotentiary, but over the course of 1937 and 1938, when the volume of arrested staff grew by orders of magnitude, special groups were formed from members of various departments. Uspenskii gave to Pertsov— at that time Deputy Secretary of the Party Committee of the Ukrainian republic NKVD and thus privy to all manner of "signals" coming from vigilant Communist Chekists regarding suspicious colleagues—the responsibility of managing these investigations. For his part, Pertsov, in an 11 March 1938 presentation to a closed general meeting of the Ukrainian republic NKVD Communist Party organization, attributed all responsibility for the unsatisfactory waging of the fight against enemies of the people to the former secretary of the Party committee, Viktor Bliuman (who had chaired a team of investigators focused on arrested staff) and the former NKVD Commissar, Leplevskii.[28]

The special investigative group began its work on 21 February 1938. Sergei Smirnov, the head of the Third Department of the Kharkov UNKVD, would later recount the particulars of its organization: "A few days after a meeting with Ezhov, I was called by telephone to Pertsov's office. . . . Upon my arrival, several [of my] colleagues were already assembled. . . . Pertsov informed us that per Uspenskii's decree a special investigative group was to be formed to conduct investigations into the cases of NKVD staff. . . . At this same point, Pertsov invited us to come the following morning not to the [NKVD offices] but to premises designated specially for the group's work in the new [NKVD] building, presently occupied by the Council of People's Commissars of Ukraine."[29] Entrance to the premises on Sadovaia Street was permitted only to members of the special investigative group; other staff were barred from entry. All detained NKVD staff were now held in this newly outfitted prison.[30]

The search for incriminatory evidence regarding NKVD officials was conducted by inspectors of the Personnel Department of the Ukrainian republic NKVD, after which the inspectors reported to Uspenskii who would then decide the fate of the "suspect employee" [*podozritel'nyi sotrudnik*].[31] On a number of such reports, Uspenskii wrote, "arrest and unravel" [*arrestovat' i razmotat'*].[32]

According to Smirnov, Pertsov, on the basis of these incriminatory materials, gave commands to investigators regarding the direction interrogations of detained Chekists should take. If, for example, a report or other materials indicated that the detained had relatives living abroad, Pertsov would suggest an interrogation premised on espionage. If the materials indicated a connection between the accused and Trotskyists, it would be suggested to ground the interrogation around Trotskyist activities. From the very outset and until the conclusion of the group's work, Pertsov systematically passed between investigators' offices and took part in interrogations. Starting roughly with the second day of the group's work, investigators began to apply "physical measures of influence"—that is, torture. These measures were sanctioned by Pertsov and always with reference to directives from the head of Ukrainian republic NKVD or his deputy, Aleksandr Radzivilovskii.[33]

Those among the victims of these interrogations who were lucky enough to survive later testified to Pertsov's personal participation. One of these victims, the former chief of the Poltava Oblast UNKVD, Andrian Peters, wrote that Pertsov on more than one occasion entered the office of the investigator assigned to his interrogation and demanded a confession; "in response to my appeals for a declaration of what exactly I was accused of, Pertsov would respond 'write [your] confession. You will be shot in any case, you'll be torn to shreds against a wall, but you will give us information.' . . . Pertsov refused my demand for a piece of paper to write a petition to the Central Committee of the Communist Party and gave me a deadline of 7 March for my confession, threatening to 'tear' me to shreds should I refuse."[34]

The former operative plenipotentiary of the Fourth Department of the Kharkov Oblast UNKVD, Zinovii Babushkin testified that "after being beaten by investigators, I was lying on the floor. At this point, Pertsov entered the room, and I addressed him with a request to hear me out. Instead of this, he ordered that I be lifted off the ground. As I could neither sit nor stand, these so-called investigators positioned me to stand by a chair, and Pertsov picked up a club and with the words, 'I'll hear you out' began beating me. . . . After several days, unable to tolerate the beatings, I was forced to give Pertsov testimony against myself."[35]

The later account of the prison chief and official executioner, Ivan Nagornyi, sheds further light on the situation at the special prison on Sadovaia Street. He said, "Doing my rounds of the cells as head of the prison, I saw detainees delivered from interrogations by the operative-investigatory group in a difficult state on account of beatings. Moreover, walking through the corridor along which detainees were interrogated, on multiple occasions I heard detainees' screams in investigators' offices. . . . That detainees were brutally beaten by this investigatory group is evidenced by the cases where detainees, having returned from interrogation, died literally in a matter of hours, never mind that certain detainees were unable to walk back from interrogations on their own."[36]

Among those detainees Nagornyi mentioned as having died during investigation were the Chief of the Lokhvytsa District Department of the Poltava Oblast UNKVD, Ivan Taruts, the Chief of the Administrative-Economic (administrativno-khoziaistvennyi) Department of the Ukrainian Police, Vladimir Antonovich, the Chief of the Resettlement Department of the Ukrainian republic NKVD, Mikhail Shor, and the Buildings Manager of the Administrative Department of the Ukrainian republic NKVD, Mikhail Frenkel'.[37]

Pertsov was directly involved in the death of Frenkel'. Babushkin recalled that Frenkel' was brought back from his first interrogation having been beaten to the point of unconsciousness. When he came to, Frenkel' recounted to his cellmate that Pertsov had beaten him during interrogation, in the course of which he had broken his wrists as he defended his upper legs, while taking blows from the stick-wielding chief of the investigatory group. Frenkel' was brought to his cell from his second interrogation on 8 March 1938 in such a condition that he labored to breathe, could barely speak, and after a short period of time began to lose consciousness, letting out screams in the throes of his pre-death agony. He was carried out of the cell with almost no sign of life and did not return.[38] Pertsov categorically refused to allow Frenkel' any kind of medical attention. Frenkel' died without regaining consciousness. On the basis of an order from the Deputy People's Commissar Razdilovskii, a death certificate was compiled without the participation of a doctor, and his corpse was buried.[39]

On 4 April 1938, Uspenskii signed a decree appointing Pertsov to be acting deputy chief of the Kharkov Oblast UNKVD.[40] The reasons for Pertsov's transfer to Kharkov are not entirely clear, but there are at least two possible explanations. First, Grigorii Teleshev, appointed on 3 March 1938 as chief of the Kharkov Oblast UNKVD (previously serving as chief of the Tambov Oblast UNKVD), had never worked in Ukraine and lacked local know-how.[41] Second, Pertsov, having served as one of the leaders of the Secret Political Department under Leplevskii, may have failed to meet expectations (*ne obespechil nuzhnuiu liniiu*) in the unraveling of cases under investigation and was thus sent off to the provinces.[42]

Familiarizing Pertsov with the operations of the UNKVD, Teleshev indicated that his staff was penetrated to a significant degree by Trotskyists, Zionists, and other suspect elements, that he had already arrested a whole series of employees suspected of Trotskyist activity, and that it was necessary to uncover a Trotskyist group among the NKVD staff in Kharkov. For this purpose he had organized a special investigatory group headed by Ivan Kriukov, whom he personally trusted and knew from previous work.[43] Commenting on Teleshev's decision, Pertsov noted entirely correctly that the investigation of cases of NKVD staff was always handled solely by the staff of the Special Plenipotentiary (*osoboupolnomochenyi*) of the NKVD headed by Grigorii Mordukhovich, "but Teleshev did not consider it possible to entrust this investigation to him and created an investigatory group. . . . Teleshev indicated that he had selected trustworthy workers for the group. I believed Teleshev that [those] selected by him were in fact experienced workers worthy of trust."[44]

Once ten cases had accumulated, Kriukov told the chief of the NKVD Administration that "the work is difficult and I am not physically in condition to manage it on my own." Subsequently, Teleshev subordinated to him the former chief of the Miropol District Department of the NKVD, Iakov Petrovich Sereda, who had been working on an investigation in Kharkov for several months.[45] Sereda not only had an unimpeachable reputation, but he had worked throughout his entire Chekist career on the periphery and did not have any connections within the local NKVD Administration. Thus,

Teleshev summoned Sereda, telling him that within the organs of the NKVD
a major counterrevolutionary organization had been uncovered, in response
to which special operative-investigatory groups had been created, and ordered
him to work in the group under Ivan Kriukov. Teleshev added a warning that
"an enemy having managed to penetrate the [security] organs was an enemy
within, and so it [was] necessary to work actively and hold all [information]
in confidence."[46]

Aleksei Pavlovich Kopaev, a former Communist Party organizer at the A-
7 Shop of the Stalin Plant in Kharkov, was mobilized on 31 March 1938 to
work for the NKVD. He joined Sereda in the special investigatory group.[47]
Later he would declare that he recoiled from the very start at the humiliations
and beatings of detainees under interrogation. Kopaev spoke out about his
displeasure to a colleague, who then immediately reported the conversation
to the chief of the Kharkov UNKVD. Teleshev summoned the new recruit
and pronounced that "You were sent here to work not whine, and if you are
going to go easy on the enemy [*liberal'nichat's vragami*], then there is no place
for you, not in the NKVD and not in the Party either. . . . Following such a
telling off I [Kopaev] was forced to come to peace with the circumstances
around me."[48]

At the end of the hallway on the fourth floor of the Kharkov UNKVD
building, three rooms were cordoned off as the offices of the special investigatory group. At Kriukov's suggestion they were separated from other
offices by a special partition with passage categorically denied to other staff.[49]
According to Mordukhovich, the group "immediately established extreme secrecy and I was not even allowed behind the partition and if I did enter once
or twice then the case files laying on the table were immediately covered up
and I . . . was not apprised of the work of the investigatory group."[50]

The cases of detained Chekists were under the special control of
Teleshev, who would occasionally include particularly trusted figures in their
interrogations. The first interrogations of Evdokim Glebov, the chief of the
Chuguev District Department of the NKVD, were conducted by Sergei
Moskalev, Inspector under the Kharkov UNKVD, who had come with
Teleshev from Tambov. Moskalev declared to one detainee that "Teleshev has
his orders from Ezhov such that if enemies of the people like you are not
disarmed then in the UNKVD a special troika is to be established headed by
Teleshev, and this troika is already functioning and you're going to be shot.
All of this depends on us!"[51]

A few days after his arrival in Kharkov, Pertsov carried out a series of operational meetings in the various departments. He lambasted Fifth Department

special plenipotentiary Petr Bol'shunov, who had inserted an ill-considered phrase into the transcript of an interrogation. The party organizer of the UNKVD party organization, Chief of the First (German) Section of the Third Department Grigorii Dresher, decided to have a conversation with Pertsov about Bol'shunov, stating "that Bolshunov did not deserve such slander."[52] In Dresher's words, "Pertsov sharply interrupted me, saying 'You've come to teach me morals have you? If that's all, then away with you.' I noted that I did not expect such an attitude toward a well-intentioned person to which Pertsov retorted, 'And I, then, will try to keep an eye out for you, maybe I could teach you a thing or two' " [*ne pridëtsia li mne koi chemu pouchit' vas*].[53] It is worth noting that Bol'shunov's colleagues recalled him as having "fairly widely applied measures of physical coercion to detainees."[54]

A few days after this conversation, Pertsov, at an operational meeting of the Third Department, declared that following the departure of the official German representative from Kharkov, there undoubtedly remained an extralegal German consul.[55] He added that fascist assault squads (*shturmovye otriady*) planted by German agents had been uncovered in a series of oblasts and that without question analogous groups existed in Kharkov and the surrounding districts where there were high concentrations of Germans, though local Chekists had not exposed them yet. Dresher, chief of the First (German) Section, declared that there was no informational basis for the uncovering of such formations in Kharkov Oblast, as no one apprehended on the basis of the division's work had said anything about assault squads. Indignant, Petr Barbarov, Chief of the Third Department, began to interrupt his subordinate. Pertsov remained silent all the while, writing something down, and asked that the speaker not be interrupted.[56] Dresher reminded his listeners that mass operations had been underway for nine months, over the course of which all actionable information had been exhausted; on the basis of the German section's work, approximately 1,560 people had already been arrested.[57]

In their own comments, Pertsov and Barbarov noted the presence of German settlements in Kharkov Oblast. For them, the underlying question was not whether the Germans had been crushed, but instead whether the Germans were exploiting counterrevolutionary elements among various other nationalities, including Ukrainians, among whom it would be possible to create assault squads.[58] But Dresher held steadfastly to his point of view, "so long as there are no adequate prospects, especially within the oblast, for the uncovering of underground assault squads." A discussion ensued during which Pertsov pulled answers out of Dresher like teeth ("*bukval'no vytiagival otvety u Dreshera*"). At the end of the meeting, Pertsov and Barbarov set a goal for the counterespionage agents to uncover underground command structures, assault squads, and extralegal consulates in the oblast.[59]

Pertsov was outraged by Dresher's insubordination and summoned Vul'f Skralivetskii, an operative plenipotentiary, to obtain incriminatory material on Dresher. Skralivetskii refused. Following this, Pertsov ceased acknowledging Skralivetskii and was soon able to engineer his dismissal.[60] In fairness, in 1935, Skralivetskii—then serving as chief of the Second Sector of the Economic Department of the Kharkov Oblast UNKVD—had been slated for dismissal on account of his non-party status. However, the leadership at that time had kept him on in his role "as [a] particularly valuable" cadre, although he was formally classed among the supporting auxiliary (*neoperativnye*) departments and did not have any special title or assignment.[61] Skralivetskii was distinguished by a particular cruelty and sadism during interrogations, beating confessions out of detainees and leading dozens of innocent people to their deaths.[62]

More accommodating to the collection of incriminatory material on Dresher was Barbarov, with whom Pertsov had served in the Foreign Department of the Ukrainian republic NKVD. They became friendly in Kharkov and even visited each other at home.[63] Viktor Rybalkin—assistant to the Chief of the Third Department of the UNKVD and a confidant of Teleshev, having worked with him in Stalingrad and Tambov—also joined in the discrediting of Dresher. On 16 April, Barbarov and Rybalkin submitted a report on the "political infirmness of Dresher" to the Chief of the Kharkov UNKVD, who turned to Uspenskii for a warrant for Dresher's arrest, which took place on 21 April.[64]

Among other duties in Kharkov, Pertsov was responsible for the interrogations of detained NKVD cadres. He later recalled that at the end of April, Teleshev came to his office and stated that he had intended to personally interrogate and "lay into Shchegolevskii" (the former head of a sector within the UNKVD) for his refusal to give a correct confession, but that, as chief, he did not have the time for this. Pertsov remembered that

> he ask[ed] me to summon Shchegolevskii and interrogate him using measures of physical coercion as Shchegolevskii was concealing the presence of a Trotskyist-Zionist organization within the UNKVD. I remember that Teleshev put it that way. Kriukov talked to him and it was impossible to get anything out of Shchegolevskii the easy way. Kriukov... had a measure of disdain for me and [consequently] I do not know anything about his investigation of the Shchegolevskii case as he

did not brief me. As directed by Teleshev, I summoned Shchegolevskii who came together with Kriukov and offered that he should confess. Measures of physical coercion were applied to Shchegolevskii by Kriukov and myself. The interrogation lasted 30 minutes after which Kriukov left with him. I reported to Teleshev this interrogation's fruitlessness.[65]

Zinovii Shchegolevskii later narrated the details of this interrogation:

At 1 A.M. on 14 April, on the fifth floor, I was summoned to Pertsov's room (a lounge). After 10 minutes, Pertsov came in. Pertsov addressed me, stating that I was hardly the leader of a Ukrainian Zionist Center but [the leader] of the Zionist Center in Kharkov, and that a whole slew of evidence incriminates me in this matter [and] that I must confess. I responded to Pertsov that I was innocent [and] that he knows me as a colleague and decent person since 1932. At this, Pertsov knocked me from my chair with a blow and began kicking me while Kriukov took a club from the windowsill and beat me with it. . . . Pertsov kicked me all over my body with his boots and when I became sick from the blows, Pertsov grabbed me by my head and began shoving my face into the vomit.[66]

Following this interrogation, Pertsov interrogated Shchegolevskii several more times, in reference to which the latter recalled, "On 8 June instead of the chief of the UNKVD, Pertsov came. I declared that I would not sign a false transcript [of the interrogation]. Pertsov spat in my face, declaring that they would bring me to such a state that I would sign anything put in front of me, and left."[67]

On 30 April 1938, Teleshev unexpectedly left for Kiev and was quickly appointed First Secretary of the Odessa Oblast Committee of the Ukrainian Communist Party. Pertsov effectively became the head of the UNKVD, though he formally remained in the role of deputy chief. Under Pertsov's leadership, the UNKVD continued dismantling the so-called Polish Military Organization. Pertsov demanded that only ethnic Poles be arrested in the course of this operation and sanctioned the arrest of members of other nationalities only in those instances where evidence "very firmly" held them to be participants in Polish espionage or counterrevolutionary groups.[68] The course of the earlier stages of the Polish operation in Kharkov was later recounted by Dresher. According to Dresher, in April 1938, the Chief of the Second (Polish) Section of the Third Department, Rafail Aizenberg, went around the city with a group of workers arresting people on the street, at establishments, and in residential buildings without any kind of basis, subjected them to beatings on the same day, obtained confessions, and convicted them basically on the following day. "I myself was a witness to this and Aizenberg told me about it."[69]

It was possibly for this reason that Pertsov attempted to bring relative order to the implementation of the Polish operation, although the attempt did not last long. In mid-March 1938, having learned through telephone conversations about the arrest of seven hundred people in Kiev as part of the Polish operation, he ordered Barbarov to "immediately launch a wide-reaching operation against the Poles" [po poliakam]. The chief of the Third Department knew well that he lacked materials sufficient for the arrest of a large number of people, but notwithstanding this he announced to his subordinates, "It is necessary to arrest several hundred people." For the task of preparing arrest warrants, the Third Department employed an inexperienced assistant operative plenipotentiary, Kagan, who over the course of several days provided to Nikolai Pogrebnyi, the new chief of the Polish Section, writs for [the arrest of] between 200 and 250 people.[70]

The new stage of the Polish operation began under new management. On 20 May 1938, Captain of State Security Grigorii Kobyzev became the new chief of the Kharkov UNKVD. He was formerly the chief of the Personnel Department of the Ukrainian republic NKVD, who until 1937 led the Personnel Department of the Sokol'niki District Communist Party Committee in Moscow and viewed himself as a "party worker" [partrabotnik].[71] The chiefs of the oblast UNKVD administrations in Ukraine noted his "particular closeness to Uspenskii," while Kharkov Chekists remarked upon his "careerist orientation" and inclination "to be a showman" [pokazat' tovar litsom].[72]

The former assistant head of the Third Department of the UNKVD, Boris Polishchuk, who had fallen into the hands of his former colleagues, later testified to Kobyzev's "showmanship" in Kharkov:

> All though May, June, and part of July [1938], the constant screams in the night from the internal prison of the UNKVD could be heard from the UNKVD Administration building, one could hear how the "fight" [boi] was going. The entire situation psychologically conditioned [nastraivala] one in such a way that you waited and desired

only one thing—a swift death, and you did everything that was wanted of you, awaiting the promised execution.[73]

At one Party meeting, Grigorii Perevolchanskii, assistant to a section chief of the Third Department of the UNKVD, who had been mobilized to work within the organs of State Security by the Central Committee of the Ukrainian Communist Party in March 1938, reported that when he addressed his direct superior Dresher—who had at that point turned out to have been an "enemy of the people"—with respect to a certain question he received the response that "You would only understand a stick over the head" [*Vam nuzhno govorit' palkoi po golove, togda poimëte*]. In response to this, UNKVD chief Kobyzev retorted that "Dresher deserves to get one in the face for that." He then phoned Pertsov who recalled, "Kobyzev called me on the telephone and suggested that we should interrogate Dresher together. I accompanied him to Kriukov's room where we interrogated Dresher, applying physical measures of persuasion."[74]

In Dresher's recounting, the details of this interrogation were as follows:

From about ten at night to five in the morning Ivan Kriukov, lying on a couch, cursed at me, offering up for my pleasure the inhuman shouts of beaten [NKVD] workers emanating from the two oppo-site rooms where Sereda and Kopaev were conducting interrogations. Around six in the morning when the staff of the administration had already dispersed, Kriukov came into the room along with Pertsov and Kobyzev. Sereda was also in the room, having remained at Kriukov's suggestion. Kobyzev sat on the couch. Pertsov came up to me and asked whether I was going to give information about treason in the UNKVD. I declared to him that I would not do so either now or in the future. Following this, Pertsov began to torture me, his fists punching me in the face, neck, and chest and his legs, or rather his boots, kicking me in the stomach. I leaned on the wall to keep myself from falling. Pertsov shouted to Sereda to bring a club. Sereda quickly brought a thick round club from his office. Pertsov kept hitting me with the club in the head, face, and torso. Telling Pertsov to knock me over, Sereda took me by the hair and pulled me down. Following this, Pertsov, Sereda, Ivan Kriukov, and Kobyzev proceeded to stomp on me lying on the ground, at which point I rolled toward the couch. I began to lose consciousness as Pertsov and Kobyzev walked out ordering: "Beat him with death blows until he gives information, don't let him down-stairs, don't give him food or drink."[75]

Pertsov also initiated the beating of detained NKVD operatives himself. When he was unsatisfied with the responses of the detained Chekist Sandler, he declared that "he had barely gotten it, [and that they] needed to give it [to him] such that his ribs would poke out," demanding information on the counterrevolutionary sabotage efforts ordered by Polish, German, and English security services. In order to get this information, Kriukov ordered Sereda to beat Sandler with the wooden stick that members of the investigatory group had fondly named the "Roly-Poly" or the "Oaken Interrogator."[76]

In June, relations between the chief of the UNKVD and his deputy became tense. Pertsov recalled:

> Kobyzev and I began to diverge on a number of matters concerning active investigatory work, including the cases of [NKVD] staff. I considered it imperative to conduct operations more carefully, while Kobyzev felt that mistakes might be resolved over the course of investigation. . . . My disagreement with Kobyzev regarding the cases of [NKVD] staff resulted in the following: considering it possible, just as he did, that there existed a Trotskyist group or organization among the workers of the UNKVD. . . . At the same time I felt and told him that insofar as their testimony about membership in an organization of Trotskyist employees was unsupported by incriminatory material some skepticism was warranted and we should not rush with arrests without adequate scrutiny. Kobyzev found in this sentiment of mine an attempt to defend such people. Meanwhile, he, as always, referred to his experience resolving cases in Moscow.[77]

According to Pertsov, Sereda suggested that he arrest Solomon Reznikov, a deputy section chief within the Third Department; Anatolii Burkser, an operative plenipotentiary of the same section; as well as Mikhail Livshits, an operative plenipotentiary of the Fifth Department.[78] (The last of these "was known [among his colleagues] in the Special Department as one of the investigators who applied coercive measures toward the majority of his detainees."[79]) Pertsov looked over the materials and came to the conclusion that he did not have grounds to arrest them. Sereda remained unfazed and passed the materials on to Kobyzev, who spoke to Pertsov in a brusque manner about his disagreement with the latter's defense of the suspects.[80] Even so, no one among this threesome was arrested. Meanwhile, according to Livshits, Sereda was "rude and impertinent with his colleagues," for which reason the former challenged his candidacy in the Party Committee election. Pertsov came to Sereda's defense and gave Livshits a dressing-down, but, regardless, Sereda did not make it onto the Committee.[81]

Pertsov also doubted the guilt of the seasoned senior section chief of the Third Department of the UNKVD, Ivan Avdeev. He spoke with the staff of the Personnel Department of the Ukrainian republic NKVD regarding the arrested Avdeev and, upon failing to receive confirmatory incriminatory material, personally interrogated him and decided to release him. Approaching Kobyzev with this suggestion, his superior did not hear him out, but instead bluntly said that it was necessary to uncover the counterrevolutionary underground among the staff rather than be so quick to release detainees. Pertsov persisted in his opinion, to which Kobyzev declared that he would take over the matter. Shortly thereafter, Avdeev was freed and appointed an inspector subordinated to the chief of the UNKVD.[82]

According to Pertsov, "As a result of Kobyzev's choice of approach and my disagreement with him, he dismissed me from my position in Kharkov. The rectitude of my allegations against Kobyzev was later confirmed."[83] Pertsov departed from Kharkov in July 1938. By all accounts, he had not lost Uspenskii's trust. Moreover, his brother-in-law, Isaak Shapiro, was at that point Deputy People's Commissar of Internal Affairs of the Ukrainian republic NKVD for Auxiliary Departments (*neoperativnye otdely*).[84] Pertsov was soon appointed to a position in Odessa as Chief of the Naval Department of the NKVD. Notably, this appointment was not formalized through personnel decrees of NKVD USSR, NKVD Ukraine, or the Kharkov UNKVD. It is also not recorded in his personnel file.

Pertsov was relatively at ease in Odessa. Pavel Kiselev, his former chief at the Third Sector of the Foreign Department of the Ukrainian republic NKVD, was serving as the chief of the UNKVD and Grigorii Teleshev as the First Secretary of the Odessa Oblast Committee of the Ukrainian Communist Party.[85] It is entirely possible that it was Teleshev who facilitated Pertsov's transfer to Odessa.

Pertsov took to his work in the Naval Department with his inherently cruel manner, which later prompted his onetime subordinate, Girshman, to say, "there's a rotten smell in the department; Uspenskii's henchman Pertsov summoned [some] young fellows and reduced them to tears."[86] The Chief of the Eleventh (Seaborne) Department of the Odessa UNKVD, Semen Karutskii, testified that as a rule those arrested by Pertsov's subordinates were detained for extra-statutory periods, without petitions for extensions of their detention. Charges were never filed on time, and everything was done at the close of the investigation.[87]

When he was working in Odessa, Pertsov attempted to purchase property confiscated in Kharkov for 1,200 to 1,300 rubles, but in fact valued at between 15,000 to 18,000 rubles; however, the intervention of Assistant Chief of the Kharkov UNKVD, Vladimir Demin, and Kharkov NKVD Inspector Nikolai Kriukov spoiled this illicit deal. Kriukov later stated that Pertsov "acted like a petty haggler attempting to take for himself as much as he could from the staff expense accounts, which aroused more than just my own indignation."[88]

Pertsov notably feuded with Kriukov, whom he appointed Inspector of the UNKVD in May 1938. The issue was that, aside from his proper responsibilities, Pertsov tasked Kriukov with visiting the canteen to pick up foodstuffs, which aroused the latter's fervent protest leading him to bring "to Pertsov the matter of categorically freeing [him] from such a distinguished mission as it conflicted with the responsibilities accruing to an inspector subordinated to the management." Pertsov was forced to find a new inspector, which fell to one Bol'shunov who, following earlier excoriations, was obedient and accommodating.[89]

A sharp turn in Pertsov's fate was brought about by the flight of People's Commissar Uspenskii. On the evening of 14 November 1938, Uspenskii disappeared after leaving the following note on his office desk: "Farewell my dear comrades! Should it be necessary, search for my corpse in the Dnepr. This as it's surer to shoot oneself and [go] into the water... without a misfire."[90] No one believed that Uspenskii had committed suicide and an immediate search began. Members of his inner circle were arrested for "abetting" his flight. On 16 November 1938, Pertsov himself was arrested.[91] He was immediately sent to Moscow as a "participant in a counterrevolutionary Right-Trotskyist organization and antisoviet conspiracy in the Ukrainian republic NKVD."[92] There, according to family lore, the new People's Commissar of Internal Affairs of the USSR, Beria, personally participated in his interrogation.[93]

The details of the investigation of Pertsov conducted at the Lubyanka in Moscow are presently impossible to establish, as his criminal case file is held by the Federal Security Service of the Russian Federation and is inaccessible to Ukrainian (and other) researchers. We can, however, obtain a sense of the contours of his time there from his own statement to the procurator Pankrat'ev, which indicated that he was accused of aiding Uspenskii in his escape. Pertsov said:

Two scoundrels revealed themselves in the persons of Iaraliants, the First Deputy People's Commissar of Internal Affairs in Ukraine, and Tushev, the Chief of Uspenskii's secretariat, who gave testimony against me in my presence at a face-to-face deposition. Iaraliants and Tushev testified that Uspenskii had for precisely that purpose nominated and eventually transferred me to Odessa—seeing as how I knew the border—so that I would lay a path for him to cross it, which I, as they declared in my presence at the face-to-face deposition, carried out. . . . They were believed and not me. After the face-to-face depositions it was demanded of me that I name the country and by which steamboat—Soviet or forcign—I had illegally sent Uspenskii over the border. I was cruelly tortured. My calves and heels were beaten with a rubber club. I urinated blood, partially lost my sight, but did not satisfy this brazen accusation. When Uspenskii was caught, the deposition transcripts disappeared from my file, but I was not released from custody.[94]

Themselves under arrest, Kobyzev and the Deputy People's Commissar of the NKVD of Moldavia, Nikolai Malyshev, accused Pertsov at a face-to-face deposition of participating in conspiratorial activity, but, according to Pertsov, their "testimonies were so dishonest that neither of them could answer a single one of the questions that I posed to them. I exposed Kobyzev's deceit to such a degree that he refused to testify in person against me in front of the Military Collegium."[95]

On 15 August 1939, the Military Collegium of the Supreme Court of the USSR tried Pertsov.[96] He was accused of having

subjected workers of the Oblast NKVD apparatus, leaders from the Party, Soviet, and economic organizations—citizens guilty of no crime against Soviet power—to persecution. Under the guise of waging battle against counterrevolutionary elements [he] applied perverse methods of investigation, contrived fake counterrevolutionary structures, and shrouded from detection actual enemies of the people.[97]

Pertsov was convicted according to statute 206-17 (a) of the criminal code of the Ukrainian SSR and sentenced to four years' imprisonment, without a forfeiture of privileges and without the initiation of a motion to strip him of either the Order of the Red Star or the special title of Senior Lieutenant of

State Security.[98] He served his sentence in the NKVD's Northeastern Labor
Camp in the city of Magadan in Khabarovsk Krai.

While Pertsov was being dealt with in Moscow, investigators in Kharkov
were hot on the trail of his illicit collaborators. On 22 March 1939, Iakov
Sereda, Chief of the First Sector of the Special Department of the NKVD of
the Kharkov Oblast Military District, was detained. On 2 April 1939, a general
meeting of the Communist Party organization of the Kharkov UNKVD issued Barbarov a strict reprimand with a notation to the effect in his personnel
file that he, "to the benefit of the enemy of the people Pertsov, drafted a report serving as the basis for the arrest of Dresher, thus helping Pertsov dis-
pense with Dresher and ... blindly trusting Pertsov, executed his treacherous
orders." Three days later, the bureau of the Kaganov District Committee of
the Communist Party endorsed this decision, reprimanding Barbarov for the
"dampening of Bolshevik vigilance manifested in [his] servility to Pertsov
(subsequently) arrested by the organs of the NKVD."[99]

Ivan Kriukov was arrested on 17 November 1939. He had been veri-
tably showered in honors after Pertsov's departure, receiving the title of
Senior Lieutenant of State Security, the Badge of Honored Worker of the
Cheka-GPU (XV), and appointment as head of the newly created Eighth
(Industrial) Department of the Kharkov UNKVD. At the end of October
1938, he was sent to Odessa where, owing to the favor of the First Secretary of
the Oblast Committee of the Party, Teleshev, he was in short order appointed
acting Oblast Procurator. On 26 December 1939, Kopaev, then serving as
Chief of the Grun' District Department of the Sumy NKVD, was arrested.
He would write in a letter to the First Secretary of the Central Committee of
the Ukrainian Communist Party, Nikita Khrushchev, that the

> former Secretary of the party oblast committee, Osipov, declared at an
> operational meeting that "It is better to beat an enemy well and later
> answer for having beaten him rather than to leave him untouched and
> bear guilt before the Party." So I was taught from my very first days of
> work. I beat those for whom there was a sanction. In the presence of
> the Chief of the Fourth Department, Ginesin, I beat section chiefs and
> others.[100]

In the course of the investigation of the cases against Sereda and Kopaev,
"new circumstances" were "uncovered" and it was decided that it was necessary to continue the investigation of Pertsov. In April 1940, Pertsov was
brought back to Kharkov where new charges were levied against him, largely

pertaining to the beatings of NKVD cadres. Pertsov declared to his interrogator, Deputy Chief of the Investigatory Section of the Kharkov NKVD
Mikhail Kuznetsov, that

> in the Dresher case I was in agreement with Teleshev and Kobyzev,
> suspecting him to be an agent of German intelligence on the basis of
> Barbarov and Rybalkin's reports. . . . My fault here is that I trusted
> Barbarov and Rybalkin and failed to personally check the [under-
> lying] materials, to which I testified before the Military Collegium of
> the Supreme Court of the USSR.[101]

Sereda echoed the version of events according to which Pertsov had not
been the instigator of Dresher's arrest: "Materials concerning Dresher were
collated under the direction of Teleshev and the employees of the Third
Department, Rybalkin and, allegedly, Barbarov."[102]

Interestingly, over the course of the second investigation, questions concerning "violations of socialist legality" in regard to ordinary Soviet citizens
were generally not posed to Pertsov. However, he did state that

> I was aware of the massive baseless arrests. [Cases were based] solely
> on the confessions of the arrested in the Radio Committee case, in
> the Partisans case; I knew that physical measures of influence were
> being applied but did not take measures to stop them, for which
> I was convicted by the Military Collegium. Yes, in order to make
> judgments about the correctness of the arrests and beatings one
> ought to have personally studied the materials regarding the arrested.
> Both I and Kobyzev limited ourselves to the information provided
> by investigators and endorsed their opinions regarding the framing
> of crimes as counterrevolutionary, as enemies of the people, and from
> this everything else followed. I do not deny that I myself beat four
> people as enemies of the people—we beat them in a group, we used a
> club also.[103]

At its 27–30 September 1940 session, the Military Tribunal of Kharkov
Military District convicted Ivan Kriukov, Iakov Sereda, and Aleksei Kopaev
under statute 206-17 (a) and sentenced them to four years' imprisonment.

A 12 December 1940 decree of the Supreme Court of the USSR canceled
Pertsov's conviction and sentence, and his case was remanded to be investigated
anew.[104] Unfortunately, the Ukrainian archives do not contain the case file for

the third investigation of Pertsov, only the verdict. The case was tried from 5 to 6 June 1941 by the military tribunal in Kiev. The verdict read:

> the preliminary and judicial investigation established that PERTSOV, working in the organs of the NKVD, was closely connected with the previously unmasked enemy of the people USPENSKII and was moved [up] through the ranks by the latter.
>
> The unmasked and convicted enemy of the people USPENSKII, knowing of PERTSOV's proximity to LEPLEVSKII, decided to use PERTSOV for conducting his treacherous activity. For this purpose USPENSKII first promoted PERTSOV and then tasked him to lead an investigatory group created by him—by USPENSKII—among the purposes of which was to stymie the best Chekist cadres by means of mass and baseless arrests and ensuing convictions of NKVD staff, who stood in the way of USPENSKII's implementation of his treacherous activities.
>
> Leading a special operational-investigatory group, PERTSOV, directly and through his subordinates, countenanced perverse methods of investigation against detained NKVD staff against whom there was no incriminatory material and . . . forced them with the use of physical measures of persuasion to give knowingly false confessions about belonging to counterrevolutionary groups.
>
> Over the course of the existence of this group, i.e., from 21 February to 30 April 1938, 241 NKVD employees were arrested and, as a result of the application of physical measures of persuasion by investigators of the investigatory group chaired by PERTSOV and by him directly, some detainees were not able to tolerate the torture and died during interrogations (Frenkel', Shor, Taruts, et al.)[105]

The "best Chekist cadres . . . who stood in the way of Uspenskii's implementation of his treacherous activities" had, it must not be forgotten, actively engaged in the same measures under the previous leadership, namely, Leplevskii's. Over the last two months of 1937 alone, the troika of the Poltava UNKVD under the leadership of Peters had convicted 4,087 people, 1,279 of whom were sentenced to capital punishment.[106]

The sentencing document read further:

> Promoted in April 1938 to the post of Deputy Chair of the Kharkov UNKVD, upon his arrival in Kharkov, PERTSOV subsequently

headed up a special operational-investigatory group which was organized on the example [of the one in] Kiev.

This group arrested 18 members of the NKVD staff who had worked 15 to 18 years within [the security] organs and under the direct management of PERTSOV likewise applied perverse methods of investigation, producing information about their participation in counterrevolutionary organizations even though the investigatory group did not possess any incriminatory materials regarding these employees.

Each of these 18 people was freed after a lengthy period of detention and their cases closed on the basis of the absence of any crime.

Thus, under the guise of waging battle against counterrevolution and by applying perverse methods of investigation, the investigatory group headed by PERTSOV artificially manufactured nonexistent counterrevolutionary groups.[107]

Unlike most Chekists sentenced at this time, Pertsov was charged with "counterrevolutionary crimes" (Article 54-17 of the Ukrainian criminal code) for his participation in a "counterrevolutionary conspiracy" supposedly led by Uspenskii. The sentence read:

David Aronovich PERTSOV on the basis of statute 54.7 and 27.1 of the Criminal Code of the Ukrainian SSR [is sentenced] to imprisonment in a labor camp for a term of 15 years with a forfeiture of rights according to points (a), (b), and (v) of statute 29 of the Criminal Codex of the Ukrainian SSR for three years and, likewise, to relieve him of the title of Senior Lieutenant of State Security.[108]

Pertsov served his sentenced in the Southern Ural NKVD camp. On 21 July 1945, on the basis of his highly productive output and excellent behavior, his sentence was commuted by six months. He was, however, not fated to see freedom. On 28 April 1948, he died at his place of confinement.[109] According to his relatives, Pertsov perished in a logging accident.[110]

Notes

1. RGASPI (Russian State Archive of Social and Political History). (All-Soviet [Bolshevik] Communist Party Registration Form No. 2323823).
2. HDA SBU Kharkiv (Kharkiv Sectoral Archive of the Security Service of Ukraine), os. spr. 9918, ark. 49.

3. RGASPI, f. 17, op. 99. (All-Soviet [Bolshevik] Communist Party Registration Form No. 2323823.)

4. HDA SBU Kharkiv, os. spr. 9918, ark. 63.

5. HDA SBU Kharkiv, os. spr. 9918, ark. 17, 63. The so-called Spring case targeted a supposed "all-union counterrevolutionary military officers' organization" within the Red Army. In Dnepropetrovsk Oblast alone, 558 people were arrested and, among those, 21 were shot. HDA SBU, f. 6, d. 67093 fp (fond prekrashchennykh del), tom, l. 9.

6. "Sprava 'Ukrains'koi filii Trudovoi selians'koi partii,'" in Reabilitovani istoriieiu, ed. T. F. Grigor'iev and V. I. Ocheretianko (Kyiv: AN Ukraini, 2010), 20. The fictive "Laboring Peasants' Party" was supposedly preparing an armed uprising against the Soviet Union and consisted mainly of agricultural specialists and scholars as well as more prosperous peasants.

7. "Sprava 'Ukraïns'koï filiï,'" 280–81.

8. HDA SBU Kharkiv, os. spr. 9918, ark. 63.

9. HDA SBU Kharkiv, os. spr. 9918, ark. 63.

10. "Prikaz NKVD SSSR po lichnomu sostava No. 18 ot 9 fevralia 1936, A GUVD U KhO (Archive of the Main Administration of Internal Affairs of Ukraine in Kharkov Oblast), Kollektsiia dokumentov NKVD SSSR za 1936, tom 1, ark 114.

11. HDA SBU, f. 13, spr. 408, tom 1, ark. 92.

12. O. G. Musienko, ed., Z porohu smerti: pys'mennyky Ukraïny—zhertvy stalins'kykh represii (Kyiv: Radians'kyi pys'mennyk, 1991), 291–93.

13. "Prikaz NKVD Ukraina po lichnomu sostavu No. 308 ot 8 avgusta 1937," A GUVD U KhO, Kollektsiia prikazov NKVD Ukraina po l/s za 1937, tom 2, ark. 61.

14. "Prikaz NKVD Ukraina po lichnomu sostavu No. 308 ot 8 avgusta 1937," A GUVD U KhO, Kollektsiia prikazov NKVD Ukraina po l/s za 1937, tom 2, ark. 61–64.

15. "Protokol dopytu Dmytra Vasyl'ovycha Konovalova, 1956 VII.6," Nashe mynule 1, no. 6 (1993): 61–62.

16. Reabilitovani istoriieiu. Kyivs'ka oblast' (Kyiv: Osnova, 2011), 3:394.

17. "Prikaz NKVD SSSR po lichnomu sostavu No. 2227 ot 17 noiabria 1937," A GUVD U KhO, Kollektsiia prikazov NKVD SSSR za 1937, tom 4, l. 205.

18. Pravda, 20 December 1937, 3.

19. "Prikaz NKVD Ukraina po lichnomu sostavu No. 43 ot 3 fevralia 1938," A GUVD U KhO, Kollektsiia prikazov NKVD Ukraina po l/s za 1938, tom 1, ark. 18.

20. "Prikaz NKVD Ukraina po lichnomu sostavu No. 117 ot 4 aprelia 1938," A GUVD U KhO, Kollektsiia prikazov NKVD Ukraina po l/s za 1937, tom 1, ark. 79.

21. HDA SBU, f. 16, op. 31, spr. 81, ark. 91.

22. O. Loshyts'kyi, "'Laboratoriia': Novye dokumenty i svidetel'stva o massovykh repressiiakh 1937–1938 godov na Vinnichine," Z arkhiviv VUChK-GPU-NKVD-KGB, nos. 1–2 (1998): 215.

23. TsDAHO (Central State Archive of Public Organizations of Ukraine), f. 1, op. 1, spr. 544, ark. 476.

24. HDA SBU, f. 16, op. 32, spr. 71, ark.3.

25. V. V. Chentsov, *Tragicheskie sud'by: politicheskie repressii protiv nemetskogo naseleniia Ukrainy v 1920–1930-e gody* (Moscow: Gotika, 1998), 107.

26. S. M. Bohunov, "Chystky chekists'kykh kadriv v Ukraini v period 'iezhovshchyny,'" in *Ukraina v dobu "velykoho teroru 1936–1937,"* ed. Yuri Shapoval et al. (Kyiv: Lybid, 2009), 47.

27. HDA SBU, f. 16, op. 31, spr. 6, ark. 44–45.

28. "Vytiah iz protokolu No. 8 zahal'nykh partiinykh zboriv partorhanizatsiï UDB NKVS URSR 10-11 bereznia 1938 r.," in *Ukraïna v dobu "velykoho teroru" 1936–1938 roky*, 257–58.

29. HDA SBU, f. 6, d. 49855 fp., tom 1, ark. 65.

30. HDA SBU, f. 6, d. 49855 fp., tom 1, ark. 67.

31. "Stenograma vystupiv po zvitnii dopovidi partiinoho komitetu NKVS URSR, 10 hrudnia 1938 r.," *Ukraïna v dobu "velykoho teroru,"* 299.

32. HDA SBU, f. 16, op. 3, spr. 95, ark. 5.

33. HDA SBU, f. 6, spr. 49855 fp., tom 1, ark. 65–66.

34. HDA SBU, f. 5, spr. 51645, tom 1, ark. 68.

35. Bohunov, *Chystky chekists'kykh kadriv*, 52.

36. HDA SBU, f. 6, spr. 49855 fp., tom 1, ark. 67.

37. O. B. Khrystenko, "Sprav, shcho zasluhovuiut' na uvahu, ne mav," in *Reabilitovani istoriieiu* (AN Ukraini. Institute istorii Ukraini), ed. P. T. Tron'ko et al. (Kyiv: Ridnyi krai, 1992), 367–68; HDA SBU, f. 6, spr. 49855 fp., tom 1, ark. 67 zv.

38. HDA SBU, f. 6, spr. 49855 fp., tom 2, ark. 226.

39. HDA SBU, f. 6, spr. 49855 fp., tom 1, ark. 67–67 zv.

40. "Prikaz NKVD Ukraina po l/s No. 117 ot 4 aprelia 1938," A GUVD U KhO, Kollektsiia prikazov NKVD Ukraina po l/s za 1938, tom 1, l. 79.

41. "Prikaz NKVD Ukraina po l/s No. 190 ot aprelia 1938," A GUVD U KhO, Kollektsiia prikazov NKVD Ukraina po l/s za 1938, tom 1, ark. 141.

42. HDA SBU, f. 6, spr. 701117 fp., tom 1, ark. 121.

43. HDA SBU, f. 5, spr. 67398, tom 6, ark. 8. Lieutenant of State Security Ivan Ivanovich Kriukov was born into a middle peasant family (*seredniak*) in Saratov Gubernia. A member of the Communist Party since December 1930, he graduated from the Leningrad University of Soviet Law in 1926. From 1932 to 1937, Kriukov worked as a special plenipotentiary in the Stalingrad Oblast NKVD. Up to June 1937, he was the chief of the Sixth Sector of the Fourth Department of the Stalingrad Oblast UNKVD; after that, he became the chief of the Khoperskii District Administration within Stalingrad Oblast. From 14 December 1937, he was the head of the Fourth Sector of the UGB of the Kharkov UNKVD. In February and March 1938, he was assigned to a special investigatory group in the Ukrainian republic NKVD for the cases of arrested NKVD staff. He subsequently returned to Kharkov, where Teleshev assigned to him the investigation of arrested Chekists. (HDA SBU, f. 5, spr. 67398, tom 10, ark. 165.)

44. HDA SBU, f. 5, spr. 67398, tom 10, ark 29 zv; HDA SBU, f. 5, spr. 67398, tom 6, ark. 28.

45. HDA SBU, f. 5, spr. 67398, tom 10, ark. 165. Sereda was born in 1903 in the settlement of Borki [ukr. Birky] (Borkovskaia Volost, Zenkov Uezd, Poltava Gubernia) to the family of a Ukrainian peasant. From his youth he worked as a hired laborer for wealthy peasants and German settlers and in 1915, upon graduation from a village primary school in Borki, relocated to the Northern Caucasus where he worked for three years as a repairman on the Vladikavkaz Railroad in Rostov-on-Don and Yekaterinodar. In autumn of 1918, Sereda returned home and worked as Secretary of the Borki Volost Committee of Poor Peasants. When Denikin's troops moved through the area, Sereda fought as a partisan in the Gadiach and Zenkov Uezds of Poltava Gubernia and, following the Bolshevik occupation of the Poltava region, worked as the Secretary of the Land Department of the Borki Volost Executive Committee. From July 1921 to February 1922, Sereda was an artilleryman of a special group fighting banditry in the Gadiach and Zenkov Uezds. From February 1922 to June 1930 he was a plenipotentiary for the distribution of nationalized lands under the Borki Volost Executive Committee, cadet-student of the Piriatin Soviet-Party School, secretary of the Komsomol cell in the village of Kovalevka [ukr. Kovalivka] (Kovalevka District, Poltava Okrug), Chair of the Borki Village Council (sel'sovet), cavalryman of the Red Army's Third Bessarabian Division in Berdichev, Political Inspector of the Zenkov District Executive Committee, Chair of the Zenkov District Committee of Poor Peasants, and instructor of the Organizational Department of the Poltava Okrug Consumers' Cooperative (potrebsoiuz). In June 1930, Sereda became a member of the Communist Party, having been transferred beginning in May 1926 into the ranks of the organs of State Security, where he engaged in active work in Karlovka, Sakhnovshchina [ukr. Sakhnovshchyna], and Khorol Districts. In April 1933, he was appointed the Chief of the Miropol District UGB, which he headed until 1938. (RGASPI, f. 17, op. 99, All-Soviet (Bolshevik) Communist Party Registration Form No. 0425595.)

46. HDA SBU, f. 5, spr. 67398, tom 9, ark. 30–31.

47. Aleksei Pavlovich Kopaev was born in 1907 into a family of poor Ukrainian peasants in the village of Verbliuzhka (Verbliuzhka Volost, Aleksandriia Uezd, Kherson Gubernia) and became a member of the Communist Party in 1932. At twelve years old, Kopaev began work as a hired laborer and at twenty-two began his career in earnest.

48. HDA SBU, f. 5, spr. 67398, tom 10, ark. 113.

49. HDA SBU, f. 5, spr. 67398, tom 10, ark. 401.

50. HDA SBU, f. 5, spr. 67398, tom 10, ark. 362.

51. HDA SBU, f. 5, spr. 67398, tom 10, ark. 36; HDA SBU, f. 5, spr. 67398, tom 10, ark. 185; HDA SBU, f. 5, spr. 67398, tom 2, ark. 226. The growing sweep of repressive behavior within the Kharkov Oblast NKVD was richly on display in Teleshev's order of 9 April 1938 about the dismissals "under investigation" of the

chief of the Chuguev District Department of the NKVD Evdokim Glebov, operative plenipotentiary of the Fourth Department Zinovii Babuskin, Chief of the Special Mixed Air Brigade Division of the NKVD Iosif Krul'fel'd, Chief of the Special Tank Brigade Division of the NKVD Ivan Ptashinskii, chief of a sector in the Fifth Department Aleksandr Pandorin, chief of another sector within the Fifth Department Zinovii Shchegolevskii, Regiment operative plenipotentiary of the Fifth Department Boris Sandler, and operative plenipotentiary of the Fourth Department Stefan Burlakov. ("Prikaz po UNKVD Khar'kovskoi oblasti No. 213 ot 9 aprelia 1938," A GUVD U KhO, Kollektsiia prikazov UNKVD po Khar'kovskoi oblasti za 1938 g., tom 2, ark. 9.)

52. HDA SBU Kharkiv, spr. 023528, ark. 129.
53. HDA SBU Kharkiv, spr. 023528, ark. 129–30.
54. HDA SBU Kharkiv, spr. 023528, ark. 188.
55. HDA SBU Kharkiv, spr. 023528, ark. 68.
56. HDA SBU Kharkiv, spr. 023528, ark. 45.
57. HDA SBU Kharkiv, spr. 023528, ark. 41–42 zv.
58. HDA SBU Kharkiv, spr. 023528, ark. 68.
59. HDA SBU Kharkiv, spr. 023528, ark. 53.
60. HDA SBU Kharkiv, spr. 023528, ark. 53.
61. HDA SBU, f. 5 spr. 67398, tom 2, ark. 153.
62. V. P. Lebedeva, E. A. Uzbek, and N. A. Dziubenko, "My est'. My byli. Budem my," in *"Grecheskaia operatsiia" NKVD v Khar'kove* (Kharkiv: A. N. Timchenko, 2009), 225.
63. HDA SBU Kharkiv, spr. 023528, ark. 113.
64. HDA SBU Kharkiv, spr. 023528, ark. 116.
65. HDA SBU, f. 5, spr. 67398, tom 6, ark. 16–17.
66. HDA SBU, f. 5, spr. 67398, tom 8, ark. 144; HDA SBU, f. 5, spr. 67398, tom 10, ark. 173.
67. HDA SBU, f. 5, spr. 67398, tom 8, ark. 145.
68. HDA SBU Kharkiv, spr. 01893, ark. 6.
69. HDA SBU Kharkiv, spr. 023528, ark. 41 zv.
70. HDA SBU Kharkiv, spr. 01893, ark. 6.
71. "Prikaz NKVD Ukraina po l/s No. 281 ot 22 maia 1938," A GUVD U KhO, Kollektsiia prikazov NKVD Ukraina po l/s za 1938, tom 1, ark. 231; TsDAHO, f. 1, op. 1, spr. 559, ark. 117; HDA SBU Kharkiv, spr. 8201, ark. 37. For more on G. M. Kobyzev, see V. Zolotar'ov, *ChK-DPU-NKVS na Kharkivshhy'ni: lyudy' ta doli 1919–1941* (Kharkov: Folio, 2003), 312–29.
72. HDA SBU Poltava, spr. 19533, tom 1, ark. 114; HDA SBU Kharkiv, spr. 106796, ark. 22.
73. HDA SBU, f. 5, spr. 67398, tom 8, ark. 160.
74. HDA SBU, f. 5, spr. 67398, tom 6, ark. 17.
75. HDA SBU, f. 5, spr. 67398, tom 4, ark. 6.

76. HDA SBU, f. 5, spr. 67398, tom 2, ark. 90–91.

77. HDA SBU, f. 5, spr. 67398, tom 6, ark. 9.

78. HDA SBU, f. 5, spr. 67378, tom 6, ark. 9.

79. HDA SBU Kharkiv, spr. 014567, ark. 188.

80. HDA SBU, f. 5, spr. 67378, tom 6, ark. 9.

81. HDA SBU, f. 5, spr. 67378, tom 1, ark. 264.

82. HDA SBU, f. 5, spr. 67378, tom 6, ark. 9–10.

83. HDA SBU, f. 5, spr. 67378, tom 6, ark. 9.

84. For more on Isaak Shapiro, see Oleg Bazhan and V. Zolotar'ov, "'Nesu moral'nu vidpovidal'nist' za vykryvlennia v orhanakh MVS,' abo Istoriia pokarannia ekzekutora 'masovoho teroru' I. A. Shapiro u chasy 'khrushchovs'koï vidlyhy,'" *Kraieznavstvo3* (2013): 165–75.

85. HDA SBU, f. 16, op. 31, spr. 94, ark. 135.

86. HDA SBU, f. 16, op. 31, spr. 93, ark. 152.

87. HDA SBU, f. 16, op. 31, spr. 94, ark. 95.

88. HDA SBU, f. 5, spr. 67398, tom 8, ark. 339.

89. HDA SBU, f. 5, spr. 67398, tom 8, ark. 338.

90. HDA SBU, f. 16, op. 1, spr. 80, ark. 1.

91. HDA SBU, f. 5, spr. 67378, tom 10, ark. 24.

92. HDA SBU, f. 6, spr. 701117 fp., tom 3, ark. 151.

93. HDA SBU, f. 5, spr. 67378, tom 10, ark. 25.

94. Uspenskii had been in hiding in the city of Miass in Chelyabinsk Oblast and was apprehended on 15 April 1939. HDA SBU, f. 5, spr. 67378, tom 10, ark. 25.

95. HDA SBU, f. 5, spr. 67378, tom 10, ark. 25 zv.

96. HDA SBU, f. 5, spr. 67378, tom 10, ark. 42 zv.

97. TsDAHO, f. 263, op. 1, spr. 51894 fp., tom 45, ark. 187.

98. HDA SBU, f. 5, spr. 67378, tom 1, ark. 310; HDA SBU, f. 5, spr. 67378, tom 10, ark. 24.

99. DAKhO (State Archive of Kharkov Oblast), f. 23, op. 1, spr. 114, ark. 57.

100. HDA SBU, f. 5, spr. 67378, tom 10, ark. 204.

101. HDA SBU, f. 5, spr. 67378, tom 6, ark.10.

102. HDA SBU, f. 5, spr. 67378, tom 8, ark. 80.

103. HDA SBU, f. 5, spr. 6 7378, tom 10, ark. 170.

104. TsDAHO, f. 263, op. 1, spr. 51894 fp., tom 45, ark. 187–187 zv.

105. HDA SBU, f. 6, spr. 36991 fp., ark. 124.

106. L. L. Babenko et al., eds., *Orhany derzhavnoï bezpeky na Poltavshchyni (1919–1991)* (Poltava: ASMI, 2005), 70.

107. HDA SBU, f. 6, spr. 36991 fp., ark. 124. This part of the sentencing document was full of inaccuracies. First, the investigatory group focused on the cases of arrested staff was created by Teleshev. Second, the majority of Kharkov Chekists were arrested even before Pertsov's arrival. Third, the accusatory assertions regarding Pertsov's management of this investigatory group do not fully comport

with reality. Sereda testified that the "chief of the special group, Kriukov, was appointed before the arrival in Kharkov of Pertsov, who came . . . and was partially linked into the management of the group, and then after Teleshev's departure, the special group was managed by Pertsov alone, and subsequently—[by] Pertsov and Kobyzev" (HDA SBU, f. 6, spr. 36991 fp., tom 3, ark. 248). Fourth, not all Kharkov Chekists arrested in the spring of 1938 were released. Burlakov, having embezzled funds from a detainee, and Sandler and Pandorin, who had in the findings of the court violated socialist legality during their work between 1937 and 1938, were all convicted and sentenced to various terms (Zolotar'ov, *ChK-DPU-NKVS na Kharkivshchyni*, 334; HDA SBU Kharkiv, spr. 014567, ark. 187). Fifth, some number of detained Kharkov Chekists had their own skeletons in the closet, for which they should have, by rights, been at the very least sacked from the NKVD. The Ukrainian Sergei Vorontsov, senior inspector of the personnel department of the Kharkov Oblast UNKVD, turned out to be Mark Cherniak. In 1919 he had deserted the Red Army amid the advance of the Whites and then, in 1920, when the Bolshevik victory was already beyond doubt Cherniak became Vorontsov in order to cover up his desertion and obtain a Party card (HDA SBU, f. 5, spr. 67398, tom 2, ark. 156). Shchegolevskii, for his part, was forced to admit that he had falsely inserted into his biography a leg wound, his arrest by Germans in 1918, his subsequent flight from a German prison by way of arson, and his service in the Red Guards (HDA SBU, f. 5, spr. 67398, tom 2, ark. 77–78). Sixth, all "illegally arrested staff-members" themselves applied illegal investigational methods and participated in illegal mass repressions. Shchegolevskii had in 1937 managed between 110 and 120 cases pertaining to the statute on treason to the Motherland and supposedly uncovered a series of groups of saboteur-wreckers within the Kharkov Military District, for which, at the end of that year, he was presented with the Badge of Honored Worker of the VChK-GPU along with yet another in a series of special titles (HDA SBU, f. 5, spr. 67398, tom 2, ark. 77–78). Not only did Babushkin systematically beat detainees, he also affixed fascist swastikas to their chests or forced them to clutch black pennants (HDA SBU Kharkiv, spr. 08839, ark. 87). Seventh, far from all Kharkov Chekists who beat their colleagues were brought to justice. According to the testimony of Polishchuk, he was beaten by stick and by fist not only at the hands of Ivan Kriukov, who promised "We'll organize a 'dance [*tantsul'ka*]' for you, like Pertsov says," but also by Nikolai Kriukov (HDA SBU, f. 5, spr. 67398, tom 8, ark. 157)

108. HDA SBU, f. 6, spr. 36991 fp., ark. 125–26.
109. HDA SBU, f. 5, spr. 67398, tom 1, ark. 308 zv.
110. HDA SBU, f. 5, spr. 67398, tom 1, ark. 313.

5

——————

"Under the Dictation of Fleishman"

THE NKVD IN SKVIRA

Lynne Viola

THE MILITARY TRIBUNAL convened from 3 to 8 August 1940 at the NKVD club in the small city of Skvira, some 75 miles from Kiev.[1] Oskar Savel'evich Fleishman and Mikhail Mikhailovich Krivtsov were the defendants, each charged with Article 207-17 of the Ukrainian criminal code, Fleishman with the more serious point "B" and Krivtsov with point "A."[2] Fleishman was the former head of the Skvirskii district NKVD office in Kiev Oblast.[3] Krivtsov worked in the regular police, but had been mobilized to serve as an NKVD investigator-interrogator during the mass operations, a common phenomenon at this time.[4] Both were part of a larger interdistrict NKVD operational group, whose headquarters were located in the town of Belaia Tserkov, roughly halfway between Skvira and Kiev.[5]

The charges against the two were the familiar violations of socialist legality.[6] Both men were charged with the falsification of investigative files and the use of physical methods of influence (torture) against arrested suspects. Fleishman was additionally charged with forcing the members of the district's village *aktiv* (e.g., collective farm chairmen, rural soviet secretaries, and village communists) to provide witness testimony and false information describing the social and political profile of suspects under arrest. In other cases, the charges continued, he simply demanded blank signed and stamped official forms that he personally filled in.[7] The chief and most damning result of these activities was the artificial creation of a counterrevolutionary group of 39 people, five of whom had been put to death by the time the trial began.[8]

Lynne Viola, *"Under the Dictation of Fleishman"* In: *Laboratories of Terror*. Edited by: Lynne Viola and Marc Junge, Oxford University Press. © Oxford University Press 2023. DOI: 10.1093/oso/9780197647547.003.0006

Although somewhat less detailed than other cases, the provenance of this case at the district and village levels makes it particularly interesting. The case demonstrates the trajectory of the contrived master plot of the Great Terror, while at the same time illuminating the terror at the lowest level of society, within the much-beleaguered collective farms. Less burdened with contrivances than other cases, the defense rested upon varying combinations of belief, ignorance, and orders from above.

The Case of the "39"

The case of the "39" was the centerpiece in the accusations against Fleishman and Krivtsov. The two were charged with the arrests of a "series of honest communists and collective farmers" in the summer of 1938.[9] The case originally went directly to the troika for sentencing. The troika sentenced five of the 39 to death, but sent the rest back to the Skvirskii district NKVD. Fleishman then "unsewed" the case—literally (the pages were sewn together into a file) and figuratively—and created a series of new cases based on smaller groups from the original 39 and organized according to the villages where group members lived.[10]

Fleishman and Krivtsov's criminal file contains many of the documents pertaining to the case of the 39, thus permitting a backward glance at the original case. The 39 were caught up in mass operation 00447. The accused, all men, included nine agricultural specialists, seven people from strong kulak farms and/or dekulakized families, and ten men with previous criminal convictions, ranging from anti-collective farm activities during collectivization to famine-related theft or "sabotage" during the famine. Some fell into multiple categories and almost all were tainted by accusations of Ukrainian bourgeois nationalism and/or ties to petliurists (members of the anti-Bolshevik army led by Ukrainian nationalist Petliura during the civil war).[11] Fleishman also arrested a group of Skvirskii district school teachers who fell outside of the group of 39.[12] The dragnet basically pulled in a combination of technical elites and collective farmers with a suspect past. Fleishman placed the already arrested Skvirskii District Party Committee secretary, Fedor Grigor'evich Kokhanenko, at the head of the group of 39 and then linked the group to a larger Ukrainian nationalist operation supposedly led by Vasilenko, already under arrest and said to be the former head of the Kiev Oblast Soviet Executive Committee.[13]

Thirty-seven of the 39 confessed to the charges leveled against them.[14] Their confessions were extracted forcibly, either through beatings or prolonged periods of standing. The original charge against the group was both exceedingly general yet somehow all-inclusive, and it reflected a Ukrainian version of the master plot of the Great Terror:

> On the assignment of the Ukrainian counterrevolutionary bourgeois nationalist center and through it the participation of the former chair of the Kiev oblast [soviet] executive committee, Vasilenko (arrested), was set up a Ukrainian counterrevolutionary nationalist insurrectionary organization led by the former secretary of the Skvirskii district party committee, Kokhanenko (arrested), and subsequently by the boss of the district land department, Zalevskii (arrested), with the aim of overthrowing the socialist system and government of the USSR and resurrecting capitalism and breaking off Ukraine from the USSR and establishing a fascist dictatorship. The organization united antisoviet petliurists and repressed kulak elements with tasks to prepare insurrectionary-diversionary cadres in the event of war against the USSR [in order] to raise an uprising in the rear; to carry out harmful activities in agriculture; to create material difficulties in order to stimulate unrest among the masses; to be prepared to destroy food warehouses in the event of war; to draw in new members from kulaks, petliurists, antisoviet elements; to carry out antisoviet propaganda among the population in the aim of discrediting the collective farms and breaking Ukraine from the USSR and orienting Ukraine to the fascist countries of Poland and Germany.[15]

This relentlessly and sullenly repetitive diatribe represented the worst Fifth Column nightmares of the Communist regime, reflecting fears based on the realities of popular protest during the civil war and collectivization, especially in Ukraine, and the tense international situation of the times, but in no way reflected current realities.

The troika and the NKVD special plenipotentiary who later reviewed the case were dismayed by what they considered to be the overly general nature of these charges and the lack of clear evidence.[16] The case against the medical worker Fedor Mikhailovich Iashchenko was the only one with concrete charges. He was accused of making incorrect diagnoses of illnesses and ignoring the unsanitary conditions of the village, thus creating "possibilities" for contagion among children.[17] Anything could be politicized within the context of the Great Terror, including what perhaps were the negligent actions or unpopular personality of the village medic. The remaining cases, however, were completely fanciful, requiring forced confessions and willing or coerced witness testimony. Fleishman would have had to have been far more resourceful to present a more specific case within the overall fiction of the Great Terror and the targeting of specific political, economic, and social categories of the population in the mass operation.

Fleishman did try. To bolster the case against the former members of the 39, he sought witness testimony to solidify the confessions.[18] He needed damning information not only about his prisoners' current, vague activities, but, more important, about their social, economic, and political pasts, which virtually determined hostile activities in the Communist worldview of that time. According to the NKVD special plenipotentiary, Fleishman "planted" the fiction of the story of the 39 in his witnesses' testimony. He provided his investigators, mainly simple policemen, with a text and a standard set of questions and answers. He also instructed his investigators to compile witness testimony in such a way that it was to contain not concrete facts but general phrases designed around the master plot. This would also allow Fleishman to make "corrections" in the witnesses' testimony. In most cases, witnesses did not read their testimony, but signed blank papers in advance. Fleishman made use of a set of regular, official witnesses within each village. He and Krivtsov told them they would not be required to appear in court (a common promise made to witnesses at the time) and therefore need not worry about "incorrect testimony" or confronting the accused. Fleishman instructed his investigators to label all witnesses as rank-and-file collective farmers and nonparty.[19]

Fleishman then sent the cases on to the NKVD *Osoboe soveshchanie* (the NKVD's highest sentencing board), where the accused were sentenced to varying lengths of time in the labor camps. Before long, however, many of the accused as well as the witnesses began to retract their confessions and testimony.[20] This was a fairly widespread phenomenon following the November 1938 scaling-back of mass operations. By November 1939, the NKVD issued a directive to halt the cases against the former members of the 39, particularly singling out the district party secretary, Kokhanenko, who retracted his confession and told of the "incorrect methods" used during his interrogations. Kokhanenko also reported that he and Fleishman had poor mutual relations and that Fleishman had told an NKVD colleague that he would "ruin" him.[21] On 16 January 1940, the NKVD called for the re-examination of all of Fleishman's cases.[22] Within months, most of the original 39, minus those no longer alive, were freed, and Fleishman and Krivtsov were behind bars.

The Trial

The trial took place at the height of a scorching Ukrainian summer in early August 1940. By this time, Fleishman had sat in prison for six to seven months and Krivtsov for four.[23] At the outset of the trial, Fleishman denied all guilt, retracting a partial admission of guilt from his March interrogations, likely made under torture. Krivtsov pleaded guilty.[24]

Fleishman was the first to speak before the tribunal. He was an old NKVD operative, having served in the organs for eighteen years, rising to the level of lieutenant. Born in 1899 in Kielce, a Polish town within the Russian Empire, his family moved to Mogilev-Podol'skii when he was an infant. He came from a working-class family. He had a primary education and was a typesetter by profession. He fought with the Red Army during the Russian civil war and entered the Cheka in 1921. He joined the party in 1931, received a reprimand in 1934 (which was lifted in 1935), and was married with two children.[25] At the beginning of his trial, Fleishman declared that "nothing I did was for mercenary ends. In eighteen years of work in the organs of the NKVD, I never violated revolutionary legality and always honorably carried out my assigned duties."[26]

From Fleishman's testimony and others, it appears that 1937 was a relatively calm year for the NKVD in Skvirskii district. Repression heated up only in 1938, stimulated by deliberate turnover among the leaders of the interdistrict operational group in Belaia Tserkov and the visits of a series of high-level oblast officials. I. M. Pivchikov was the head of the group until sometime in the summer of 1938 when Ivan Ignat'evich Babich arrived. Ivan Babich then served as leader of the group for about one month, during which time the terror steeply escalated. He was followed by Mikhail Mikhailovich Tsirul'nitskii, who ran the group in August, September, and December 1938.[27]

In his interrogations and in a handwritten confession, Fleishman documented the escalation of the terror and the role he claimed was played by higher-level officials in the summer of 1938. Still under Pivchikov, Fleishman arrested one Nastevich. In his confession, Nastevich literally implicated the entire district's rural officialdom—every collective farm chair, every rural soviet secretary, and many communists and district officials. Fleishman said he told Pivchikov that, according to Nastevich's confessions, he would have to arrest every official in the district. Fleishman also said that he told Pivchikov that they had no compromising evidence on the majority of these people. Pivchikov then told Fleishman to wait for the arrival of Dolgushev, the head of the Kiev Oblast NKVD, who was scheduled to get there that evening.[28]

As soon as he arrived, Dolgushev called an operational meeting at which Pivchikov reported that the Belaia Tserkov interdistrict operational group had uncovered a branch of a Ukrainian insurrectionary organization in Skvirskii district. According to Ivan Babich, Dolgushev called for their "immediate arrest."[29] He mocked Fleishman, telling him, "You will work, Fleishman, or do you think that the operational group will work for you?" Fleishman later claimed that "Dolgushev harshly cursed me and said if there is not a radical change in work then he would be forced to raise the issue of my loyalty to the party."[30] Then Pivchikov intervened, telling Dolgushev that Fleishman said that they would have to arrest the entire district and village *aktiv* if they followed Nastevich's lead. At that point, Dolgushev changed his tune, hesitating somewhat, and asked Fleishman whether they had compromising evidence for all of the newly accused. Fleishman said they had no compromising material on the majority of suspects.[31] Dolgushev gave Fleishman 48 hours to collect the requisite evidence for the cases to proceed. Fleishman then mobilized all of his cadres, sending them out to gather incriminating evidence. Initially, they only arrested seven people, but from these seven, they received additional names, leading to the arrest of the 39. Fleishman claimed that it was Ivan Babich who had the idea to link the 39 to the already-arrested Vasilenko, the former head of the oblast Soviet executive committee (*ispolkom*), and to make him the group's "leader."[32] The arrest list for the troika would be signed by both Fleishman and Ivan Babich.[33]

Fleishman also claimed that the orders to press for confessions came from above. Sometime after Dolgushev's visit, the head of the Fourth Department of the Kiev Oblast NKVD arrived with an order to make use of the infamous *stoiki*—the process by which prisoners were forced to stand uninterruptedly, sometimes for days at a time, until they "confessed." The order for forced standing, according to Fleishman, came from Dolgushev.[34] At his trial, Fleishman would claim that Ivan Babich gave the order to use physical force on individual suspects.[35] Fleishman only admitted to striking someone for what he described as "slander" and another person apparently because he was a priest.[36]

Fleishman told the tribunal at his trial that he had closely "studied" the district from early 1937 when he became the head of its NKVD branch. He said that he knew that there were many petliurists and remnants of other "bands" in villages. Following the operational meeting with Dolgushev, Fleishman sent out his investigators, mainly local policemen seconded to the NKVD, to collect witness testimony and the political and social profiles—especially from the past (meaning prerevolutionary times and the civil war)—of the villagers under arrest. He admitted to the tribunal that he told his investigators to write that witnesses were rank-and-file collective farmers and not to indicate that they were in fact party members or other village and collective farm officials; otherwise, however, he claimed that he asked them to obtain "truthful testimonies." He denied that he had used official witnesses—that is, the same select group of witnesses to testify multiple times. And he claimed that he had no idea that his investigators falsified witness testimony.[37] As far as the actual interrogations of suspects were concerned, Fleishman said that there was "a standard protocol, according to which the interrogator questioned his suspect. I personally gave the interrogators this form of protocol."[38] When he was questioned in March 1940, he also admitted to giving orders to his investigators to include the following in each of their interrogation protocols of the arrested: antisoviet agitation, defeatist agitation, and terrorist manifestations. He then said, "I gave these instructions on the basis of orders from the oblast."[39] In fact, throughout his trial, he used the excuse that he was following the orders of the various heads of the interdistrict operational group who, he claimed, were really in charge of investigations.[40]

Krivtsov was up next before the tribunal. Like many of his fellow policemen, he was a local. He had been born into a Ukrainian family in a village in the district in 1905. Too young to fight in the civil war, he joined the Red Army in 1923. After he left the army in 1933, he returned to Skvirskii district, working first in a *Politotdel* (Political Department, most probably, in the Skvirskii Machine-Tractor Station), and then in a series of other positions before becoming a policeman in April 1937. In September of the same year, he was seconded to work under Fleishman in the district branch of the NKVD. He worked both in Skvira and Belaia Tserkov until the fall of 1938. He became a member of the Communist Party only in 1938. By October of that year, he had been fired from the regular police on corruption charges. Krivtsov was married with three children.[41]

Krivtsov began his testimony by denying any guilt. He told the tribunal that prior to his mobilization into the NKVD, he had no experience in investigative work. He said, "In general, I did everything on Fleishman's orders," and he had no idea that he was violating socialist legality. His ignorance could only have been based on sheer stupidity or a justified sense that everything was permitted in the brutal culture of those times. He went on to say that Fleishman taught him, along with three other policemen (Romanov, Beregovoi, and Antonets), how to conduct interrogations at one of their operational meetings. Fleishman told them what to write. According to Kritsman, "all interrogation protocols were one and the same tract. . . . In general, as a rule, in all cases, I wrote in the interrogation protocol about the defeatism and antisoviet activities of the arrested."[42]

Krivtsov denied using physical force during interrogations despite accusations from his colleagues. He did freely admit to making suspects stand for prolonged periods of time, but justified this by saying that everyone in the operational team did the same. Moreover, he was under orders from Fleishman to complete his cases "in not more than 40 to 50 minutes." As a seeming corroboration of Fleishman's testimony, he said the arrest of the 39 only occurred after criticism at an operational meeting, "that in Skvira there is nothing," meaning there had been insufficient arrests up to that time. The arrests began directly after this meeting, he said, on the order of Pivchikov, the head of the Belaia Tserkov interdistrict operative group before Ivan Babich.[43]

Earlier, at his own interrogation, Krivtsov had presented somewhat more detail on some of the practices used in Skvira and Belaia Tserkov. In particular, he explained to his interrogator how they gathered witness testimony. In the first instance, he claimed "not to remember" falsifying witness testimony; yet all his testimony pointed precisely to falsification. He said that Fleishman ordered them to write the protocols of the witness testimony "in general terms [*ne konkretno*]" and, most of all, to write about antisoviet agitation, agitation against the Supreme Soviet elections, and rumors about the coming war with Germany. This material, according to Krivtsov, had to figure in all witness statements. Further, Fleishman instructed his investigators "that it was necessary preliminarily to select and converse with [members of] the village *aktiv* and only afterward to question them formally. In cases when a witness did not want to give testimony, they were to find someone else." Fleishman then checked each witness statement, making the necessary "corrections."[44]

Krivtsov then moved on to the actual arrests. These were made at night.[45] Fleishman "gave an order to write general, non-specific [*ne konkretnye*] protocols" when writing up cases for arrest.[46] He would later "correct" them. On one occasion, he cursed Krivtsov "with vulgar words" when the "facts" of a case did not correspond with the suspect's age. Fleishman yelled at Krivtsov: "What? Don't you have a brain?" and then "corrected" the suspect's date of birth.[47] Krivtsov also said that Fleishman had beaten a priest with a ramrod and another victim with his fists.[48] Krivtsov said that everyone was afraid of Fleishman. At the same time, he said that he did not understand that "such methods were incorrect." He explained, "I thought as a member of the party and the organs, Fleishman could not be incorrect." Fleishman had also told him that their directions came from the center and the oblast. Finally, Krivtsov told his interrogator that he and the other policemen were strictly warned never to talk about these methods of investigation and had to sign a secrecy agreement, a standard practice in the NKVD.[49]

To this point, Fleishman and Krivtsov denied any or almost any personal wrongdoing, attributing their actions to orders from above. Krivtsov had the additional excuse that he lacked experience, not to mention intelligence. At the end of his interrogation, he did volunteer additional testimony, in which he suddenly admitted that he had had doubts about the guilt of a number of the 39 as well as doubts about the methods of interrogation.[50] However, it would be up to their co-workers and superiors, along with a handful of witnesses and a few victims, to complete the story of what happened in Skvirskii district in 1938.

"There is nothing terrible about this"

Fleishman and Krivtsov worked closely with three other former policemen from Skvira: Nikolai Alekseevich Romanov, Ivan Mikhailovich Beregovoi, and Avtonom Sidorovich Antonets, the last of whom was originally supposed to stand trial with Fleishman and Krivtsov.[51] Each of them had been mobilized from the regular police to work in mass operations in 1938. None had more than a primary education, if that. Like Krivtsov, they had no prior experience working in investigative-interrogation work and received no prior training. Antonets told the tribunal that he was sent to Belaia Tserkov to lead the interrogation of those arrested in Skvirskii district on his second day of work.[52]

They were all afraid of Fleishman. Romanov said, "Fleishman related very crudely to the workers, cursing us with vulgar swear words and threatening arrest and court if we did not fulfill his orders."[53] "Fleishman yelled at everyone," Romanov told the tribunal, "saying, 'what, you are sitting surrounded by bands, counterrevolutionaries, and you do nothing.'"[54]

They all testified to Fleishman's use of physical force in his dealings with the prisoners. Romanov said, "Going by Fleishman's office door, I often heard moans and blows. Besides this, I personally saw how Fleishman beat with a ramrod the arrested Spiridon Gavva while he was lying on the ground. . . . In my presence, he also beat the arrested Korinnyi."[55] Beregovoi admitted that "the beating of prisoners who refused to confess was widely practiced among us in the district branch of the NKVD." He witnessed Fleishman beating confessions out of prisoners and noted one prisoner who was forced to stand continuously for eight days.[56] He told the tribunal that Krivtsov also beat a prisoner.[57] Beregovoi added that Fleishman had arrested a collective farmer with whom Beregovoi had served in the Red Army. Beregovoi said that he knew this man was not a counterrevolutionary and knew at least five others who were also innocent.[58]

Antonets, who said nothing about whether Krivtsov beat anyone, claimed to know of only two cases of prisoners being beaten. He saw Fleishman beat one prisoner "with his fists." And he saw one Grigorevich, presumably a fellow interrogator, beat someone. When Antonets asked Grigorevich about his actions, Grigorevich responded, "There is nothing terrible about this," neatly highlighting the tenor of the times.[59] Another policeman, Fedor Leont'evich Adamchuk, who stood watch over prisoners subject to prolonged standing, remembered Fleishman beating a priest and forcing him to join in.[60]

The collective farmer Petr Pavlovich Gutsalo also testified about the violence in Skvira and Belaia Tserkov. After he was arrested in June 1938, Fleishman and Romanov interrogated him, accusing him of belonging to a counterrevolutionary organization. Gutsalo stood his ground, refusing to confess or sign the interrogation protocols. Fleishman then kicked him in the stomach. After that, Fleishman handed him over to a group of six policemen "and ordered them to do with me what they wanted." The six men beat him with the "butt of a rifle, a revolver, and with their hands," then forced him to stand for three days, after which he finally capitulated and signed. Gutsalo said the other people in his cell had also been beaten. He later retracted his confession. He told the tribunal that he had been in his collective farm since its founding in 1929, had received awards for good work, and only fought with Petliura's forces for five days under duress.[61]

Kalistrat Viktorovich Korinnyi was a collective farmer who had been caught up in the group of 39. He told of how Fleishman beat him with the leg of a chair and forced him to stand uninterruptedly when he refused to slander himself. In the end, this simple collective farmer, who had never before been arrested and who fought in the civil war, was forced to incriminate ten innocent people. He said that Fleishman and Krivtsov had also beaten his cellmates. The oblast court freed Korinnyi from prison in March 1939.[62]

Fedor Grigor'evich Kokhanenko, the district party secretary in Skvira, testified that Fleishman held a grudge toward him because he had refused Fleishman 2,000 rubles to repair his apartment. Soon after this refusal, at a party meeting, Fleishman accused Kokhanenko of traveling drunk to the villages, corruption, and connections with alien elements. Kokhanenko was arrested in Kiev on 5 June 1937 and subsequently turned into the leader of the 39. He told the tribunal, "I consider that testimony about me given by the arrested was obtained under force" and that the real reason for his arrest was his "bad relations with Fleishman." Fleishman confirmed that he had asked Kokhanenko for money to repair his apartment, but said that when he first came to the district he heard that Kokhanenko was "closely tied to kulak elements." He continued, "I wrote several reports for the oblast NKVD administration [in Kiev] about the leading composition of the district and their links with unreliable elements, in particular I wrote this about Kokhanenko." Kokhanenko then told the court that he received a reprimand for his rude relations with several people and connections with alien elements, but that the reprimand was lifted under appeal. When he received the reprimand, he realized "that Fleishman played in this a role of the first order."[63]

Beregovoi, Antonets, and Romanov testified to the use of standard forms for prisoner interrogations and witness statements, as well as to standard content. Romanov said he regularly rewrote interrogation protocols under Fleishman's dictation.[64] He also said that Fleishman ordered all interrogators to write in their protocols that the prisoner carried out antisoviet agitation and—this was "mandatory"—discussed the defeat of the USSR in war.[65] Romanov continued that, if they did not write what Fleishman dictated, Fleishman "screamed at us, saying we were playing into the hands of the enemy."[66] Beregovoi said that Fleishman threatened to arrest him if he did not provide the correct protocols.[67] Antonets added that since he knew nothing about conducting an interrogation, he was given a model of a protocol of interrogation and told to question his prisoners according to a standard form.[68]

Ivan Babich, the head of the interdistrict operational group in Belaia Tserkov in the summer of 1938, corroborated the use of a standard pattern, not for the interrogation protocols, but for the indictment of the case (the *obvinitel'noe zakliuchenie*), compiled after interrogations and used to present the case and charges before the troika. During the trial, Ivan Babich told the tribunal, "In general, they sent from Kiev a standard model form, according to which to write indictments. In this form, they indicated the aims and tasks of the counterrevolutionary organization and in general if I corrected the introduction to the case summary on the group case [of the 39], I took data from the material of the case."[69] Mikhail Mikhailovich Tsirul'nitskii, who took over as the head of the operational group from Ivan Babich, told the tribunal that he had initially expressed surprise at how quickly Krivtsov interrogated his prisoners. Krivtsov responded that "he only rewrote or wrote under dictation. And some interrogation protocols were simply signed [forged] by Fleishman."[70]

Fleishman was surely dictating charges in Skvira and Belaia Tserkov, but the master plot was from Kiev and Moscow. The fiction of the Great Terror was grafted on to the victims of the mass operations, in the best of cases people with some kind of suspect past, in the worst of cases completely innocent individuals. And everyone was forced to play along—the policemen who had known some of the "enemies" from their youth, as well as the village and collective farm officials and activists who were forced or otherwise influenced to tell lies about their neighbors in their capacity as "witnesses."

Witnesses

Witnesses provided two types of evidence for the NKVD investigations in Skvira and Belaia Tserkov. This evidence laid the groundwork for the arrests and interrogations of the 39, although it generally followed rather than preceded the arrests. The first type of document was the *kharakteristika*, paperwork that provided a political and social profile of the suspects, including information about their activities during the civil war and before the revolution. The second was a *spravka*, which included the witnesses' descriptions of a suspect's antisoviet activities, past and present. In practice, these two types of documents were interchangeable. In almost all cases, the past prevailed over the present in determining a suspect's guilt. It was a matter of not what he did but who he was. The genealogists of the NKVD were particularly interested in a suspect's prerevolutionary past and his political affiliations in the civil war.[71]

Policeman Beregovoi explained: "As a rule, the district branch of the NKVD required from the rural soviet a form about the social past of each of the arrested."[72] As for testimony, he continued, "As a rule, we had permanent official witnesses who testified in multiple cases. Such witnesses gave whatever testimony the interrogator wanted. Generally, in each village, there was a group of witnesses who testified in all cases of [people] arrested from the given village."[73] Beregovoi's colleagues, Romanov and Antonets, corroborated his testimony on the use of official witnesses.[74]

In many cases, perhaps most cases, all the interrogator needed to do was to call in the rural soviet secretary and order him to bring with him official stationery along with the official stamp and press. Beregovoi admitted to this practice, as did the fire warden and former policeman Adamchuk.[75] Romanov told the tribunal that once Fleishman told him, "your protocol [of witness testimony] is worthless, you need another one." Fleishman sent him back to the village two to three times to obtain the "correct" results. Finally, rural soviet secretary Nikolaichuk told Romanov, "I have no time. How about if I just give you a signed blank form and then you can write what you need?"[76]

In order to disguise the fact that he forced village and collective farm officials to serve as witnesses, Fleishman ordered his investigators to describe the witnesses as rank-and-file collective farmers.[77]

The official witnesses followed the script of the Great Terror under the dictation of one or another NKVD investigator. Witnesses testified to antisoviet agitation, conversations about the defeat of the USSR in war, the coming of the fascist order, and so on.[78] Investigator Antonets went so far as to say that they sent witnesses to Belaia Tserkov to give testimony according to the "standard form," including information on antisoviet conversations, terrorist moods, and the like.[79]

The witnesses themselves also had an opportunity to testify at Fleishman and Krivtsov's pre-trial investigation and, in some cases, even at the trial. Nikolai Luk'ianovich Nikolaichuk, who had given Romanov a signed blank form, was the secretary of a rural soviet and, at the time of his testimony, the head of the Skvirskii MTS (Machine-Tractor Station). He testified: "I remember that Fleishman called me into the district-level NKVD two times with my stamp and press in order to provide a certificate for people arrested in [the village of] B. Erchika. Fleishman demanded that I write under his dictation a certificate about the antisoviet activities of these people. However, I refused to do this and wrote about [their] positive activities. Then Fleishman threatened me, declaring that I was defending the enemy. However, I paid no attention to these threats."[80] Although it is unlikely that Nikolaichuk both freely offered Romanov blank forms and stood up to Fleishman, the basic thread of the story is clear.

Another rural soviet secretary, Antonina Nikiforovna Matusevich, a people's judge at the time of her testimony, was also called into the Skvirskii NKVD office in 1938. She told the tribunal, "They called me into the district office of the NKVD and told me to provide a certificate on Tishchenko, where it could be indicated that Tishchenko was an antisoviet individual. I then said that I knew Tishchenko only from the positive side and knew nothing bad about him. After this, they suggested that I give them blank forms with the stamp and press, but I didn't do this. I went home and told my husband that they had demanded blank forms . . . my husband answered to me, 'give them anything they want, if you don't, they'll arrest you.'" So Matusevich returned to the NKVD where she ran into Beregovoi. She asked him, "can one issue a certificate on Tishchenko if it is not true?" Beregovoi told her to go home, that they no longer needed her. Matusevich added to her testimony: "I knew the Tishchenko family well. They all worked well in the collective farm. Now, Tishchenko leaves behind a family of 8." Tishchenko had been executed.[81]

Andrei Feofanovich Antonik and Domna Mikhailovna Orlova provided witness testimony about Dmitri Ivanovich Ianchuk. Antonik chaired a collective farm. He said he knew nothing about Ianchuk's antisoviet agitation, but that the interrogator Antonets "persuaded me and urged me to sign and I signed." He added that he only knew that when Ianchuk returned from exile in 1934, having most probably been exiled as a kulak in 1930 or 1931, "he worked well in the collective farm, he was the best collective farmer."[82] Orlova, who was apparently an actual rank-and-file collective farmer, testified that she "had quarreled with Ianchuk's wife and that Ianchuk's children did all sorts of harm in the collective farm," but she said nothing about Ianchuk's antisoviet activities since she knew nothing about this. "I knew Ianchuk worked well in the collective farm." She added, "The investigator did not read me the protocol and I could not sign my testimony since I am completely illiterate and don't know how to write."[83]

Another witness, Andrei Andreevich Dieskul', told the tribunal that Krivtsov did not read the protocol questions to him, but that he signed three blank forms.[84] The witness M. K. Klimas, a rural soviet secretary, admitted that "part of his testimony did not correspond to reality," while other witnesses denied their testimony or claimed never to have said what was contained in their interrogation protocols.[85]

The entire district bore witness against Fleishman. His non-local status, perhaps his Jewish background, may have contributed to his lack of popularity. At the same time, the entire district was implicated in the Great Terror, whether by force or not.[86] Within the villages of the Soviet Union, the terror was, by necessity, far more public. It was simply not possible to make arrests without the village's knowledge. Furthermore, the machinery of the mass operations required widespread participation beyond the closed corridors of the NKVD. In part, such participation was based on a feeble and perverse show of socialist legality that sought to highlight its "evidence" beyond the all-important confession and assumed the aspect of a legal, or, more accurately, administrative fetishism carried to the extreme. In part, the NKVD needed local witnesses who knew the social and political profile of the village, for, after all, there were a handful of witnesses—mainly those called by Fleishman—who stuck with their stories about petliurists and former kulaks in the village.[87] Above all, the witnesses—whether coerced or not—played a key role in the elaboration of the fiction of the Great Terror's master plot.

Back to Fleishman

On the face of it, all roads in this trial lead back to Fleishman and, to a much lesser degree, to Krivtsov. Yet Fleishman also claimed that he was only following orders—the orders of the successive heads of the interdistrict NKVD group, Pivchikov, Ivan Babich, and Tsirul'nitskii, and the head of the Kiev Oblast NKVD, Dolgushev.

Fleishman told the tribunal that all arrests occurred only on the orders of the oblast NKVD.[88] He said that the group of 39 was sent to the troika not by him but by Ivan Babich, something Babich immediately denied.[89] When the troika returned the case to him, Fleishman claimed that Dolgushev ordered him to "unsew it" (take apart the file) and form new cases based on eight to ten people each, and to direct these cases to the *Osoboe Soveshchanie*. When Fleishman asked Dolgushev if he should free several of the group's members, Dolgushev said, "do not free even one person."[90] Fleishman also claimed that Ivan Babich had indicated to him that it was permitted to use physical force in interrogations and that the permission to use forced standing came down from the oblast NKVD in Kiev.[91]

Fleishman insisted that he had warned his underlings to carefully check the evidence provided by witnesses.[92] He called his own witness—fire inspector Illiarion Iosifovich Levakovskii, who worked in the NKVD in 1938— to back him up on this point.[93] Fleishman admitted to falsifying only one case, the case of an individual named Dement'ev. He said that he did this out of fear that "they" would tie him to Dement'ev, for reasons left unclear, and arrested Dement'ev to "convince" the oblast NKVD. He knew the information gathered on Dement'ev was not true.[94]

Still, he held firm in his protestations of innocence. He declared, "I do not admit guilt in the creation of a counterrevolutionary nationalist insurrectionary organization, since all of the arrested confessed"—a rather circular argument. He did admit that he had used "illegal methods in conducting interrogations" and had instructed his subordinates to make use of forced standing. He also admitted to telling his underlings the fictive content of the case, although he added that the interrogators soon learned how to write their protocols on their own. However, he said, "In general, I received orders from the [oblast] NKVD to implement everything that occurred in the district-level NKVD."[95]

Fleishman's final statement to the tribunal began on the usual revolutionary autobiographical note, proceeded to his defense, and ended with an appeal for mercy. He said:

I want first of all to talk about myself. I came from a working-class family. I grew up in poverty and hunger. Already in 1914, I went to work for hire since my father was away in the army.

In 1917, I was among the first to enter the ranks of the Red Guard, and then the Red Army and on 4 January 1921 I was sent to work in the *Osobyi otdel* ["Special Department" of the internal security police]. Thus I worked uninterruptedly in the organs of the NKVD until 1939. In this time, I had not one reprimand, always honestly relating to my work. . . .

After I was fired from the NKVD organs, I was directed by the party committee to responsible work as the director of the state factory Dietfabrika in Odessa, where I also worked honestly, and for good results in work, I, together with the factory's collective, was awarded 10,000 rubles.

I didn't think I was committing a crime. Being at the operational meeting, they gave us various orders, how to lead investigations and whom to arrest. If I committed a mistake, then this did not depend on me, but on other circumstances.

I indisputably committed a series of gross mistakes but individual facts are the inventions of the investigators and not my orders.

For seven months, I have been under guard . . . this is for me a big punishment.

I ask that you take into account all circumstances in the determination of my fate.

Dependent upon me are my father and mother and two small children who will remain without any means of existence.

And therefore I again plead for a just sentence.[96]

Krivtsov followed Fleishman to the stand to give his final statement to the tribunal. Initially, Krivtsov had denied all guilt. Over the course of the trial, however, he admitted that he had fabricated several interrogation protocols, but added, significantly, that "all this I did only on the orders of Fleishman."[97] His final statement was brief in comparison to Fleishman's. He said, "I request [the tribunal] take into account that I never in my life had to carry out an investigation. Completely not knowing the methods of work and considering the orders of Fleishman to be correct, I see now that I committed a crime. . . . I violated revolutionary legality not because I wanted to, but because they forced me."[98] Krivtsov based his defense on ignorance and orders from above.

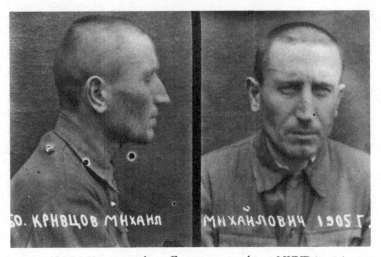

FIG. 5.1 M. M. Krivtsov, police officer, in 1937 and 1938 NKVD investigator-interrogator in Skvirskii district, Kievan Oblast NKVD. Prison photo from 1940, HDA SBU, f. 5, spr. 57637, kontrol'no-nagliadova sprava (KNS), ark. 50. By exclusive permission of the State Archive of the Security Services of Ukraine.

The tribunal found both of the defendants guilty. Fleishman was sentenced to eight years in a corrective labor camp. Krivtsov received a lesser sentence of six years. The documents do not say whether they served out their terms or were released to fight in the war, nor is the subsequent fate of Fleishman known. Krivtsov, however, lived long enough to petition for his rehabilitation in the late 1950s. Then and again in the late 1990s, the courts confirmed the original sentence.[99] The fate of Pivchikov, Ivan Babich, and Tsirul'nitskii is not clear; Dolgushev was arrested in early 1939 and stood trial roughly one week after Fleishman and Krivtsov.[100]

Following Orders

Fleishman and Krivtsov were following orders. There is no doubt about that, nor about the role of senior NKVD officers like Dolgushev in pushing the terror forward. The orders came from Moscow through Kiev. Yet Fleishman in particular certainly believed there were enemies. He not only believed, he knew there were enemies. He had fought in the civil war and knew it still cut a swath through Soviet territory. And he knew, or thought he knew, or lied that he knew who the enemies were. This is not to say that the enemy was real. In almost all cases, the civil war had ended long ago for the defeated; moreover, many had had no choice regarding which side they served in the civil war, being the objects of forced conscription by all sides. For the victors, however, the civil war remained very real, perhaps nowhere more so than in the small and isolated outposts of "Soviet power" in the countryside like Skvira.

Whether out of fear or vengeance, Stalin and the NKVD leadership also believed in the enemy.[101] In the countryside, people knew who had fought on which side during the civil war and collectivization. The logic of the mass operations was such that it did not matter what former enemies had done in the interval between the end of the civil war and the start of mass operations. When witnesses in the Fleishman case told of neighbors who were good collective farm workers, this did not matter for the NKVD. Their very existence (or survival) remained a threat. Political and social profiles were unchanging in the minds of the executors of the mass operations.

The master narrative of the Great Terror reflected the paranoia of the top leadership. It also captured the fears of a generation of NKVD officials, like Fleishman, who had fought in the civil war and understood enmity. Their fears were not just based on the civil war—indeed, many were in territories far from where they fought—but also on their actions in the years since then. Many of these NKVD officials and policemen had served in the violent collectivization and dekulakization campaigns. In Ukraine, they remembered well the famine of 1932–1933. Guilt and memory may have consolidated their fears, thereby helping to shape their actions during the Great Terror. A combination of orders from above and local creativity, not to mention ignorance, however, were requisite conditioning factors in Skvira.

Notes

1. HDA SBU, f. 5, spr. 57637 (sledstvennoe delo Fleishmana, O. S. i Krivtsova, M. M.), ark. 50. Unless otherwise noted, all archival references will be from this fond and spravka, and identified further only by the volume (tom) and page numbers (ark).
2. Tom 3, ark. 50, 52 (Protokol sudebnogo zasedaniia—further, PSZ).
3. Tom 1, ark. 2 (Postanovlenie na arrest. 1 February 1940); tom 3, ark. 50 zv (PSZ).
4. Tom 3, ark. 50 zv (PSZ).
5. Tom 3, ark. 52–53, 67 (PSZ).
6. Tom 1, ark. 33 (Zakliuchenie. 16 January 1940).
7. Tom 1, ark. 34 (Zakliuchenie. 16 January 1940).
8. Tom 1, ark. 35 (Zakliuchenie. 16 January 1940); tom 2, ark. 227–36 (Obvinitel'noe zakliuchenie. 27 June 1940).
9. Tom 1, ark. 33 (Zakliuchenie. 16 January 1940).

10. Tom 2, ark. 198–9 (Obvinitel'noe zakliuchenie po obvineniu zhitelei sela Kalennaia Skvirskogo raiona Kievskoi oblasti. November 1938); ark. 205–6; ark. 227–28 (Obvinitel'noe zakliuchenie. 27 June 1940); tom 3, ark. 107 (PSZ).

11. Tom 2, ark. 112–13 (Spravka po sledstvennomu delu no 146430. n.d.); ark. 114–52 (Povestka zasedaniia Osoboi troiki Kievskogo oblastnogo upravleniia NKVD Ukraine. Belotserkovskaia opergruppa. Raion Skvirskii. n.d.); ark. 153–70 (Obvinitel'noe zakliuchenie. July 1938).

12. Tom 2, ark. 27–28 (Protokol dopros Sverinenko, Z. E., Jan. 1940); tom 3, ark. 76–78 (PSZ).

13. Tom 2, ark. 112–13 (Spravka po sledstvennomu delu no 146430, n.d.).

14. Tom 2, ark. 112–13 (Spravka po sledstvennomu delu no 146430, n.d.); ark. 114–52 (Povestka zasedaniia Osoboi troiki Kievskogo oblastnogo upravleniia NKVD Ukraine. Belotserkovskaia opergruppa. Raion Skvirskii, n.d.).

15. Tom 2, ark. 112–13 (Spravka po sledstvennomu delu no 146430. n.d.).

16. Tom 2, ark. 227–36 (Obvinitel'noe zakliuchenie. 27 June 1940).

17. Tom 2, ark. 124 (Povestka zasedaniia Osoboi troiki Kievskogo oblastnogo upravleniia NKVD Ukraine. Belotserkovskaia opergruppa. Raion Skvirskii, n.d.).

18. Tom 3, ark. 81, 107 (PSZ). (He had not sought witnesses before the case was returned by the *troika*.)

19. Tom 2, ark. 228–29 (Obvinitel'noe zakliuchenie. 27 June 1940).

20. Tom 2, ark. 174–79 (Postanovlenie o prekreshchenii sledstviia. 29 November 1939); 181–85 (Zaiavlenie Zalevskogo. 19 August 1939); 188 (zaiavlenie Chetverika. 16 January 1940).

21. Tom 1, ark. 39 (Zakliuchenie. 16 January 1940); tom 2, ark. 174–79 (Postanovlenie o prekreshchenii sledstviia. 29 November 1939).

22. Tom 1, ark. 43 (Zakliuchenie. 16 January 1940).

23. Tom 1, ark. 32 (Postanovlenie. 1 June 1940); tom 3, ark. 2, 32 (PSZ). Fleishman was arrested on 1 February 1940—tom 1, ark. 2 (Postanovlenie na arrest); and Krivtsov on 29 March 1940—tom 1, ark. 17 (Postanovlenie na arrest).

24. Tom 1, ark. 30 (Postanovlenie. 25 March 1940); tom 3, ark. 52 (PSZ).

25. Tom 1, ark. 2–3 (Postanovlenie na arrest. 1 February 1940); tom 3, ark. 50 zv (PSZ).

26. Tom 3, ark. 52 (PSZ).

27. It is not clear who ran the group in October. Tom 1, ark. 152 (Dopolnitel'noe-ob"iasnenie o metodakh vedeniia sledstviia v 1937–38 gg. 14 January 1940, from Krivtsov); tom 2, ark. 78–79 (Protokol doprosa Tsirul'nitskogo. 16 December 1939); tom 3, ark. 152, 161–62 (PSZ). My thanks to Vadym Zolotar'ov for information on Pivchikov. Note also that there were *two* NKVD officers named Babich—Ivan Ignat'evich (who is noted here) and Isai Iakovlevich, a much more senior NKVD officer.

28. In Dolgushev's *sledstvennoe delo* (spr. 38237, tom 3, ark. 42. (Protokol sudebnogo zasedaniia. 10–13 August 1940), NKVD operative L. M. Pavlychev, who worked as deputy head of the Kiev NKVD, said that Dolgushev went to Belaia Tserkov

several times to deal with the *"lipa"* (falsification, forgery) and as a result several prisoners were freed.

29. Tom 3, ark. 61 (PSZ).

30. Tom 3, ark. 63 (PSZ).

31. Tom 3, ark. 156 (Vypiska iz protokola doprosa Fleishmana. 18 June 1940).

32. Tom 3, ark. 52–53 (PSZ); tom 3, ark. 155 (Vypiska. Sobstvennoruchnye pokazaniia Fleishman).

33. Tom 2, ark. 114–52 (Povestka zasedaniia osoboi troiki Kievskogo oblastnogo Upravleniia NKVD Ukraine. Belotserkovskaia opergruppa. Raion Skvirskii).

34. Tom 3, ark. 54 (PSZ).

35. Tom 3, ark. 64 (PSZ). Babich denied this and also said Dolgushev did not give such an order.

36. Tom 3, ark. 54 (PSZ).

37. Tom 3, ark. 54–55 (PSZ).

38. Tom 3, ark. 53, 56 (PSZ).

39. Tom 1, ark. 72–73 (Protokol doprosa. 9 March 1940).

40. Tom 3, ark. 153 (Protokol doprosa. 2 March 1940); tom 3, ark. 154 (Vypiska iz protokola doprosa Fleishmana. 9 March 1940).

41. Tom 1, ark. 17 (Postanovlenie na arrest. 29 March 1940), ark. 18 (Postanovlenie. 29 March 1940), 121 (Protokol doprosa. 10 December 1939); tom 3, ark. 50 zv (PSZ).

42. Tom 3, ark. 56–59 (PSZ).

43. Tom 3, ark. 56–59 (PSZ. 3–8 August 1940); on Pivchikov, see tom 3, ark. 61 (PSZ).

44. Tom 1, ark. 121–23 (Protokol doprosa. 10 December 1939); ark. 139–41 (Ob"iasnital'naia zapiska po voprosu metodov vedeniia sledstviia v 1937–1938 gg. ot byvshego sotrudnika militsiia Krivtsova M. M. 13 January 1940.)

45. Tom 1, ark. 139 (Ob"iasnital'naia zapiska . . .).

46. Tom 1, ark. 122 (Protokol doprosa. 10 December 1939).

47. Tom 1, ark. 123 (Protokol doprosa. 10 December 1939).

48. Tom 1, ark. 121 (Protokol doprosa. 10 December 1939), l. 141 (Ob"iasnitel'naia zapiska . . .).

49. Tom 1, ark. 139–41 (Ob"iasnitel'naia zapiska . . .).

50. Tom 1, ark. 146–52 (Dopolnitel'noe-ob"iasnenie o metodakh vedeniia sledstviia v 1937–38 gg. ot Krivtsova. 14 January 1940).

51. Tom 1, ark. 32 (Postanovlenie. 1 June 1940); tom 1, ark. 49–51 (Zakliuchenie, 14 June 1940)

52. Tom 3, ark. 67 (PSZ).

53. Tom 2, ark. 3 (Protokol doprosa Romanova. 13 January 1940); tom 3, ark. 75 (PSZ).

54. Tom 3, ark. 75 (PSZ).

55. Tom 2, ark. 1 (Protokol doprosa Romanova. 13 January 1940).

56. Tom 2, ark. 9a–11 (Protokol doprosa Beregovogo. 13 January 1940).

57. Tom 3, ark. 78 (PSZ). Antonets and Romanov said nothing about Krivtsov beating anyone.

58. Tom 3, ark. 77 (PSZ).

59. Tom 3, ark. 68 (PSZ).

60. Tom 2, ark. 25 (Protokol doprosa Adamchuka); tom 3, ark. 79 (PSZ). Also see the testimony of policeman, Z. E. Sverinenko in tom 2, ark. 27–8 (Protokol doprosa), where he describes the torment unleashed upon a series of teachers during *stoiki*.

61. Tom 2, ark. 60–61 (Protokol doprosa Gutsalo. 13 January 1940); tom 3, ark. 85 (PSZ).

62. Tom 2, ark. 56–75 (Protokol doprosa Korinnogo. 13 January 1940); tom 3, ark. 84–85 (PSZ).

63. Tom 3, ark. 72–74 (PSZ).

64. Tom 2, ark. 2 (Protokol doprosa Romanova. 13 January 1940); tom 3, ark. 75 (PSZ).

65. Tom 3, ark. 75 (PSZ).

66. Tom 2, ark. 9–11 (Protokol doprosa Romanova. 11 January 1940).

67. Tom 2, ark. 16–17 (Ob"iasnitel'naia zapiska from Beregovoi to the deputy of the oblast procurator. 12 January 1940).

68. Tom 3, ark. 67 (PSZ).

69. Tom 3, ark. 61 (PSZ).

70. Tom 3, ark. 65 (PSZ).

71. On this type of evidence, see M. Iunge and R. Binner, "Spravki sel'soveta kak faktor v osuzhdenii krest'ian," *Stalinizm v sovetskoi provintsii, 1937–1937 gg.* (Moscow: Rosspen, 2009), 613–23. On the use of village "genealogy" to purge collective farmers (or to settle scores), see Lynne Viola, "The Second Coming: Class Enemies in the Soviet Countryside, 1927–1935," in *Stalinist Terror: New Perspectives*, ed. J. Arch Getty and Roberta T. Manning (New York: Cambridge University Press, 1993), 65–98.

72. Tom 2, ark. 11 (Protokol doprosa Beregovogo. 13 January 1940).

73. Tom 2, ark. 10 (Protokol doprosa Beregovogo. 13 January 1940).

74. Tom 3, ark. 68–69, 75 (PSZ).

75. Tom 2, ark. 11 (Protokol doprosa Beregovogo. 13 January 1940); tom 3, ark. 80 (PSZ).

76. Tom 3, ark. 76–77 (PSZ).

77. Tom 2, ark. 3 (Protokol doprosa Romanova. 13 January 1940); tom 3, ark. 77 (PSZ).

78. Tom 2, ark. 10 (Protokol doprosa Beregovogo. 13 January 1940).

79. Tom 3, ark. 69 (PSZ).

80. Tom 2, ark. 48 (Protokol doprosa Nikolaichuk. 13 January 1940).

81. Tom 3, ark. 80–81 (PSZ).

82. Tom 2, ark. 89–90 (Protokol doprosa Antonika. 13 January 1940). Ianchuk had been exiled for three years for "sabotage" in the collective farm in 1933, certainly a famine-related "crime" (tom 2, ark. 147, Povestka Zasedaniia Osoboi Troiki Kievskogo oblastnogo Upravleniia NKVD Ukraine. Belotserkovskaia opergruppa. Raion Skvirskii. Approx. July 1938).

83. Tom 2, ark. 87 (Protokol doprosa Orlovy. 13 January 1940).

84. Tom 3, ark. 102 (PSZ).

85. Tom 3, ark. 100–7 (PSZ).

86. On this point, see Junge and Binner, "Spravki sel'soveta," 622.

87. For example, see tom 3, ark. 97–99 (PSZ), where one witness went so far as to accuse another witness of being a gendarme under the tsar.

88. Tom 3, ark. 72 (PSZ).

89. Tom 3, ark. 63 (PSZ). Also see Fleishman's testimony to this in tom 3, ark. 155 (Vypiska. Sobstvennoruchnye pokazaniia Fleishman).

90. Tom 3, ark. 107 (PSZ).

91. Tom 3, ark. 64, 76 (PSZ).

92. Tom 3, ark. 96 (PSZ).

93. Tom 3, ark. 96 (PSZ).

94. Tom 3, ark. 93 (PSZ).

95. Tom 3, ark. 108 (PSZ).

96. Tom 3, ark. 110 (PSZ).

97. Tom 3, ark. 83, 109 (PSZ).

98. Tom 3, ark. 111 (PSZ).

99. Tom 3, ark. 169–72 (Zaiavlenie to Vorshilov from Krivtsov. 20 December 1958), ark. 173 (Zaiavlenie to Voroshilov from Krivtsov. 15 August 1959), ark. 218–33 (Postanovlenie. 23 November 1959, with detailed investigation into the case); ark. 324 (decision of the Ukrainian courts from 1998).

100. See HDA SBU, f. 5, spr. 38237, ark. 31–47 (Protokol sudebnogo zasedaniia. 10–13 August 1940).

101. Oleg Khlevniuk is correct when he postulates that Stalin launched mass operations in order to eliminate a potential Fifth Column in the event of war. See his *Master of the House: Stalin and His Inner Circle*, trans. Nora Seligman Favorov (New Haven, CT: Yale University Press, 2009), 173.

6

"The Situation at the Time"

THE NKVD IN ZHITOMIR

Serhii Kokin
Translated by Aaron Hale-Dorrell

THE PURGE OF the Zhitomir UNKVD began with the arrival of Aleksandr Uspenskii in Kiev in early 1938, when he began the systematic removal of NKVD cadres associated with his predecessor Izrail' Leplevskii. It continued after Uspenskii's flight, when the tables were turned on his own appointees. The Chekists were first accused of "counterrevolutionary crimes" (Article 54 of the Ukrainian criminal code) for their participation in a "counterrevolutionary conspiracy." Then in spring 1939, the charges in their cases were suddenly changed to "violations of socialist legality" (Article 206-17 of the Ukrainian criminal code). In both instances, the charges included unwarranted arrests, fabrications of confessions, the torture of prisoners, and atrocities at the site of execution.

The Zhitomir Oblast, along with the new Zhitomir Oblast UNKVD, was created on 22 September 1937.[1] Captain of State Security Lavrentii Iakushev, who had previously served as deputy director of the Kiev Oblast UNKVD, was named acting director. Senior Lieutenant of State Security Grigorii Grishin, was transferred from the position of director of the Third Department of the State Security Administration (Upravlenie gosudarstvennoi bezopasnosti, UGB) of the Odessa Oblast UNKVD, to become Iakushev's deputy. Both were appointments made by then head of NKVD Ukraine, Leplevskii, who wrote that "Iakushev is weaker than Grishin in operational matters, but has other qualities," while Grishin was to supply qualified leadership for the operational activities of the UNKVD.[2]

Serhii Kokin, *"The Situation at the Time"* In: *Laboratories of Terror*. Edited by: Lynne Viola and Marc Junge, Oxford University Press. © Oxford University Press 2023. DOI: 10.1093/oso/9780197647547.003.0007

After Uspenskii's appointment as the Ukrainian republic People's Commissar of Internal Affairs, on 26 February 1938, Iakushev was removed from his post and, on 15 March, reassigned to the All-Union NKVD. His place was taken by Captain of State Security Grigorii Viatkin, who had been director of the Sixth Section of the Sixth Department of the All-Union NKVD Main State Security Administration in Moscow. At the same time, Senior Lieutenant of State Security Mikhail Fedorov became the new head of the UNKVD Third Department. On 1 April 1938, Sergei Golubev was confirmed as temporary acting special plenipotentiary of the Zhitomir Oblast UNKVD and soon was elected secretary of the party committee for the UNKVD.[3] Joining together these two important posts in the service and party hierarchies of the UNKVD, Golubev reported to the UNKVD director, Viatkin, and became someone trusted by him. In April 1938, Grigorii Grishin was transferred to Kiev and replaced by Andrei Luk'ianov, who served as the new deputy director of the UNKVD until September 1938 when the post was left vacant.[4] On 16 November 1938, the second day after Uspenskii disappeared from Kiev, Viatkin, one of his closest collaborators, was arrested and transported under guard to the All-Union NKVD in Moscow.[5] This is the story of the unraveling of the Zhitomir UNKVD.

The Beginning of the Investigation (April–October 1938)

From 21 January 1938, reports of the beatings of detainees, mass shootings, and the looting of property during executions began to trickle in with the proceedings of a Military Tribunal trial of Boris Davidovich, an officer of the Zhitomir Oblast police (militia) administration.[6] From the trial, it emerged that the Zhitomir UNKVD lacked strict accounting for the personal effects of detainees. UNKVD execution squads had looted with impunity the possessions of their victims. The military lawyers sent the trial proceedings to the Ukrainian republic NKVD. From there, the documents were transferred to the Zhitomir Oblast UNKVD for investigation. UNKVD director Viatkin immediately recognized the danger in the case. On 4 April 1938, he dispatched a note to Uspenskii, telling him that the accusations were unwarranted.[7]

Temporary acting UNKVD special plenipotentiary Sergei Golubev began the internal investigation. He questioned many UNKVD personnel. They explained that, after the completion of each operation, every individual who had taken part in shootings and the disposal of bodies took for himself the property of the executed. They acted with the authorization of the head of the Fifth Department, Vasilii Lebedev, who directed the executions, and UNKVD chief Lavrentii Iakushev.[8] Approximately twenty UNKVD personnel took part in the looting with the knowledge of the leadership. The looted items were purportedly returned to the UNKVD and destroyed according to an 11 May 1938 directive.[9] Zhitomir UNKVD boss Viatkin approved the conclusions of the investigation, which indicated that "the looting of detainees' effects was facilitated by the previous UNKVD leadership." Arguing that the looters "had carried out significant tasks for the UNKVD prison commandant" and that the majority of the items had supposedly been recovered, Viatkin limited the punishments to only seven individuals, six of whom were detained for periods from three to fifteen days, and one of whom received a formal reprimand.[10]

On 7 September 1938, Viatkin sent to the Ukrainian republic NKVD a letter that effectively concealed the actual situation. He portrayed widespread looting as "isolated instances of misappropriation of items," and he made the twenty looters appear to be "a few UNKVD personnel." The UNKVD boss considered "the specific circumstance of the work" to be a mitigating factor. The execution squad needed to "swap" their clothing and footwear, which was splattered with the blood of the executed, for the clothing and footwear of their victims. He reported that he had issued administrative punishments to those who had stolen goods.[11] At the time, colleagues in Kiev met these explanations with understanding, but another opinion about this issue soon materialized.

A letter dated 13 October 1938, from the head of the Novograd-Volynskii city NKVD department, Grigorii Artem'ev, to Viatkin, reported that Vladimir Girich, the driver for the NKVD Special Department of the Red Army's 12th Mechanized Brigade, had traveled on several occasions since the autumn of 1937 to Zhitomir using an official automobile. Upon his return, he "brought back in sacks the effects of executed people, which he and his wife then sold in the town market of Novograd-Volynskii at speculative prices." Among the items were leather and woolen overcoats, jackets, boots, suits, as well as military tunics, overcoats, and belts. Given the shortages of goods characteristic of Soviet life, a person with such resources could quickly become wealthy by the standards of the day. According to Artem'ev, Girich had explained at the Novgorod-Volynskii city NKVD that in the autumn of 1937 he had worked for the UNKVD prison commandant, where team members were paid 50 rubles per execution. Artem'ev then accused Girich of divulging "state secrets." He recommended his dismissal from the NKVD and his arrest.[12] It would be up to Viatkin to make the final judgment.

On 31 October 1938, Viatkin made his decision, stating that the looting was a result of the "situation at the time" and sanctioned by the previous UNKVD leadership. Girich received an administrative punishment of fifteen days' detention without pay.[13] Thus, for a second time, Viatkin limited himself to insignificant punishments of the guilty, thereby becoming an accomplice in covering up these crimes.

After Viatkin's own arrest, the Ukrainian republic NKVD demanded the documents from the investigation. Reviewing them, they concluded that the administrative punishments imposed by Viatkin were insufficient, constituting "a sheer glossing over" of crimes defined in Article 207-6 (B) of the Ukrainian republic criminal code. Acting Zhitomir UNKVD director Ivan Daragan was ordered to conduct a thorough investigation, to arrest the culprits, and to hand them over for trial to the Military Tribunal.[14]

By this time, the climate in the UNKVD had begun to change. During a closed meeting of the UNKVD Communist Party organization on 16 December 1938 following Stalin's November directive to curtail the mass operations, NKVD personnel began to level a variety of accusations against Golubev, who had conducted the initial investigations, and Viatkin. The meeting expelled Golubev from the party for conducting affairs according to the "hostile line of the enemy, Viatkin, and in close cooperation with him," and "for systematically covering up crimes." A 13 June 1939 order from the All-Union NKVD dismissed him from the NKVD without severance pay.[15]

Following this meeting, on 21 December 1938, a preliminary inquiry began in the case of the former UNKVD prison commandant Grigorii Timoshenko, warden Feliks Ignatenko, Vladimir Girich, and other individuals accused of looting.[16] During a search of Ignatenko's apartment, thirty-seven gold crowns were discovered, some of which were still attached to teeth. The investigation established that in December 1937, Ignatenko, Timoshenko, and inspector of the UNKVD Manasha Sosnov had used pliers to tear "gold teeth and crowns from the mouths of the executed for illicit gain."[17]

In the meantime, on 15 December 1938, the Ukrainian republic NKVD dispatched to Zhitomir its representative, Sergeant Timofei Golubchikov, an agent of the Second Section of the Third Department of the UGB, to take part in the investigation. He familiarized himself with the documents of the investigation and reported on its results to the Ukrainian republic NKVD leadership. In December 1938, investigations into the cases of Zhitomir UNKVD personnel entered a new phase.

The Case of Grigorii Grishin
(30 May–October 1938)

On 30 May 1938, the former deputy director of the UNKVD, Grigorii Grishin, was arrested in Kiev. Grishin was accused of being an agent of foreign intelligence agencies and of having carried out espionage.[18] Somewhat later, he would also be accused of participating in an "antisoviet Trotskyite organization."[19] Although this case was pursued after Grishin left Zhitomir and before the November 1938 directive curtailing the mass operations, the accusations would shed further light on the NKVD's activities in Zhitomir. The case file contained testimony from the director of the Third Section of the Third Department of the Ukrainian republic NKVD, Senior Lieutenant Moisei Detinko. He characterized Grishin's service activities while "a member of the organization":

> Under the outward cover provided by the large number of detainees, Grishin tried to extract testimony from them about their individual counterrevolutionary activities and finish up the cases against them, but without revealing all activities of the counterrevolutionary underground, and without unmasking and repressing the fascist agent network. In this respect, Grishin in many instances sent case files against detainees to Moscow five to ten days after their arrest.[20]

NKVD personnel were required to "uncover" the entire "underground" and "fascist agent network," but Grishin apparently limited himself to repressing "lone wolves," an accusation often made during the Uspenskii purge of Leplevskii cadres. He did not see the necessity of artificially creating underground structures.

On 31 July 1938, the deputy director of the Third Department of the UNKVD, Daniil Man'ko, gave testimony about Grishin's "enemy activities" during the Polish Operation, one of the component parts of the mass operations of the Great Terror. Man'ko stated that Grishin "with hostile intent" ordered the mass arrest of the wives of individuals repressed under All-Union NKVD Order No. 00485, which mandated the Polish Operation. Moreover, Grishin ordered "the rapid sale of the effects of the wives of the repressed and dispersal of the children among the local orphanages." As a result, more than eight hundred wives and relatives of those repressed under Order No. 00485 were arrested.

After the change in the UNKVD leadership and the arrival in Zhitomir of Viatkin, these arrests were halted and more than 350 individuals were freed. The released wives of "enemies of the people" began to appeal to the UNKVD, the procuracy, and other organizations, demanding back their unlawfully confiscated property and their children.[21]

The second part of the accusation against Grishin came from the opposite direction. He was accused of insufficient zeal in carrying out repression. Man'ko stated that when Ezhov arrived in Ukraine in February 1938, he ordered the preparation of documents against so-called Polish-nationalist counterrevolutionary elements in Zhitomir. In Man'ko's opinion, many such "elements" existed, but Grishin argued instead that in Zhitomir Oblast such elements as indicated by surveillance records (*operativnye uchety*) were insignificant. When the UNKVD leadership changed, "a large organization of the POV [the Polish Military Organization] was 'discovered' in Zhitomir Oblast, numbering more than 3,000 individuals."[22] Man'ko judged that "Grishin, with hostile intent, had attempted to save the POV cadres."[23]

Another witness in the Grishin case was Aleksei Tomin, the temporary acting head of the NKVD Special Department for the 68th Aviation Brigade, which was based in Zhitomir.[24] On 14 August 1938, he attested:

> Grishin was dissatisfied with the number of arrests carried out, admonishing that the investigations were criminally dragged out in length and that absolutely all wives of those Poles and Germans condemned under Order No. 00485 must be arrested. He gave me the following order: every investigator must bring to the Special Session [of the All-Union NKVD–author] a minimum of 30 cases against wives of traitors to the motherland per day.... Notwithstanding that the special receiving centers for housing the children of those repressed were already overcrowded, Grishin gave the order to arrest the mothers, that is, the wives of traitors to the motherland, and to leave the children in the custody of collective farms.[25]

The deputy director of the UNKVD, Andrei Luk'ianov, also accused Grishin of "energetic hostile activities." He clarified that 820 wives of individuals repressed under Order No. 00485 had been arrested.[26] The subtext of Luk'ianov's deposition was that all of this was done with the intent to discredit the actions carried out by the NKVD organs.

The investigation sought to use the friendly relations between Grishin and the arrested former head of the Berdichev city NKVD department, Vsevolod Martyniuk, to reveal the "counterrevolutionary organizational connections" between them. According to Martyniuk's deposition, Grishin ordered the arrest of "the leadership of counterrevolutionary armies and the bosses of the counterrevolutionary nationalist underground," but left the rank-and-file participants in these "armies" and "underground" not subject to arrest. These assertions referred to the Army of the Ukrainian People's Republic and the Polish Military Organization of the period from 1919 to 1921, which by 1938 were little more than an illusion.

The head of the UNKVD Fourth Department, Matvei Lesnov, added to the portrait of the "hostile activities" of Grishin. Lesnov explained that during the mass operations Grishin required subordinates to close cases more quickly. At the same time, according to Lesnov, "Grishin more than once gave orders to personnel to 'more carefully' interrogate the arrested, to not pressure them in demanding confessions, but to scare [them] with criminal liability, which in practical terms demoralized the entire apparat of the oblast administration [i.e., the UNKVD]."[27]

In testimony about his enrollment by Grishin in the "organization," Martyniuk conveyed notable details: "In our conversations, Grishin expressed his dissatisfaction with the mass arrests that were being carried out, supporting this with the fact that the policy of the Communist Party was incorrect, as a result of which arose mass dissatisfaction among the working people, and from this, that the arrests and repression [proceeded] without any scrutiny of how and against whom [they were carried out]. I fully shared and approved of the views of Grishin."[28]

Subsequently, Grishin became aware of the fact that he could be held accountable for the mass repression. A certain psychological breakdown among the perpetrators of the repressions was associated with this. Many of them understood that they were doing wrong, but they saw no way out. Clearly trying to mollify themselves, they called on their subordinates to be careful and warned them about their responsibility, but at the same time pushed them relentlessly forward in the search for enemies. The psychological pressure on subordinates was a defensive reaction by the leaders. On 13 October 1938, Grishin was informed of the testimony of Martyniuk about his "enrollment" by Grishin in an "organization." Grishin denied this.[29] Then the investigation paused for a period that lasted until the end of December 1938.

Expansion of the Investigation
(November 1938–May 1939)

In November 1938, the investigation in Zhitomir entered a new phase. Its most important actor was the representative of the Ukrainian republic NKVD Military Procuracy for Border and Internal Troops, Military Judicial Officer, First Class, Morozov, who quickly ascertained the criminal bacchanalia inside the UNKVD. The violations included crimes such as beating detainees, including to the point of death, committed by UNKVD personnel during investigations; violations of the regulations governing the special troika, although the troika's legitimacy as an extrajudicial organ was not questioned; falsification of UNKVD record-keeping, or "counterfeiting," on the part of the leadership, operational personnel including investigators, the technical apparatus, and UNKVD medical personnel; and humiliating the condemned prior to their execution, as well as property theft following executions.

During the investigation, many UNKVD personnel were questioned or gave statements. One of these was the head of the UNKVD First Special Department, Nikolai Zub, who was subsequently arrested on 8 January 1939. He stated that Viatkin, after receiving a coded telegram from the Ukrainian republic NKVD on 16 September 1938 about organizing a special troika within the UNKVD for reviewing the case files of arrestees, assigned the responsibilities of secretary of the troika to him (Zub). Beginning with the first troika session on 20 September 1938, however, Viatkin amended the functions of the perpetrators of repression. Zub was not present at the troika sessions. The investigatory files were presented in the sessions primarily by Daniil Man'ko, who was arrested on 8 January 1939. Present at the first session were: Viatkin, as chairman of the troika; second secretary of the Zhitomir Oblast Party Committee Mikhail Grechukha, substituting for the absent first secretary, Maksim Didenko; and the oblast procurator, Vasilii Rasput'ko. Man'ko read aloud to the troika members the indictment in a group case, and then began to present the background reports on the accused. Once he had reported on forty or fifty people, Viatkin proposed ending the readings. Members of the troika then began only to skim the information and pass decisions. The oblast party committee secretary and the oblast procurator, moreover, made no comments on the documents at all. Then, the UNKVD chief personally marked with a pencil on the background reports (on condemned individuals) a note about punishment—the letter "R," which indicated *"rasstreliat'"* (to shoot).[30]

After the troika session, Viatkin ordered Zub not to await completion of the sentencing protocols, which, because the volume for 350 to 500
individuals was so large, the typists had been unable to complete before the
troika session. Instead, Zub was to write up orders for UNKVD commandant Mitrofan Liul'kov to immediately implement the troika decisions by
executing all those that Viatkin had condemned to death with his "R" in the
book of background reports. This practice meant that, by the day of the arrest
of Viatkin, on 16 November 1938, out of the thirteen session protocols of the
special troika, six remained unsigned by the members of the troika, which
included the cases of 2,178 individuals. Of these, 2,114, had been shot. The
rulings of the troika had not been implemented in the cases of a mere twenty
individuals, who at the time of selection were not in the local jail.[31]

Grechukha took part in the special troika sessions one more time, but
still made no notes on the documents. The oblast procurator, Rasput'ko,
did the same. During all remaining troika sessions, the first secretary of the
oblast party committee, Didenko, along with Viatkin, made notes about
the judgments rendered in the books of background reports and in the
indictments. However, the oblast party committee secretary and the oblast
procurator did not even glance over the cases. Moreover, Didenko signed the
minutes of troika sessions in which he, having been on work assignment, did
not participate. This was a blatant violation of the special troika operational
procedures.

These violations were connected to the enormous disproportionality in
the severity of the "sentences," that is, the judgments imposed by the special
troika. In accordance with the protocols of sessions between 27 September
and 3 November 1938, the following sentences were imposed: first category,
that is, execution—2,134 individuals, and second category, imprisonment—
42 individuals.[32] If the troika members had delved into the substance of each
case, the proportions of judgments they imposed might have been different,
and many people might have survived. As it turned out, in some of these cases
the investigations were not even formally concluded.

In a 17 December 1938 report to the then de facto head of the Ukrainian
republic NKVD, Senior Lieutenant Amaiak Kobulov, the representative of
the Ukrainian republic NKVD, Timofei Golubchikov, called attention to
this fact and charged that the special troika members had exceeded their
authority. "The UNKVD special troika chaired by Viatkin," Golubchikov
wrote, "imposed judgments in cases not under its jurisdiction, against Red
Army commanders, engineers, agronomists, teachers, and the like, reviewing
a whole host of cases without any investigatory documentation, cases of

[people] long deceased, and cases of accused [who had been] murdered during interrogation."[33]

Similarly, Zub recounted the case of the former head of the Korosten town police, Vasilii Skrypnik, who was arrested on 27 April 1938, as an "active participant in a counterrevolutionary insurrectionary organization." The case against him was handled by Maluka. On the night of 26 June 1938, Maluka called Skrypnik in for questioning and beat him. Skrypnik died after returning to his cell. On 16 December 1938, as a result of an investigation into Skrypnik's murder, military procurator Morozov sanctioned the arrests of Maluka, warden of the UNKVD jail Feliks Ignatenko, and senior jail overseer Daniil Levchenko.[34]

However, that was all in the future. In September 1938, Maluka stated to Zub that Viatkin had ordered the inclusion of the Skrypnik case in the final protocol of a session of a troika convened by the UNKVD in May 1938. Only later was a document attesting to the implementation of the troika's decision recorded. To this end, the signed final sheet of the troika session protocol was torn out and retyped with the addition of the case against Skrypnik. At the request of Viatkin, Zub later wrote an order to UNKVD commandant Liul'kov to implement the troika decision to execute Skrypnik as if it were from May. However, according to Zub, he did not complete the document attesting to the implementation of the sentence. Later, Maluka explained to him that Skrypnik had died.

Military procurator Morozov concluded—as was wholly in keeping with investigations carried out in other regions at that time—that "a gang of enemies had insinuated themselves" into the UNKVD leadership.[35] He did not, however, stop there. He deemed it necessary to arrest and bring to trial— in addition to Viatkin—Fedorov and Man'ko, who were arrested on 8 January 1939, as well as the first secretary of the oblast party committee, Didenko, and the oblast procurator, Rasput'ko, both of whom were arrested at the end of December 1938. The majority of the violations stipulated were not unique to Zhitomir Oblast. What was unusual was the arrest of the first secretary of the oblast party committee and the oblast procurator, in addition to UNKVD personnel. Nowhere else in Ukraine had this happened.

Fedorov provided his own rationalization of the situation in the UNKVD. In 1938, four inter-district operational-investigatory groups were created: in Zhitomir, Berdichev, Novograd-Volynsk, and Korosten.[36] At the end of June 1938, the groups for Korosten and Novograd-Volynsk were eliminated. All case files from these groups, along with the detainees, were transferred to the UNKVD for completion of investigations. Personnel of the UNKVD Third

Department composed reports about each person implicated in a case based on the case files received. Subsequently, the reports and the case files on which they had been based were reviewed by personnel from the oblast and military procuracies. They collated the contents of the reports with the investigation documents.[37]

The case files were then sent to the Ukrainian republic NKVD for verification, after which they were returned to Zhitomir, and protocols—albums— with the reports on the accused and with the proposed punishments were sent to Moscow for approval by a two-member commission, or "*dvoika*," comprising the All-Union People's Commissar of Internal Affairs and the All-Union Procurator. At some later point, the All-Union NKVD returned these albums to the UNKVD with a proposal that the special troika created within the UNKVD review them.[38]

Fedorov's explanation exhibits an effort to shift responsibility for violations onto the leaders and personnel of the operational-investigation groups, the oblast and military procuracies, the central apparatus of the Ukrainian republic NKVD, and even the All-Union NKVD. The orders to the perpetrators regarding their further actions, which made possible all that occurred in the oblast, did, indeed, come from Moscow and Kiev.

Maluka disclosed the mechanism in the UNKVD for fabricating case files. Many detainees were held in jail for up to a year without questioning. Accordingly, a bureaucratic conveyor belt of falsified procedural documents was created for more than one thousand case files. From five to eighteen formulaic resolutions on extending the period of detention for the arrestees were inserted into each file, and junior personnel signed these documents with dates predating their service in the NKVD.[39] According to Maluka, Lesnov had demanded from each investigator a daily quota of between five and eight "confessions." Maluka said: "Naturally, to fulfill this norm, the investigators quickly resorted to wholesale beatings of detainees and, by this method, managed to get confessions from them."[40] Lesnov offered the excuse that, after the disbanding of the Korosten and Novograd-Volynsk groups, approximately eight hundred detainees wound up in the UNKVD Fourth Department. It had only between fifteen and twenty investigators and temporarily assigned personnel, who were "exclusively junior comrades, recently recruited into the organs [the NKVD]." For this reason, they were unable to keep up with such a large workload.[41]

Returning to earlier events, Lesnov recounted how, at the end of January 1938, Uspenskii had called a meeting to brief the heads of oblast NKVD administrations, where he spoke of the existence of a "Ukrainian

Military-Insurrectionary Underground," which must be liquidated as quickly as possible. Returning from Kiev, UNKVD chief Iakushev called a meeting of the NKVD operational staff in the oblast and conveyed to them the commissar's directive. Carrying out this order, the personnel of the district NKVD organs traversed the villages and established operational records for former "political bandits," "Petliurists," members of the Volynsk Insurrectionary Army (VPA), and other individuals with "dark" pasts.[42] Subsequently, personnel composed operational folios with lists of individuals marked for arrest and then brought these folios to Zhitomir to receive approval for the arrests. Iakushev, Grishin, Luk'ianov, Lesnov, and other UNKVD leaders each received documents from several districts and, on the basis of reports on the individual given by the head of the district department, sanctioned their arrest. "Undoubtedly," acknowledged Lesnov, "many mistakes were made then."[43]

In this way arose a system of arrests carried out according to lists without the existence of incriminating evidence against the individuals. The tragedy both in this situation and in general was that baseless arrests were made, and then they snowballed. Lesnov judged that the earlier arrests were insufficiently justified, but the later ones carried out according to the testimony of "those who had acknowledged their participation in the organizations" had a more substantial basis and were primarily arrests of "actual enemies." This was far from the case.

Even Lesnov himself understood this. Acknowledging his own guilt, he said, "In meetings in the department, I often warned about taking a critical approach to testimony, that they [investigators] should, prior to arrest, confirm the profile of the person who was to be arrested, his actions, whether they were clearly hostile, and so on."[44] The majority of NKVD personnel were realistic about what was happening but continued to play by the rules established by the leadership, either out of hope of ingratiating themselves or as a method of self-preservation. This was the social-psychological situation within Chekist circles at that time.

Lesnov identified the application of unlawful investigation methods, that is, the beating of detainees, as one of the fundamental violations. He explained that Viatkin "introduced a system in which every investigator was required to personally report to him about investigative cases, and he gave orders about how to interrogate, that is, to whom to apply unlawful methods of questioning." In answer to the question of why this occurred, Lesnov responded, "Because Viatkin always was co-opting everyone, including myself, into error. He—Viatkin—gave instructions to the effect that the party Central Committee and Comrade Ezhov permitted, to enable the quickest crackdown on the enemies, streamlined methods of investigation [i.e., torture] to be sure that it was established that he [the arrested] was an enemy."[45] Such an explanation was typical during the investigations then being carried out. Lesnov acknowledged his participation in the beating of detainees in March and April 1938, "but only under orders from Viatkin and only with respect to those clearly established as enemies." But who were "those clearly established as enemies"?

Lesnov first named Pavel Postoev. Before the revolution, he had been director of the Zhitomir teachers seminary and head of the provincial department of education. At the time of his arrest in November 1937, however, he was head of the Department of Physical and Economic Geography of Ukraine at the Institute of Popular Education in Zhitomir. Postoev was confronted with the accusation that he was one of the leaders of the "Ukrainian counterrevolutionary nationalist military-insurgency organization," which was supposedly created to sabotage the railway.[46] Lesnov beat Postoev in order to get from him testimony about the existence of weapons caches, which, he claimed, had been confirmed by other suspects.[47] On 10 May 1938, the UNKVD troika approved a resolution to execute Postoev, and he was shot.[48]

Lesnov named as the second victim of his beatings the former second secretary of the Chudnovskii District Party Committee, Viktor Voiteru, supposedly an active participant in "a Trotskyite organization" and the POV. Lesnov did not indicate a reason for beating him because he had "already been sufficiently unmasked and had been convicted by the Military Collegium."[49] The third individual beaten by Lesnov was the director of the historical archive in Zhitomir and "leader of the Socialist Revolutionary underground," Vladimir Iur'ev-Byk. Lesnov considered the primary reason for his beating was that he had concealed "the existence of counterrevolutionary literature received from the Kiev Center for the SR underground."[50] On 10 May 1938, the Zhitomir UNKVD troika approved the decision to execute him as "an enemy of the people."[51] Years later, all these people were rehabilitated.

Lesnov similarly related that in two instances detainees in the Fourth Department were murdered. The first was Vasilii Skrypnik, but Lesnov did not remember the surname of the second victim, although he had reported it to Viatkin. Clearly, the murder of a detainee during investigation was not an extraordinary event at a time when the UNKVD daily carried out "legitimate" murders, that is, executions, in which many agents took part. Possibly, among the perpetrators of repression there existed some sort of dual consciousness that psychologically explained both the prosaic character of mass terror and the hidden desire to escape memories of its "unpleasant" and bloody details.

Completing the Investigation into the Crimes of the "Iakushevites" (January–May 1939)

In the investigation of UNKVD personnel during Iakushev's leadership, Vasilii Lebedev, the head of the Fifth Department, was deemed the most brutal of the NKVD investigators. In Grishin's opinion, when it was necessary to organize mass shootings by the UNVKD, Iakushev "correctly decided the issue." "Neither of us," Grishin stated, "knew this work well, and a specialist was needed. Lebedev was named the director [of the execution brigade]." It was said that he was "a veteran Chekist,"[52] who as early as 1921 had earned the Order of the Red Banner and was known as "a serious agent."[53]

The investigation established that the "specialist," Lebedev, systematically beat those sentenced to execution and introduced into the system the expropriation and resale of personal items by members of the execution teams. In December 1937 and January 1938, Lebedev, in collaboration with the former UNKVD commandant, Grigorii Timoshenko, sold to the jail (in the name of another organization) six truckloads of the clothing of the executed. The money they received, some 37,000 rubles, was spent on their apartments, with the rest distributed among the brigade members. Lebedev ordered that those to be executed—they did not know their fate until the penultimate moment—sign a voucher for the storage of money and valuables.[54]

Lebedev was subject to criminal prosecution. At that time, he was head of the Third Department of the Krasnodar Oblast UNKVD. The documentation on him was diverted into a separate case file and dispatched to the Ukrainian republic NKVD. It has been impossible to document his subsequent fate. However, in 1939, Lebedev was not arrested and was not one of the main suspects in the cases against Zhitomir UNKVD personnel.[55]

The head of the UNKVD auto park, Ivan Panshin, testified that under Lebedev's leadership virtually the entire operational staff took part in the UNKVD commandant's "operations," that is, the executions. UNKVD boss Iakushev "proposed that this be a test of the fortitude of personnel." There were two permanent brigades: one was composed of operational agents and the second of technical staff.[56] Clearly, participation in the shootings was "to temper" the personnel and connect them to a bloody circle of collective responsibility.

The head of the UNKVD Department of Corrective Labor Colonies, Nikolai Klimov, recounted what the "test of fortitude" meant to him:

In the final days of December 1937 or else early in January 1938, I don't now recall precisely, [Mitrofan] Liul'kov called me into the garage at night, telling me that the call was made on the orders of UNKVD deputy chief Grishin. When I entered the garage, I saw sitting on the floor fifty or sixty people sentenced to *VMN* [acronym for "supreme measure of punishment," i.e., the death penalty]. When I entered the next room, there was Grishin, and in the same room about thirty or forty detainees were restrained, having been prepared for execution. It was suggested that I take off my coat, and at that time they led eight individuals into the next room. Operational Agent Blank gave me a small caliber rifle, with which I carried out the sentences.[57] When I left following the implementation of the sentences, Blank stated that "I had passed the exam."[58]

Panshin recounted the consequences of an escape by eleven prisoners sentenced to execution from the UNKVD jail on the night of 11–12 February 1938: "All were captured within 15 days and they were delivered to the garage for implementation of their sentences. This operation was directed by Iakushev, Lebedev, Timoshenko, and Grishin alone." Panshin was struck by the fact that after the implementation of the sentences, "no signs of bullets" were visible on the escapees' bodies: "the bodies were undressed and burned, with their necks scorched and blackened."[59] The UNKVD commandant, Liul'kov, confirmed the words of Panshin. The burns on the victims struck him as abnormal.[60] The group escape from the UNKVD jail carried enormous danger for the leadership. If even one of the escapees had not been caught, the leaders themselves would be under threat of arrest. This explains the executioners' unusual cruelty toward the escapees.

Instances of humiliation of prisoners of a sexual nature also occurred. According to the testimony of Feliks Ignatenko, "There were many instances when, prior to the execution of women, especially those on the younger side, they stripped them naked to humiliate them, to ogle their bodies. Others did this pretending to prepare them for a medical examination or for bathing in 'the bathhouse,' most often this was done by Grishin and Lebedev."[61] Grigorii Timoshenko confirmed the fact of this practice of stripping the prisoners, recalling other instances of sadistic, sexual humiliations of prisoners.[62]

In face-to-face confrontations, Grishin strove to counter almost all the accusations against him by former subordinates.[63] Grishin had developed some hope of a favorable outcome of his case. He declared that he was not a participant in an antisoviet Trotskyite organization and had committed no hostile deeds.[64] He explained that he had confirmed the false testimony he had previously given because he saw no exit from the situation: "From conversations with a host of leading Ukrainian republic NKVD personnel, I could see that they did not believe me, and therefore I had to stand by my testimony about participation in an antisoviet organization."[65]

This is a very important detail. Anonymous leaders of the Ukrainian republic NKVD were conversing with Grishin. Although there is no documentary confirmation in the case file, it suggests that someone had hinted to him how to conduct himself during the investigation: namely, not to confess to anything. Grishin disavowed his own previous testimony about espionage for foreign intelligence agencies.[66] The account of his membership in "an antisoviet Trotskyite organization" faded after the addition to the case file of a report that the former head of the Third Department of the Ukrainian republic NKVD, Arkadii Ratynskii, had been convicted in Moscow but had not given testimony against Grishin.[67]

Nonetheless, on 26 April 1939, Ukrainian republic NKVD personnel completed the indictment, charging Grishin under Article 54-4 (B) and Article 54-11 of the Ukrainian republic criminal code for "actively participating in an antisoviet Trotskyite terrorist organization," "carrying out espionage for Romanian intelligence," "hostile, subversive activities within the NKVD organs," and for "enrolling Martyniuk in the organization."[68] On 4 May 1939, the indictment was confirmed by the Ukrainian republic deputy commissar for internal affairs, Amaiak Kobulov. The contents of the indictment did not correspond to the investigation documentation. The case had no prospects in a criminal court, but nonetheless, on 31 May 1939, the Ukrainian republic NKVD approved its transfer to the courts.

The Case of Mikhail Gluzman
(16 July 1938 to 8 February 1940)

Mikhail Gluzman was the head of the UNKVD jail between February and October 1937; from November 1937, he was the temporary acting director of the Department of Sites of Imprisonment of the UNKVD. On 16 July 1938, he was arrested on an accusation of participating in a Trotskyite organization and of recruiting other individuals into it.[69] The real reason for Gluzman's arrest, however, was that he had proved an embarrassment to the UNKVD leadership.

Within the Zhitomir UNKVD, Gluzman was responsible for a broad range of duties related to the functioning of the jails. This was a relatively exacting job, requiring attention to a great many details, as well as initiative, perseverance, and autonomy in making decisions. According to Gluzman's testimony, the jail was designed for eight hundred individuals; because of the mass operations, the number of prisoners had skyrocketed to as many as twenty thousand.

The UNKVD leadership did not know how the jail's financial and managerial mechanism functioned, but they sought to resolve many issues in their own way. Gluzman quickly understood that the UNKVD leaders broke the law with ease. He did not want to be a participant in these violations and strove to ensure his own safety whenever possible.

In December 1937, Gluzman paid 27,594 rubles to UNKVD commandant Timoshenko for clothing for the prisoners, but this money was embezzled by Lebedev, Timoshenko, and the UNKVD leadership. Therefore, in the annual report for 1937, dispatched to the finance department of the Ukrainian republic NKVD Administration for Sites of Imprisonment, Gluzman highlighted "the purchase for cash of the clothing of executed individuals," but, in his words, "nothing was received."[70]

Gluzman acted differently the next time. On 2 January 1938, he was called in by Iakushev, who said that the UNKVD could again sell the clothing of executed individuals to the jail. Gluzman was pleased because he had to deport to the north ten thousand prisoners, who lacked suitable clothing. The jail again bought several truckloads of things, but this time Gluzman refused to pay Iakushev in cash, instead transferring 27,000 rubles to the UNKVD account through the State Bank.[71]

Iakushev similarly ordered prisoners taken from the jail to the UNKVD—most to be executed—to bring their personal funds with them. Inasmuch as no directives from Moscow or Kiev appeared to exist on the issue of what to do with the money of prisoners when dispatching them in groups, Gluzman was required to follow the orders from the UNKVD boss. After individuals subject to execution arrived in the UNKVD, their money and valuables were given over to UNKVD Commandant Timoshenko and UNKVD chief Iakushev, who distributed the money among the members of the execution teams and spent it on the leadership's everyday needs.[72] The fact that the director of the UNKVD auto park, Ivan Panshin, on seven occasions received sums ranging from 350 to 500 rubles for participation in the "operations" speaks to how the money taken from the victims of repression and received from the sale to the jail of their personal effects and clothing was distributed.[73]

After the February 1938 change in the UNKVD leadership, Gluzman became a witness to new crimes committed by his colleagues. When he began to express dissent on some issues, he was quickly scolded by Viatkin. Gluzman did not retreat and, on those issues where he could prove the correctness of his stance, he continued to stand his ground, resorting to extreme measures. In April 1938, he addressed a statement to Uspenskii in Kiev, in which he wrote, among other things: "They have filled the prison, having taken two stories in two separate wings for interrogations, and the methods of interrogation violate prison operating procedures."

He later explained what he meant by "methods of interrogation": "I reported to Viatkin that the detained cannot sleep in the cells because the interrogators are beating those under interrogation in the interrogation rooms, and their cries are heard in the cells. Viatkin responded, 'Well, they can go to hell, let them not sleep.' I gave my statement about this to Kiev, to Uspenskii."[74]

Gluzman requested to be released from the NKVD. He understood that by reporting to the people's commissar about investigatory methods in violation of prison operating procedures, he had overstepped corporate boundaries. Later, he explained the situation thus: "Seeing all this abnormality and that they were forcing me to commit crimes, I . . . gave a statement with a request to be released. The natural reason provoking me to give the request to be released was that . . . I could not cope with the work."[75]

Viatkin did not like the obstinacy of his subordinate. The final straw for Viatkin was something that occurred during a visit by Gluzman to the NKVD prison in the town of Berdichev. Here, he received a complaint from a detainee that money had been taken from him, but no voucher for it had been given. The money had been taken by the operational plenipotentiary of the jail, Aleksandr Fadeev. A commission in Kiev called for by Gluzman established that Fadeev had embezzled 6,000 rubles. Gluzman also became aware that Fadeev had embezzled valuable gold items from detainees, including watches and coins. Gluzman reported this to Viatkin, but the latter, in the words of Gluzman, "Cursed [me] out and told [me] not to stick my nose in others' business." It was then that Gluzman wrote his anonymous denunciation to Uspenskii.

A few days later, the acting UNKVD special plenipotentiary Sergei Golubev showed Gluzman a large number of gold watches confiscated from Fadeev.[76] Regardless, sometime later Gluzman was arrested, and Fadeev gave testimony as a witness in Gluzman's case. He strove to portray Gluzman as an accomplice of "an important Polish woman spy," who was imprisoned in the

Vinnitsa industrial colony, the name given to the local prison. At one time, Gluzman had been an aide to the colony's warden.[77]

The zealous party members among the UNKVD personnel considered Gluzman's weakness to be that he had not steered clear of the detainees. In Zhitomir, he had petitioned the Kiev oblast court to free an individual of German nationality who, sentenced for "espionage and sabotage" to a ten-year imprisonment, had become ill with tuberculosis in prison. A former colleague of Gluzman, Riva Liubarskaia, portrayed Gluzman's efforts as anti-party activities.[78]

It is clear from the investigation documents that Gluzman was not pursuing financial interests. Moreover, as a Jew he had tried to save from certain death a German, notwithstanding the presence among his colleagues of the stereotype that "If he's a German, that means he's a fascist agent." Observation of the detainees' suffering in this and in other instances may have elicited in Gluzman a desire to ease their burdens. In the inhumane conditions of imprisonment and investigation in the UNKVD, the efforts of one person were too little, yet these efforts were not fruitless.

Gluzman had his shortcomings, but he was one of only a few who did not fear objecting to what he saw as wrong—a violation of the Cheka corporate pseudo-ethical code. During the investigation he was cruelly beaten, threatened via a staged execution, and assured that his wife would be summoned to the UNKVD and raped in his presence.[79] Gluzman was convinced of the extreme degree of the moral degradation of his colleagues, who had lost their final shreds of humanity.

On 8 January 1939, the new UNKVD leadership approved a directive to close the investigation into the accusations against Gluzman about his belonging to "an antisoviet Trotskyite organization." He was, however, indicted under Ukrainian republic Criminal Code Article 206–17 (A) for having committed workplace abuses of a financial nature.[80] As a result of the court session of the Military Tribunal for the NKVD Troops of Kiev Military District on 4 July 1939, Gluzman was found guilty of abuses of his office. In his guilty verdict, the "pressure from the criminal UNKVD leadership" and the lack of personal interest in the financial violations committed were extenuating circumstances. From this resulted a light sentence: two years' imprisonment in a general prison without deprivation of rights. The sentence was considered conditional, with the possibility of early release.[81]

On 9 October 1939, the Military Collegium of the All-Union Supreme Court confirmed the sentence of Gluzman without amendment.[82] He left Zhitomir and worked as the deputy director of the cadre department at a factory in the city of Nikolaev. On 8 February 1940, by a decision of the Military Tribunal for the NKVD Troops of Kiev Military District, the conditional sentence of Gluzman was considered to have "lapsed early" and his sentence was annulled.[83]

The Final Act: The Case of Grigorii Grishin

On 19 June 1939, the Military Tribunal for NKVD Troops of the Kiev Military District brought a new indictment, combining the cases against Grigorii Grishin and the looters. The accusations against Grishin were expanded on the basis of specific details of the case, and he was charged with "cultivating among UNKVD personnel [a culture of] looting and humiliation of the convicted, and taking part in these humiliations" out of counterrevolutionary motives.[84]

During the judicial proceedings of the Military Tribunal from 27 June to 4 July 1939, Grishin presented himself as a politically sophisticated and experienced professional in contrast to his colleagues and the prevailing disorder. Grishin explained that his transfer to the central apparatus of the Ukrainian republic NKVD was, according to Viatkin, because Uspenskii wanted to promote him to "important work." However, Grishin painted an unflattering portrait of Uspenskii, accusing him of antisemitism.[85]

Grishin denied participating in the crimes outlined in his case, at times even denying that the crimes took place. On 4 July 1939, the military tribunal session wrapped up by concluding that systematic abuses had taken place within the Zhitomir UNKVD, first under the leadership of Iakushev and his deputy, Grishin, and then later under the leadership of Viatkin and his deputy, Luk'ianov.[86] Yet some of the charges against Grishin did not hold up. Grishin rationalized his initial testimony and confession, arguing that he had been set up by "the enemy leadership of the NKVD in the person of Uspenskii," and a "fictive report" delivered to the Ukrainian republic NKVD by Andrei Luk'ianov, who was arrested on 1 July 1939. The military tribunal judged that the accusations of "hostile acts" were based on false testimony against Grishin by UNKVD personnel arrested later, and that these accusations were unproven.[87]

Most of the charges against Grishin were dropped for a variety of reasons. First, Uspenskii's ultimately unsuccessful escape played into the hands of Chekists who had been arrested during his tenure. They could present themselves as victims of lawlessness, pointing to the intrigues of the previous "enemy leadership." Second, the testimony of Man'ko and the report of

Luk'ianov about the arrest of the wives of the repressed were completely accurate, as was the testimony of Lesnov about Grishin's order to more quickly
complete investigations so as not to slow the pace of repression. However,
the fact of these witnesses' arrest for the crimes they had committed overrode
their earlier reports of their former boss's criminal activities. Their testimony
given during the preliminary investigation was now viewed as false. Third,
accusations of espionage required serious verification. This was not done
during the preliminary investigation. The confession or lack of confession by
the accused to participating in espionage therefore became the decisive argument in the courtroom.

The military tribunal found Grishin guilty only of having taken part in
the torture of people sentenced to execution, "allowing a system of abuses
by UNKVD personnel during the completion of operational assignments
for the commandant, that is plunder and humiliation of those sentenced to
VMN [the death penalty]."[88] The military tribunal ignored evidence from the
preliminary investigation that former UNKVD boss Iakushev and Grishin
had created a criminal system of abuses that went far beyond the bounds of
"completion of operational assignments for the commandant," ranging from
groundless arrests to torture during investigation and outrages against the remains of the victims.

In accordance with the military tribunal's decision, Grishin was sentenced
under Article 206-17 (A) of the Ukrainian republic Criminal Code to ten
years' imprisonment in a corrective labor camp and was stripped of his rank
as captain of state security. He was acquitted of charges under Article 51-1
(B) and 54-11.[89] On 9 October 1939, however, the Military Collegium of the
All-Union Supreme Court overturned the sentence. It came to the conclusion
that the judicial investigation had established that the looting, the beating of
detainees during investigations and of the convicted before their execution,
and the humiliation of convicted women prior to execution had occurred
with Grishin's knowledge and sanction. The Supreme Court decided to return the case for further judicial review to the same tribunal (in Kiev), but
with a different configuration of judges.[90]

From 16 to 18 November 1939, Grishin underwent a second trial by
Military Tribunal. The new configuration of the court reached the same
verdict.[91] The case was again sent to Moscow. In this instance, examination
of the files sent was completed on 22 April 1940, and this time the Military
Collegium of the Supreme Court confirmed the verdict.[92]

While Grishin awaited the decision of the Military Collegium, he served
as a witness in the court proceedings of the Military Tribunal of the NKVD

Troops of the Kiev Military District in the cases of Maksim Didenko, Vasilii Rasput'ko, Mikhail Fedorov, Daniil Man'ko, Matvei Lesnov, Daniil Maluka, Nikolai Zub, and Mitrofan Liul'kov, which took place between 13 April and 23 April 1940. His testimony facilitated death sentences for Maluka and, later, Lesnov.

On 4 May 1940, Grishin was read the decision of the Military Collegium of the All-Union Supreme Court in his case. He was held for a further two months in the NKVD prison in Zhitomir. On 9 July 1940, he was transferred to serve the remainder of his sentence at the Northern Railway Corrective Labor Camp (*Sevzheldorlag*) of the All-Union NKVD.[93]

During December 1938, the First Deputy All-Union People's Commissar of Internal Affairs, Lavrentii Beriia, and the All-Union Procurator, Andrei Vyshinskii, regularly reported to Stalin about all important cases in the investigation process within the NKVD and procuracy. The "Zhitomir Affair," however, stood out, thanks to the report by Military Procurator Morozov to Vyshinskii. In the files of the Ukrainian republic NKVD, a copy of this report is dated 17 December 1938. However, the report itself had been prepared somewhat earlier. On 16 December a memorandum based on it and addressed to Stalin and Chairman of the All-Union Council of People's Commissars, Viacheslav Molotov, had been composed in the All-Union Procuracy, where the crimes committed by the Zhitomir UNKVD personnel had been discussed.[94]

Thanks to the efforts of the procurators, the case against the Zhitomir UNKVD became one of the largest cases in the oblast organs of the NKVD of Ukraine. In just the investigation files in the cases against Fedorov, Man'ko, Lesnov, and others, thirty-four UNKVD personnel fell under suspicion of having committed crimes.[95] In total, this number ultimately exceeded fifty individuals. A major stroke of luck for Sergei Golubev and others was that they avoided arrest and expulsion from the NKVD.

In the course of the reorganization of the UNKVD, the pendulum of justice swung in different directions. A tendency to lighten the punishment of the four UNKVD bosses is evident. For a start, on 22 February 1939, Viatkin was convicted by the Military Collegium of the All-Union Supreme Court as "a participant in a conspiratorial organization," sentenced to death, and shot. Then, on 20 June 1939, Iakushev was sentenced by the same military collegium to twenty years' imprisonment in a corrective labor camp.[96] Grishin was twice—on 4 July and 18 November 1939—sentenced by the Military Tribunal for NKVD Troops of the Kiev Military District to ten years' imprisonment in a corrective labor camp. On 1 February 1940, Luk'ianov was also sentenced to ten years' imprisonment in a corrective labor camp.

In this way, justice began with the death sentence of one boss—Viatkin—after which the punishment was lightened to a twenty-year prison term for the second—Iakushev—and then further lightened to ten-year prison terms for their deputies. Moreover, after the first conviction of Grishin, the Military Collegium of the All-Union Supreme Court justifiably considered the sentence incommensurate to the severity of the crimes committed by him. Only on the second time around did the Supreme Court confirm the evidently "liberal" sentence.

A different picture is apparent for the mid-level UNKVD leaders. Sentenced on 1 July 1939, Ignatenko received ten years' imprisonment in a corrective labor camp and Timoshenko, eight years. As a result of the session of the Military Tribunal for NKVD Troops of the Kiev Military District from 19 to 22 August 1939, the former head of the Fifth Department, Naum

FIG. 6.1 N. A. Remov-Poberëzkin, from November 1937 to February 1938 assistant and then head of the Fifth Department of the Zhitomir Oblast NKVD. Photo from 1930, HDA SBU, f. 12, spr. 31602, chastina 5, ark. 3 (convert). By exclusive permission of the State Archive of the Security Services of Ukraine.

Remov-Poberëzkin,[97] was the first among the mid-level leadership to be sentenced to death and, on 29 November 1939, was executed.[98]

On 23 April 1940, the Military Tribunal for NKVD Troops of the Kiev Military District sentenced Man'ko and Maluka to death, and they were shot on 28 August 1940.[99] It sentenced Fedorov and Lesnov to ten years, Zub to five years, and Liul'kov to three years' imprisonment in a corrective labor camp.[100] However, the Military Collegium of the All-Union Supreme Court overturned the sentences in the cases of Fedorov and Lesnov because the Military Tribunal had underrated the severity of their crimes.[101] As a result of a second court proceeding by the Military Tribunal from 27 to 29 September 1940, both were sentenced to death.[102] On 18 October 1940, the Military Collegium approved the sentences and, on 4 November 1940, the men were shot.[103]

In this way, the harshest justice was visited on the mid-level leadership of the UNKVD: five implemented sentences to death in the cases of the

FIG. 6.2 M. S. Liul'kov, from November 1937 to February 1938 plenipotentiary (*operupolnomochennyi*) of the Eleventh Department of the Zhitomir Oblast NKVD, from March 1938 prison commandant in Zhitomir. Photo from 1936, HDA SBU, f. 5, spr. 67839, tom 4, ark. 170 (convert). By exclusive permission of the State Archive of the Security Services of Ukraine.

directors of the three main operational departments, the Third, the Fourth, and the Fifth. Although they were certainly the main "violators of socialist legality" in the UNKVD in practice, the role of their four leaders as agents and perpetrators of mass repression was far more serious.

During the campaign to unmask "violators of socialist legality," no one questioned the mass repression of 1937–1938, one of the most serious crimes of the twentieth century. For that reason, NKVD personnel were convinced that in the majority of cases they had repressed "actual enemies." To prove the opposite was not part of the task of Soviet justice of that time. The incoherence and unsystematic nature of the discovery of crimes committed in 1937 and 1938 by NKVD personnel, and not only by them, did not provide a reckoning with the crimes of the times and, indeed, could not have considering who was most fundamentally to blame. However, the documentation from these early investigations were used once again, between 1954 and 1956, when the Soviet leadership under Nikita Khrushchev began a partial de-Stalinization and, significantly, approved the first wave of mass rehabilitations of victims of Stalinist terror.

Notes

1. Previously, the territory of the Zhitomir Oblast had formed part of the Kiev and Vinnitsa oblasts. The new Zhitomir Oblast included all districts and towns of Korosten, Novograd-Volynskii, and Zhitomir counties, eight other districts of Kiev Oblast, as well as four districts and the town of Berdichev from Vinnitsa Oblast. *Reabilitovani istoriieiu: Zhitomyrs'ka oblast'*, tom 1 (Zhitomir: Polissia, 2006), 655–56. The document collection *Reabilitirovannye istoriei* includes seven volumes on Zhitomir Oblast. These volumes shed light on the basic trajectory of the terror and on its victims, and also contain some information about the perpetrators of the repressions. For further information on this region, also see Iu. Shapoval, G. Kuromiia, et al., *Ukraina v dobu "Velikogo teroru": 1936–1938 roki* (Kiev: Lybid', 2009), 143–45; V. A. Zolotar'ov, O. G. Bazhan, and E. R. Timiriaiev, "ChK-GPU-NKVD Zhitomyrshchiny u 1919–1941 rokakh: struktura ta kerivnyi sklad," in *Reabilitovani istoriieiu: Zhitomyrs'ka oblast'*, tom 3 (Zhitomir: Polissia, 2010), 9–23.

2. Along with the appointment of Iakushev, the new heads of the main operational departments of the UNKVD were Senior Lieutenant of State Security Abram Maslovskii of the Third Department (Counterintelligence), Lieutenant of State Security Andrei Luk'ianov of the Fourth Department (Secret-Political), and Senior Lieutenant of State Security Vasilii Lebedev of the Fifth Department (Special). On 12 October 1937, the post of chief of the Fourth Section of the Third Department was filled by Sergeant of State Security Daniil Man'ko, who on 15 July 1938 became

temporary acting deputy director of the Third Department. At the same time, Lieutenant of State Security Matvei Lesnov became the deputy director of the Fourth Department, and Lieutenant of State Security Daniil Maluka became chief of the Third Section of the Fourth Department. On 28 November 1937, Lieutenant of State Security Naum Remov-Poberëzkin was appointed temporary acting aide to the director of the Fifth Department of the Zhitomir Oblast UNKVD. On 20 December 1937, Sergeant Sergei Golubev was appointed operational plenipotentiary in the apparatus of the special plenipotentiary for the UNKVD. After the formation of Zhitomir Oblast, the county NKVD departments were transformed into town departments. Senior Lieutenant of State Security Vsevolod Martyniuk became the director of the Berdichev town department, Sergeant of State Security Moisei Gilis the director of Korosten department, and Junior Lieutenant of State Security Grigorii Artem'ev the director of the Novograd-Volynskii department. In January 1938, Lebedev was reassigned to the Ukrainian republic NKVD and then, later, to the All-Union NKVD. On 26 February 1938, Remov-Poberëzkin was named temporary acting director of the Fifth Department, but in August 1938 he too was reassigned to the Ukrainian republic NKVD. HDA SBU, f. 5, op. 1, spr. 67841, tom 3, ark. 149–50; f. 12, op. 1, spr. 31602, tom 1, ark. 16 and f. 5, op. 1, spr. 67841, tom 1, ark. 4.

3. HDA SBU, f. 12, op. 1, spr. 31601, ark. 3–4, 35 zv.

4. The post of director of the Fourth Department was taken by Matvei Lesnov. On 9 September 1938, Luk'ianov was appointed director of the Special Department of the NKVD for the Odessa Army Group. Zolotar'ov, Bazhan, and Timiriaiev, "ChK-GPU-NKVD Zhitomirshchiny," 3:18–19.

5. The director of the Special Department of the Zhitomir Army Group, Senior Lieutenant of State Security Ivan Daragan, began to fulfill the duties of UNKVD director, followed by Sergei Mashkov in January 1939 and Vladimir Trubnikov in August 1940. They became witnesses to the investigation into the crimes of their predecessors, Lavrentii Iakushev and Grigorii Viatkin, as well as of other UNKVD personnel.

6. HDA SBU, f. 5, op. 1, spr. 67841, tom 1, ark. 130–32.

7. HDA SBU, f. 5, op. 1, spr. 67841, tom 1, ark. 146.

8. HDA SBU, f. 5, op. 1, spr. 67841, tom 1, ark. 153–53 zv, 159, 165.

9. HDA SBU, f. 5, op. 1, spr. 67841, tom 1, ark. 173.

10. HDA SBU, f. 5, op. 1, spr. 67841, tom 1, ark. 177–78.

11. HDA SBU, f. 5, op. 1, spr. 67841, tom 1, ark. 180.

12. HDA SBU, f. 5, op. 1, spr. 67841, tom 1, ark. 169–71.

13. HDA SBU, f. 5, op. 1, spr. 67841, tom 1, ark. 172.

14. HDA SBU, f. 5, op. 1, spr. 67841, tom 1, ark. 184–88.

15. HDA SBU, f. 12, op. 1, spr. 31601, ark. 46 (cover), 47, 64, 65.

16. HDA SBU, f. 5, op. 1, spr. 67841, tom 1, ark. 3.

17. HDA SBU, f. 5, op. 1, spr. 67841, tom 1, ark. 43, 73.

18. HDA SBU, f. 5, op. 1, spr. 67841, tom 3, ark. 31.

19. HDA SBU, f. 5, op. 1, spr. 67841, tom 3, ark. 15.

20. HDA SBU, f. 5, op. 1, spr. 67841, tom 3, ark. 137–38.

21. HDA SBU, f. 5, op. 1, spr. 67841, tom 3, ark. 245–46.

22. The Polish Military Organization (POV) existed in the territory of Ukraine until 1921. In 1937 and 1938, the POV became one of the phantoms against which NKVD organs were ordered to combat.

23. HDA SBU, f. 5, op. 1, spr. 67841, tom 3, ark. 246–46 zv.

24. He was the brother of Aleksandr Tomin. For more on him, see Lynne Viola, *Stalinist Perpetrators on Trial: Scenes from the Great Terror in Soviet Ukraine* (New York: Oxford University Press, 2017), chap. 5.

25. HDA SBU, f. 5, op. 1, spr. 67841, tom 3, ark. 253–53 zv.

26. HDA SBU, f. 5, op. 1, spr. 67841, tom 3, ark. 258–59 zv, 19–21.

27. HDA SBU, f. 5, op. 1, spr. 67841, tom 3, ark. 248–48 zv.

28. HDA SBU, f. 5, op. 1, spr. 67841, tom 3, ark. 160–67.

29. HDA SBU, f. 5, op. 1, spr. 67841, tom 3, ark. 106.

30. E. Bednarek, V. V'iatrovych, et al., eds., *Pol'sha ta Ukraïna u tridtsiatykh-sorokovykh rokakh XX stolittia: nevidomi dokumenty z arkhiviv spetsial'nykh sluzhb*, tom 8, *Velykyi teror: Pol'ska operatsiia 1937–1938*, Kniga 2 (Kyiv and Warsaw: HDA SBU; Institut natsional'noi pam'iati—Komisiia z peresliduvannia zlochyniv proti pol'skogo narodu; Instytut politychnykh i etnonatsional'nykh doslidzhen' Natsional'noï akademiï nauk Ukraïny, 2010), 1718.

31. Ibid., 1626–32.

32. Ibid., 1716.

33. Ibid., 1712.

34. Ibid., 1708.

35. Ibid., 1724–26.

36. Arkhyv Upravlinnia Ministerstva vnutrishnikh sprav (UMVS) Ukrainy v Zhitomirs'kiy oblasti (Departmental Archive of the Ministry of Internal Affairs of Ukraine in Zhitomir Oblast), f. 2, op. 1, spr. 6751, tom 1, ark. 393.

37. Bednarek, et al., eds., *Pol'sha ta Ukraïna u tridtsiatykh—sorokovykh rokakh,* tom 8, kn. 2, 1728.

38. Ibid., 1728–30.

39. HDA SBU, f. 5, op. 1, spr. 67839, tom 2, ark. 288 zv and ark. 351.

40. Bednarek et al., eds., *Pol'sha ta Ukraïna u tridtsiatykh*, tom 8, kn. 2, 1736.

41. Ibid., 1750. Previously, this document was published in Shapoval, Kuromiia, et al., *Ukraïna v dobu "Velikogo Teroru,"* 316–22.

42. In the fall of 1922, the Volynskaia Povstancheskaia Armiia, or VPA, had prepared an armed attack on the Bolshevik regime with the goal of restoring the Ukrainian government. Two days before the planned attack, agents of the Cheka arrested the majority of the command structure of the organization, although the command staff and its protective detachment successfully crossed the border into Poland.

43. Bednarek et al., eds., *Pol'sha ta Ukraïna u tridtsiatykh*, tom 8, kn. 2, 1748.

44. Ibid., 1748–50.

45. Ibid., 1744.

46. M. Iu. Kostrytsia, "Geograf, kraenavets', pedagog (Postoev, P. G.)," in *Reabilitovani istorieiu: Zhitomirs'ka oblast'*, tom 1, 190–92.

47. Bednarek et al., eds., *Pol'sha ta Ukraïna u tridtsiatykh*, tom 8, kn. 2, 1750–52.

48. Kostrytsia, "Geograf, kraenavets', pedagog," 193.

49. Bednarek et al., eds., *Pol'sha ta Ukraïna u tridtsiatykh*, tom 8, kn. 2, 1752.

50. Ibid., tom 8, kn. 2, 1752.

51. *Reabilitovani istoriieiu: Zhitomirs'ka oblast'*, tom 3 (Zhitomir: Polissia, 2010), 60.

52. Conversational term for a member of the secret police, derived from an acronym for the civil war–era predecessor to the NKVD, the Extraordinary Commission for Combatting Counterrevolution and Sabotage, or Cherezvychainaia kommissia (Che-Ka). —*Trans.*

53. HDA SBU, f. 5, op. 1, spr. 67841, tom 5, ark. 84 zv, 85.

54. HDA SBU, f. 5, op. 1, spr. 67841, tom 1, ark. 83–84.

55. According to the Ukrainian researcher Vadym Zolotar'ov, on 14 May 1940, Vasilii Lebedev was expelled from the Communist Party "for use of depraved methods during the implementation of death sentences and unlawful arrests in Zhitomir." He was arrested and sentenced to a five-year prison term. In 1941, his sentence was overturned and he was released from prison and, on 25 August 1941, re-admitted to the party. During World War II, he was employed in the front-line activities of the NKVD-NKGB organs, twice awarded the Order of the Red Banner, in 1943 and 1945, the Order of the Patriotic War, Second Class, in 1944, and the Order of Lenin, in 1945. In 1945, he was a NKGB colonel and the head of one of the sub-departments of the All-Union NKGB.

56. HDA SBU, f. 5, op. 1, spr. 67841, tom 3, ark. 208.

57. In 1937 and 1938, Miron Blank was an Operational Agent of the NKVD Special Department for the Fifth Cavalry Division, Second Cavalry Corps, Kiev Military District, in the city of Zhitomir.

58. HDA SBU, f. 5, op. 1, spr. 67841, tom 3, ark. 200–1.

59. HDA SBU, f. 5, op. 1, spr. 67841, tom 3, ark. 27, 209.

60. HDA SBU, f. 5, op. 1, spr. 67841, tom 3, ark. 170.

61. HDA SBU, f. 5, op. 1, spr. 67841, tom 3, ark. 178.

62. HDA SBU, f. 5, op. 1, spr. 67841, tom 3, ark. 195.

63. HDA SBU, f. 5, op. 1, spr. 67841, tom 3, ark. 293–300, 301–9, 318–21, 322–27, 328–30, 331–38, 339–43, 344–48.

64. HDA SBU, f. 5, op. 1, spr. 67841, tom 3, ark. 109–10, 118–19.

65. HDA SBU, f. 5, op. 1, spr. 67841, tom 3, ark. 111–12, 121.

66. HDA SBU, f. 5, op. 1, spr. 67841, tom 3, ark. 128–30, 131–34.

67. HDA SBU, f. 5, op. 1, spr. 67841, tom 3, ark. 353.

68. HDA SBU, f. 5, op. 1, spr. 67841, tom 3, ark. 358.

69. HDA SBU, f. 5, op. 1, spr. 67841, tom 1, ark. 4, 5.

70. HDA SBU, f. 5, op. 1, spr. 67841, tom 1, ark. 278–79.

71. HDA SBU, f. 5, op. 1, spr. 67841, tom 1, ark. 85 zv–86.

72. HDA SBU, f. 5, op. 1, spr. 67841, tom 1, ark. 76.

73. HDA SBU, f. 5, op. 1, spr. 67841, tom 1, ark. 80.

74. HDA SBU, f. 5, op. 1, spr. 67841, tom 5, ark. 86 zv.

75. HDA SBU, f. 5, op. 1, spr. 67841, tom 1, ark. 280, 282.

76. HDA SBU, f. 5, op. 1, spr. 67841, tom 1, ark. 209.

77. HDA SBU, f. 5, op. 1, spr. 67841, tom 1, ark. 218–20.

78. HDA SBU, f. 5, op. 1, spr. 67841, tom 1, ark. 213–14.

79. HDA SBU, f. 5, op. 1, spr. 67841, tom 5, ark. 87 zv–88.

80. HDA SBU, f. 5, op. 1, spr. 67841, tom 1, ark. 17.

81. HDA SBU, f. 5, op. 1, spr. 67841, tom 5, ark. 202–2 zv, 209–11.

82. HDA SBU, f. 5, op. 1, spr. 67841, tom 1, ark. 279 zv.

83. HDA SBU, f. 5, op. 1, spr. 67841, tom 1, ark. 384–84 zv.

84. HDA SBU, f. 5, op. 1, spr. 67841, tom 1, ark. 4.

85. HDA SBU, f. 5, op. 1, spr. 67841, tom 1, ark. 78 and 315 zv.

86. HDA SBU, f. 5, op. 1, spr. 67841, tom 1, ark. 198 and 205.

87. HDA SBU, f. 5, op. 1, spr. 67841, tom 1, ark. 199 zv, 200, 207.

88. HDA SBU, f. 5, op. 1, spr. 67841, tom 1, ark. 20, 208.

89. HDA SBU, f. 5, op. 1, spr. 67841, tom 1, ark. 202–20bv, 210.

90. HDA SBU, f. 5, op. 1, spr. 67841, tom 1, ark. 279–79 zv.

91. HDA SBU, f. 5, op. 1, spr. 67841, tom 1, ark. 336–37 zv, 338–40.

92. HDA SBU, f. 5, op. 1, spr. 67841, tom 1, ark. 390–90 zv.

93. HDA SBU, f. 5, op. 1, spr. 67841, tom 1, ark. 485.

94. State Archive of the Russian Federation (Gosudarstvennyi arkhiv Rossiiskoi Federatsii, GARF), f. R-8131, op. 37, d. 118, ll. 19–20.

95. HDA SBU, f. 5, op. 1, spr. 67839, tom 4, ark. 108–9.

96. N. V. Petrov and K. V. Skorkin, eds., *Kto rukovodil NKVD, 1934–1941: Spravochnik* (Moscow: Zven'ia, 1999), 462–63.

97. Remov-Poberëzkin was deputy director of the Third Department of the Turkmen republic NKVD. On 16 January 1939, he was arrested and, in February 1939, transported under guard to the custody of the Ukrainian republic NKVD. HDA SBU, f. 12, op. 7, spr. 135, tom 2, ark. 75, 85.

98. Arkhiv UMVC Ukrainy po Zhitomirskyi oblasti, f. 2, op. 1, spr. 6751, tom 1, ark. 646.

99. HDA SBU, f. 5, op. 1, spr. 67839, tom 5, ark. 429a, 429b.

100. HDA SBU, f. 5, op. 1, spr. 67839, tom 5, ark. 329–30, 337–38.

101. HDA SBU, f. 5, op. 1, spr. 67839, tom 5, ark. 427–28.

102. HDA SBU, f. 5, op. 1, spr. 67839, tom 5, ark. 512–16, 518–21.

103. HDA SBU, f. 5, op. 1, spr. 67839, tom 5, ark. 537–37 zv.

7

"This Is How You Interrogate and Secure Testimony"

KOCHERGINSKII AND THE NORTHERN DONETSK RAILWAY NKVD

Jeffrey J. Rossman

WHAT MOTIVATED RANK-AND-FILE NKVD officers to commit gross violations of socialist legality—to fabricate cases, torture suspects, coerce witnesses into giving false testimony—during the Great Terror? This question has not been asked as often as one might suppose given the wealth of research on perpetrator motivation in genocide studies—above all, in studies of the Holocaust. Scholars of the Great Terror tend to focus on high-level decision makers, such as Stalin and Ezhov, on victims of the Great Terror, or on the role of the general public in fueling what at times amounted to a witch-hunt.[1] Though rarely stated explicitly, the assumption seems to be that rank-and-file NKVD operatives followed orders because they were trained to do so. The investigation and trial of Georgii Kocherginskii, who served as head of the Transportation Department (Dorozhnyi-transportnyi otdel, or DTO) NKVD of the Northern Donetsk Railway from November 1937 to August 1938, suggests that situational factors—above all, fear of punishment and a desire to secure the approbation of superiors—played a significant role in motivating NKVD operatives to participate in mass violations of socialist legality during the Great Terror. Ideology, of course, also played a role: Kocherginskii himself harbored no doubts that class enemies permeated the Soviet Union and his jurisdiction, in particular. It is not clear from the evidence, however, that his subordinates shared this world view. At the same

Jeffrey J. Rossman, *"This Is How You Interrogate and Secure Testimony"* In: *Laboratories of Terror.*
Edited by: Lynne Viola and Marc Junge, Oxford University Press. © Oxford University Press 2023.
DOI: 10.1093/oso/9780197647547.003.0008

time, situational factors—above all, fear of falling victim to the hunt for class enemies within the NKVD—played a role in motivating Kocherginskii himself.

Georgii Izrailovich Kocherginskii was born in Latvia in 1898.[2] He came from a humble background: his Jewish father worked in Riga lumber mills as a boat hookman, and his mother—who was either German or Estonian— tutored students in the German language and needlework.[3] His parents were either divorced or never married, and Kocherginskii barely knew his father and stepfather. Perhaps overwhelmed by the burden of raising two young children or seeking to help her son find a trade, Kocherginskii's mother sent him to live at the age of eight with her brother, Al'bert Leikht, an electrician at the Riga power station. Leikht soon became one of the two most influential people in the young boy's life, taking him on as an apprentice and funding his studies at vocational school. Leikht also introduced Kocherginskii to the second most influential person of his childhood, a longtime Marxist by the name of Ul'rikh who tutored young workers to take *Realschule* equivalency examinations.[4]

Although Kocherginskii participated in a *kruzhok* (a study circle) or-ganized by Ul'rikh for his pupils and came to know several members of the Russian Social-Democratic Workers Party (RSDRP), his studies occupied far more of his attention than politics. With the support of Leikht and Ul'rikh, Kocherginskii passed the equivalency examinations for the fifth and seventh classes of *Realschule*. Meanwhile, after two years of apprenticeship, he became an electrician at the Riga power station.[5]

Kocherginskii's discipline, intelligence, and capacity to overcome setbacks came into relief in 1916, when he was arrested on suspicion of distributing revolutionary May Day pamphlets at the power station. Although he played no role in the incident, he lost his job. Frightened by the loss of his liveli-hood, Kocherginskii crammed for the entrance examination to the Riga Polytechnical Institute and, three weeks later, passed.[6]

Because Riga's higher-education institutions had been evacuated during the war, Kocherginskii relocated to Moscow, where he pursued his studies and worked as a tutor and a mechanic at a match factory. At this juncture, Kocherginskii was on the path to a higher, if still modest, station in life. That trajectory was dramatically altered by the events of 1917. When the Old Regime collapsed, the Riga Polytechnical Institute closed and Kocherginskii returned to his position as an electrician at the Riga power station. In September, when the Germans entered Riga, he joined the Bolshevik Party. In early 1918, he left Riga as a rank-and-file soldier in the Karl Liebknecht International Battalion. Within six months, he was a political commissar.[7]

Little is known about Kocherginskii's experiences during the civil war, though they must have been formative. He distinguished himself and acquired responsibilities that, in normal times, would have been beyond the reach of a young Jewish electrician from Latvia. Three years after leaving Riga as a rank-and-file soldier, Kocherginskii—at the age of twenty-three—served as deputy chairman of the Revolutionary Tribunal of the Third Rifle Division of the Kharkov Military District.[8] If nothing else, his work on the tribunal acclimated him to the experience of delivering summary justice to enemies of the Bolshevik regime: foreign agents, peasant anarchists, Ukrainian nationalists, counterrevolutionaries, and class enemies.

Aside from the responsibilities that he acquired in the Red Army, another indication of the distinction with which Kocherginskii served came on the day of his demobilization in 1921. Rather than being left to make his way in the country's devastated economy, Kocherginskii was immediately hired by the Crimean Division of the Cheka.[9] Thus began his seventeen-year career in the Soviet security police.

Like many successful Chekists, Kocherginskii served in a variety of administrative positions and was relocated periodically. After four years in Crimea, he spent two years in the Far East, where he was stationed in Vladivostok and at the OGPU residency in Manchuria. In 1927, he began a nine-year stint in the North Caucasus, where he held important posts in Krasnodar, Shakhty, Rostov, and Piatigorsk. These were volatile regions, and Kocherginskii's assignments in the Operational and Special Divisions of the OGPU/NKVD placed him at the center of important operations against real and imagined enemies of Soviet power.[10]

That Kocherginskii was a Chekist who could be counted on to deal effectively with class enemies in high-priority regions was confirmed after Stalin elevated Ezhov to leadership of the NKVD in September 1936. After several months serving as head of the Kursk Oblast NKVD's Counterintelligence Division, Kocherginskii was summoned to Moscow at the conclusion of the February–March 1937 Central Committee plenum and appointed to a special NKVD brigade headed by Counterintelligence (Third Department) Chief Lev Mironov. An NKVD decree of 4 April 1937 succinctly formulated the Mironov brigade's mission: "detection and destruction of Trotskyist espionage and sabotage [formations] and other groups on the railways . . . and in the army" in Siberia and the Far East.[11]

The dispatch of the Mironov brigade signaled Moscow's concern that Far Eastern and Siberian NKVD bosses would be unable to root out class enemies believed to be ensconced in the ranks of the *nomenklatura*, or party-state officialdom. When the Mironov brigade arrived in Khabarovsk on 23 April 1937, it launched a wave of arrests, including within the NKVD, and deployed so-called new methods that became a hallmark of the mass operations of 1937–1938—such as physical and psychological torture and the falsification of interrogation protocols—to identify and liquidate covert antisoviet terrorist networks.[12]

Judging from the frequency with which he later boasted about his participation in the Mironov brigade and cited it as justification for his actions, Kocherginskii was influenced by his experience in Khabarovsk, where he headed an investigative group that wrung espionage confessions from Far East NKVD leaders.[13] Although Mironov himself came under suspicion and was arrested in June 1937,[14] Kocherginskii confided to a colleague that he was indebted to Mironov because "he taught him well" during the time they spent together in Khabarovsk.[15] When Kocherginskii left Moscow in November 1937 to assume leadership of the DTO NKVD of the Northern Donetsk Railway, he believed he had been chosen by Ezhov to achieve in

FIG. 7.1 G. I. Kocherginskii, from November 1937 to August 1938 head of the Northern Donetsk Railway NKVD sector (DTO NKVD). Photo from between 1934 and 1936. Personal archive of Vadym Zolotar'ov.

Artemovsk what the Mironov brigade achieved in Khabarovsk—that is, to transform a compromised NKVD apparatus into an effective counterterrorist organization.

Although Kocherginskii was not close to Mironov, he had powerful protectors in the NKVD. These relationships illuminate the patronage networks in which Kocherginskii was ensconced and point to formative influences on his professional identity. Kocherginskii's patrons were NKVD officials from humble, mostly Jewish, backgrounds who fulfilled critical leadership positions in Crimea and the North Caucasus during the 1920s and 1930s. The most important of these patrons was Izrail' Dagin, who managed security for Soviet leaders from 1936 to 1938. As deputy chairman of the Crimean Cheka in 1921, Dagin hired Kocherginskii on the day he was demobilized from the Red Army. The two worked together for the next thirteen years, especially during the bloody collectivization campaign in the North Caucasus. According to Kocherginskii:

> In DAGIN I always saw for myself the model of a Chekist-communist. Under the direction of DAGIN I began my Chekist career. In the North Caucasus I was nominated for the "Honorable Chekist" award, which I received in 1935. Dagin nominated me alone out of numerous NKVD deputy department heads to receive the rank of captain of national security.

Kocherginskii stayed in close touch with Dagin after the latter was transferred to Moscow, seeking his insight and advice.[16]

Kocherginskii's other patron-protectors included: Aleksandr Radzivilovskii, under whom he served in Crimea; Moisei Gatov, under whom he served in the North Caucasus; and Grigorii Gorbach, with whom he worked closely in the Shakhty-Donetsk OGPU sector during the Great Famine.[17] Gorbach, who hailed from Ukrainian peasant stock and distinguished himself under Ezhov as a particularly ruthless regional NKVD boss, thought so highly of Kocherginskii that he endeavored to recruit him on the eve of the mass operations to serve as his deputy in the NKVD's Western Siberia Region Directorate.[18]

If Kocherginskii modeled himself on tough Chekists such as Dagin, Gorbach, and Mironov, he almost certainly was also motivated by fear. After his return to Moscow from the Far East in October 1937, Kocherginskii learned that he had recently been denounced for allegedly opposing the general line and espousing Trotskyite views in 1928. After being interrogated about the accusation, Kocherginskii visited Dagin, who placed a call to Mikhail Volkov, head of the NKVD's Transportation Department. That evening, Volkov quashed the investigation of Kocherginskii and reaffirmed his appointment as the next head of the DTO NKVD in Artemovsk, Ukraine.[19] In the context of the times, knowing that he had been denounced as a Trotskyite gave Kocherginskii additional motivation to demonstrate his fealty to the Party by zealously rooting out enemies in his new post.

Kocherginskii may also have been motivated to demonstrate his zeal as a result of a more concrete vulnerability: he grew up in Latvia and had close relatives who still lived in Riga. The NKVD's mass operation against alleged spies for Latvia was launched on 30 November 1937 and extended by a Politburo decree of 31 January 1938.[20] In spring 1938, Kocherginskii recited his autobiography at a district party conference. When he mentioned his Latvian roots, delegates "became apprehensive, which to me was extremely unpleasant." Meanwhile, Ukraine's NKVD boss, Uspenskii, had ordered that NKVD ranks be purged of operatives with foreign ties. These events left Kocherginskii wondering if his days in the NKVD were numbered. He confessed his concerns in summer 1938 to Dagin, who assured him that there was no reason to panic.[21]

Kocherginskii arrived at the headquarters of the DTO NKVD of the Northern Donetsk Railway in Artemovsk, Ukraine, on November 15, 1937.[22] As of the previous month, the DTO and its branch offices—these were situated at stations along the railway—had made 165 arrests as part of ongoing mass operations.[23] At his first DTO staff meeting, Kocherginskii underscored that he was not impressed by this figure. Boasting that he was an Old Bolshevik and experienced Chekist who had been dispatched personally by Ezhov "for the 'strengthening' of the DTO," Kocherginskii notified subordinates that their shortcomings placed them in the camp of enemy "accomplices." Demanding that confessions be secured within twenty-four hours rather than three to five days, he vowed to implement the special investigative methods that he had mastered in Khabarovsk, where he claimed to have personally arrested and executed Far East NKVD boss Deribas.[24]

Kocherginskii was true to his word. Within days of his arrival in Artemovsk, a wave of arrests struck white- and blue-collar railroad workers. To secure confessions to capital crimes such as sabotage and espionage, Kocherginskii implemented the Mironov brigade's methods: systematic beating and serial interrogation of arrested individuals; the creation of special cells where those who refused to confess were made to stand for days without rest; and "editing" (falsification) of interrogation protocols. Although violations of Soviet criminal procedure occurred before Kocherginskii's arrival in Artemovsk, they now became routine.[25] "Before his arrival . . . we didn't have such interrogation practices," testified DTO plenipotentiary Ivchenko. "From November 1937 through February 1938, beatings of arrested individuals became commonplace at DTO headquarters and district branch offices."[26]

Kocherginskii secured compliance with the new investigative paradigm using a variety of tactics. First, he led by example. Almost from the day of his arrival in Artemovsk, he burst into investigators' offices and, if a confession had not been secured, he began to pummel the suspect. Sometimes he ordered investigators and arrested individuals to participate in these assaults. After repeatedly beating a suspect who refused to confess to being a member of a counterrevolutionary group, an exhausted Kocherginskii barked at a hapless investigator: "What, are you a guest here? Get beating!"[27] Although he never formally authorized wholesale beating of suspects—at some staff meetings, he carefully stated that "beatings" could only be employed with his or his deputy's permission[28]—Kocherginskii communicated his expectations by, for instance, telling subordinates who had just witnessed his handiwork: "This is how you interrogate and secure testimony." According to deputy DTO chief Matveev: "Certainly, such a display untied the hands of investigators."[29]

Second, Kocherginskii issued directives that expedited investigations and all but invited investigators to falsify cases. While leading a mass operation in Debalt'sevo in January 1938, Kocherginskii announced that socially alien individuals could be arrested without evidence of antisoviet activity; circulated a copy of what he considered to be a model kulak confession and urged investigators to use it as a template; insisted that witnesses be chosen from among the ranks of reliable party members; demanded that "witness testimonies be sharp [*rezkie*] because all cases will go to the troika"; and made clear that nothing less than conviction and a death sentence were acceptable.[30]

Furthermore, Kocherginskii gave explicit guidance when it came to securing witness testimony. Witnesses were told that the suspect had already been unmasked as an enemy of the regime and that the NKVD merely needed confirmation of the suspect's "defeatism, terroristic intentions, and acute antisoviet agitation." Reluctant witnesses were to be assured that they would not be summoned to court since all cases would be heard by an extrajudicial tribunal. Stubborn witnesses were to be told that they were "enemy accomplice[s]" whose refusal to cooperate with the NKVD's "battle with enemies" would have devastating consequences.[31]

Kocherginskii legitimized his directives by invoking Moscow's authority and created a sense of urgency by framing the mission in military terms. At more than one operational meeting with subordinates, he claimed that Ezhov had declared that Soviet proxy wars in Spain and China and the threat of attack by Germany and Japan required the USSR to purge the home front of— that is, execute—five million internal enemies in addition to the two million who had allegedly been executed in 1937.[32] The unmasking of armed insurrectionary organizations in the Far East and Kazakhstan, he averred, further underscored the need for quick and decisive action.[33]

Kocherginskii ridiculed and threatened subordinates who failed to produce results. Investigators who did not fulfill arrest quotas or secure confessions were singled out at staff meetings, accused of being enemy accomplices, and threatened with arrest and expulsion from the Party.[34] "By means of intimidation Kocherginskii compelled members of the Directorate of State Security (UGB) to carry out his . . . directives," recalled Debal'tsevo plenipotentiary Guenok.[35] "Kocherginskii's terrorization of employees was done in such a way that none of them could say anything," testified Debal'tsevo plenipotentiary Khodarev. "Kocherginskii . . . declared: 'I was sent from Moscow and have special powers. I do what I want, so carry out my orders and you can complain about me to People's Commissar [Ezhov].'"[36]

Kocherginskii used threats to silence voices of dissent, such as when a subordinate objected to an arbitrary arrest quota or raised doubts about a suspect's guilt or the veracity of a confession.[37] "Kocherginskii uniformly terrorized the employees of DTO headquarters and district branch offices," recalled deputy DTO boss Konstantin Matveev. "From his first days on the job . . . he presented himself as a person whom nobody should contradict and whose actions were beyond reproach."[38] Plenipotentiary Ivchenko echoed the point: "Kocherginskii created an oppressive atmosphere and employees were afraid to go to his office if any of them started having doubts as to the guilt of any of the arrested individuals."[39] Any investigator who concluded that a suspect should be released was derided as "a liberal," "an opportunist," or "an enemy accomplice."[40] Soon after deputy DTO chief Matveev reported to Stalino Oblast UNKVD chief Sokolinskii about mass beatings at the DTO, Kocherginskii summoned Matveev to his office and declared: "I don't understand this behavior. You don't understand Bolshevism."[41] Informed that DTO division chief Timoshek doubted the veracity of a suspect's confession, Kocherginskii "pointedly" told him: "You don't have a good mindset."[42]

Fear was a powerful motivator. "Kocherginskii placed most of the DTO and district branch office employees in a position that required unquestioning fulfillment of his orders in order to avoid abuse," recalled Matveev, "and many were frightened by his threats" of dismissal and arrest.[43] According to Timoshek, whom Kocherginskii singled out for abuse at a staff meeting for failing to procure a confession: "Under the conditions Kocherginskii created, some employees resorted to outright crime"—that is, to wholesale fabrication of cases.[44] Investigator Nikolai Kuznetsov, who was convicted alongside Kocherginskii, admitted that he began to fabricate cases after hearing Kocherginskii threaten to arrest investigators Khodarev and Bondarchuk, who had missed their quotas.[45] Plenipotentiary Aronovich gave a compelling account of the atmosphere in Debal'tsevo during the January 1938 mass operation:

> While running the operation in Debal'tsevo, Kocherginskii uniformly terrorized us and obscenely cursed everyone. His attitude toward his co-workers was terrifying, and none of us was safe from either arrest or the most frightening insults. It's impossible to convey in words what he did with us in both group and individual meetings. His behavior couldn't have been more vile. Worst of all is that he capitalized on Comrade Ezhov's name. . . .
>
> Naturally, the operational staff carried out Kocherginskii's directives and didn't take a critical look at the fate of arrested individuals— whether they were guilty or not—but snatched everyone they came upon who'd been identified as "enemies" by one person or another.[46]

An equally vivid description of Kocherginskii during the Debalt'sevo operation was offered by plenipotentiary Fadeev: "Kocherginskii came across as some sort of animal, attacking his co-workers and throwing fists, lobbing all kinds of undeserved insults at them, calling them enemies of the people, and threatening to have them thrown into the basement."[47]

DTO sub-division chiefs were both recipients and conveyers of Kocherginskii's threats. At a January 1938 assembly to discuss forthcoming mass operations, Kocherginskii announced that all Germans, Poles, Latvians, Greeks, and former kulaks were to be arrested as spies. The absence of compromising information against such individuals was to be no barrier to arrest because, Kocherginskii asserted, documents in Moscow proved their guilt. When district branch office chiefs Zaloznyi and Sin'ko protested that many such individuals held vital positions at train stations, Kocherginskii barked in reply: "You're harboring spies rather than looking for them. . . . If I discover . . . after this operation that a German or Pole is employed at one or another junction, . . . I'll arrest and interrogate you . . . instead of them." Noted the head of the DTO's second department, Omel'chenko: "After this mass lawlessness broke out: [there were] unlawful arrests without either a shred of compromising material or the procurator's sanction."[48]

Returning to his post at Kaganovich station, Sin'ko flatly told his men "not to come back without incriminating testimony." When plenipotentiary Kushvid pressed for the release of a suspect against whom there was no evidence, Sin'ko reprimanded him: "You don't know how to work and are being soft on the enemy."[49] After witnessing this encounter, plenipotentiary Voronin and others felt they had no choice but to falsify interrogation protocols. "Not wanting to earn the title 'the enemies' patron saint,'" explained Voronin, "I was compelled to act this way . . . even though I knew it was a crime."[50] Likewise, Krasnyi Liman station plenipotentiary Al'bert Rozenberg falsified witness and defendant testimony after repeatedly being ordered by station chief Matveev "to obtain compromising material about these people by any means necessary."[51]

If fear was a powerful motivator, so too was positive reinforcement. Investigators who produced confessions quickly were singled out by Kocherginskii for praise and material benefits.[52] "Kocherginskii always made an example" of investigators who fulfilled daily confession quotas, according to DTO plenipotentiary Ivchenko, even though "to complete this [task] honorably was physically impossible."[53] When DTO assistant head Antonenko called Kocherginskii during a staff meeting at Debal'tsevo during the January 1938 mass operation and reported on his success as leader of the operation at Krasnyi Liman station, Kocherginskii put down the phone and announced: "See, *this* is how to work: in one day . . . Antonenko broke twenty-eight individuals!" Picking up the phone again, Kocherginskii told Antonenko: "I'll kiss your ass for this!"[54] When the Debal'tsevo mass operation ended, Kocherginskii held a banquet at the apartment of district branch office chief Ignatov and bestowed awards on each of his investigators.[55]

Kocherginskii employed a version of socialist competition to increase pressure on subordinates during mass operations. When Sin'ko called Kocherginskii to report that Kaganovich station had arrested one hundred individuals, Kocherginskii (misleadingly) claimed that in Debal'tsevo they had arrested five times as many. Sin'ko promptly sent his men back into the field to make another hundred arrests.[56] Assistant DTO chief Antonenko likewise maintained pressure on station chiefs by telling them that they were falling behind in the race to procure confessions.[57]

Although Kocherginskii's subordinates rarely were told explicitly to violate criminal procedure, orders issued by Kocherginskii played an important role in creating the context in which mass violations of socialist legality occurred. *Nomenklatura* suspects whose cases should have been sent to the Military Collegium of the Supreme Court were intentionally dispatched to the oblast troika, apparently because Kocherginskii feared cases of severely beaten suspects were more likely to collapse if sent to Moscow for trial.[58] Arrest quotas issued on the eve of the January 1938 mass operation were based on the size of each station and the number of employees therein rather than on compromising materials.[59] During mass operations, Kocherginskii insisted that all cases be formulated so as to result in a death sentence and circulated a template confession that investigators drew upon in drafting interrogation protocols.[60] Kocherginskii also ordered the creation of special holding cells (*otstoiniki*) where suspects who refused to confess were made to stand with their face against the wall until they agreed to sign a confession.[61] While in Debal'tsevo during the January 1938 mass operation, Kocherginskii told investigators not to release witnesses until they gave incriminating testimony and declared that arrested individuals "weren't eligible for release."[62]

Summarizing Kocherginskii's culpability for the mass violations of criminal procedure that occurred during the January 1938 mass operations, the chairman of the Military Tribunal that convicted Kocherginskii, P. F. Gur'ev, wrote in an analysis of Kocherginskii's appeal to the Military Collegium of the USSR Supreme Court: "While Kocherginskii didn't give direct orders to falsify cases, he created all the conditions for this to occur, such as by demanding thirty-three cases in three days . . ., praising those who stood out for speedy 'creation' and 'cracking' of cases, setting up the *otstoiniki*, and threatening operatives for the slightest delay."[63] Endeavoring to further isolate what might be called "the Kocherginskii factor," Gur'ev added: "Force was applied less often when Kocherginskii was absent. This is clear from the files of the judicial and preliminary investigations."[64]

The "excesses" that occurred under Kocherginskii at the DTO NKVD of the Northern Donetsk Railway sector generated a stream of complaints from victims, their relatives, and Kocherginskii's subordinates to regional and central offices of the NKVD and state procurator.[65] These complaints triggered investigations by central NKVD officials in March and June 1938.[66] Although the investigations confirmed that "excesses"—including fabrication of cases, falsification of testimony, and physical and psychological torture—had occurred systematically under Kocherginskii, Ezhov did not move against him until being repeatedly pressured by USSR General Procurator Andrei Vyshinskii to do so.[67]

Per Ezhov's order, Kocherginskii was arrested on 20 August 1938 while on a trip to Moscow.[68] During the next five months, he was interrogated thirty-nine times while being held at Lefortovo prison.[69] Accused of being a Trotskyist counterrevolutionary who endeavored to discredit Soviet power by authorizing systematic violations of socialist legality, Kocherginskii insisted on his loyalty to Soviet power but conceded that excesses had occurred even as he blamed them on scheming, untrustworthy subordinates.[70] The investigation continued after Kocherginskii was sent under armed guard to Stalino, where the oblast UNKVD combined his case with that of five of his former subordinates.[71] Consistent with similar prosecutions at this time, the accusation of counterrevolutionary activity was dropped. On 20 March 1939 and consistent with the November 1938 directive, the defendants were indicted under Article 206-17 of the Ukraine SSR Criminal Code for gross violations of socialist legality.[72] A three-day trial in June 1939 before the Kharkov District NKVD Military Tribunal ended with a guilty verdict, prison sentences ranging from three to five years for Kocherginskii's former subordinates, and a death sentence for Kocherginskii.[73] Three days after his appeal to the Military Collegium of the Supreme Soviet USSR was denied, Kocherginskii was executed.[74]

The Kocherginskii case reveals the extent to which situational factors—above all, fear of punishment and a desire for approbation—motivated rank-and-file NKVD operatives during the Great Terror. This is not to say that ideology did not play an important role. Kocherginskii had no doubt that millions of class enemies threatened the existence of the USSR and needed to be eliminated prior to the outbreak of war. His experience delivering summary justice as a member of the Kharkov Revolutionary Tribunal during the civil war and as an NKVD official during the collectivization campaign in the North Caucasus, as well as his experience unmasking high-level terrorist plots as a member of the Mironov brigade in the Far East, primed him to accept the notion that the enemy was omnipresent, masked, and dangerous. Yet even Kocherginskii himself was motivated during the Great Terror by situational factors—in particular, an awareness that he had been denounced earlier as a Trotskyite and that his ties to Latvia made him vulnerable to internal NKVD purges. Based on the evidence that emerged during the investigation and trial of Kocherginskii for "gross violations of socialist legality," it is clear that situational factors were a major factor in motivating rank-and-file NKVD operatives to engage in blatant violations of criminal procedure, including wholesale fabrication of cases, torture of suspects, and coercion of witnesses. Kocherginskii motivated his subordinates by heaping praise on those who fulfilled impossible quotas and, more important, by creating a climate of terror within the DTO NKVD.

Notes

1. For a notable exception, see Lynne Viola, *Stalinist Perpetrators on Trial: Scenes from the Great Terror in Soviet Ukraine* (New York: Oxford University Press, 2017).

2. HDA SBU, f. 5, op. 1, spr. 67988, tom 5, ark. 316.

3. HDA SBU, f. 5, op. 1, spr. 67988, tom 3, ark. 20, 23.

4. HDA SBU, f. 5, op. 1, spr. 67988, tom 3, ark. 24, 40.

5. HDA SBU, f. 5, op. 1, spr. 67988, tom 3, ark. 41, 40 zv, 23.

6. HDA SBU, f. 5, op. 1, spr. 67988, tom 3, ark. 23–24 zv.

7. HDA SBU, f. 5, op. 1, spr. 67988, tom 3, ark. 25.

8. HDA SBU, f. 5, op. 1, spr. 67988, tom 3, ark. 25 zv.

9. HDA SBU, f. 5, op. 1, spr. 67988, tom 3, ark. 25 zv.

10. HDA SBU, f. 5, op. 1, spr. 67988, tom 3, ark. 43.

11. HDA SBU, f. 5, op. 1, spr. 67988, tom 3, ark. 43–43 zv.; http://www.memo.ru/history/nkvd/kto/biogr/gb327.htm.

12. Elena Nikolaevna Chernolutskaia, "Prikaz NKVD No. 00447 'ob operatsii po repressirovaniiu . . . antisovetskikh elementov.' Dal'nii Vostok, 1937–1938 gg," *Rossiia i ATR* 3 (2005): 56.

13. HDA SBU, f. 5, op. 1, spr. 67988, tom 3, ark. 246.

14. http://www.memo.ru/history/nkvd/kto/biogr/gb327.htm.

15. HDA SBU, f. 5, op. 1, spr. 67988, tom 3, ark. 103–4

16. HDA SBU, f. 5, op. 1, spr. 67988, tom 3, ark. 44. Dagin was arrested three months after Kocherginskii while still serving as head of security for Soviet leaders. Capital lettering is in the original. http://www.memo.ru/history/nkvd/kto/biogr/gb129.htm.

17. HDA SBU, f. 5, op. 1, spr. 67988, tom 3, ark. 43, 44. Radzivilovskii was arrested less than a month after Kocherginskii while serving as a division chief in the NKVD's Transportation and Communications Directorate. http://www.memo.ru/history/nkvd/kto/biogr/gb406.htm. Gatov was arrested four months after Kocherginskii while serving as a division chief in the NKVD's Main Economic Directorate. http://www.memo.ru/history/nkvd/kto/biogr/gb94.htm.

18. HDA SBU, f. 5, op. 1, spr. 67988, tom 3, ark. 43. On Gorbach, see Chernolutskaia, "Prikaz NKVD No. 00447," 58; and http://www.memo.ru/history/nkvd/kto/biogr/gb107.htm. Gorbach was arrested three months after Kocherginskii while serving as head of the NKVD's Far East-Khabarovsk Region Directorate.

19. HDA SBU, f. 5, op. 1, spr. 67988, tom 3, ark. 44–44 zv, 2.

20. "Statisticheskie itogi 'Bol'shogo terrora," http://www.memo.ru/history/y1937/hronika1936_1939/xronika.html#y1.

21. HDA SBU, f. 5, op. 1, spr. 67988, tom 3, ark. 1, 44–45. Kocherginskii lost contact with his mother and sister after leaving Riga in 1918. They spent years trying to track him down, and finally located him in 1934. After receiving a postcard from his mother, Kocherginskii replied that he was well and explained that he could not

write again. Later that year, Kocherginskii met his sister for two hours at the Kursk train station in Moscow after she notified him that she would be visiting the USSR as part of a workers' delegation. Kocherginskii received permission from superiors before replying to his mother's postcard and traveling to Moscow for the rendezvous with his sister. Other than these two instances, Kocherginskii had no contact with his relatives in Latvia. HDA SBU, f. 5, op. 1, spr. 67988, tom 3, ark. 25 zv–28.

22. HDA SBU, f. 5, op. 1, spr. 67988, tom 5, ark. 228.

23. HDA SBU, f. 5, op. 1, spr. 67988, tom 5, ark. 277–81.

24. HDA SBU f. 5, op. 1, spr. 67988, tom 3, ark. 246–47, 159–160.

25. HDA SBU, f. 5, op. 1, spr. 67988, tom 3, ark. 3, 82, 90, 1070b.; tom 5, ark. 120 zv, 161, 164, 171–73, 215.

26. HDA SBU, f. 5, op. 1, spr. 67988, tom 3, ark. 82.

27. HDA SBU, f. 5, op. 1, spr. 67988, tom 3, ark. 83–84.

28. HDA SBU, f. 5, op. 1, spr. 67988, tom 1, ark. 112–13; tom 5, ark. 227, 321; tom 3, ark. 161.

29. HDA SBU, f. 5, op. 1, spr. 67988, tom 3, ark. 107 zv.

30. HDA SBU, f. 5, op. 1, spr. 67988, tom 1, ark. 151; tom 3, ark. 98, 86, 80, 135. According to plenipotentiary Khodarev, the model kulak confession said: "I'm a kulak, I used fake documents to get a job in transportation, and I've carried out the following acts of wrecking and sabotage at the railroad." HDA SBU, f. 5, op. 1, spr. 67988, tom 3, ark. 80–81.

31. HDA SBU, f. 5, op. 1, spr. 67988, tom 3, ark. 50–55.

32. HDA SBU, f. 5, op. 1, spr. 67988, tom 3, ark. 139, 47, 286; tom 5, ark. 144; tom 3, ark. 103, 248, 110.

33. HDA SBU, f. 5, op. 1, spr. 67988, tom 3, ark. 286, 110 zv.

34. HDA SBU, f. 5, op. 1, spr. 67988, tom 3, ark. 106–7, 246–48, 159–60, 162, 51; tom 1, ark. 150.

35. HDA SBU, f. 5, op. 1, spr. 67988, tom 1, ark. 304.

36. HDA SBU, f. 5, op. 1, spr. 67988, tom 3, ark. 79.

37. HDA SBU, f. 5, op. 1, spr. 67988, tom 3, ark. 99–100, 102, 85, 110.

38. HDA SBU, f. 5, op. 1, spr. 67988, tom 3, ark. 106.

39. HDA SBU, f. 5, op. 1, spr. 67988, tom 3, ark. 85.

40. HDA SBU, f. 5, op. 1, spr. 67988, tom 3, ark. 98–100.

41. HDA SBU, f. 5, op. 1, spr. 67988, tom 3, ark. 109.

42. HDA SBU, f. 5, op. 1, spr. 67988, tom 3, ark. 102.

43. HDA SBU, f. 5, op. 1, spr. 67988, tom 3, ark. 106, 107. See also HDA SBU, f. 5, op. 1, spr. 67988, tom 5, ark. 215.

44. HDA SBU, f. 5, op. 1, spr. 67988, tom 3, ark. 101.

45. HDA SBU, f. 5, op. 1, spr. 67988, tom 1, ark. 150.

46. HDA SBU, f. 5, op. 1, spr. 67988, tom 3, ark. 145 zv, 146. Aronovich also criticized his immediate superior, Debal'tsevo district branch office chief Ignatov, for uncritically fulfilling Kocherginskii's directives during the mass operation and failing to

set a good example for his subordinates. HDA SBU, f. 5, op. 1, spr. 67988, tom 3, ark. 146 zv.

47. HDA SBU, f. 5, op. 1, spr. 67988, tom 3, ark. 150–51. See also HDA SBU, f. 5, op. 1, spr. 67988, tom 5, ark. 43.

48. HDA SBU, f. 5, op. 1, spr. 67988, tom 3, ark. 165–66.

49. HDA SBU, f. 5, op. 1, spr. 67988, tom 3, ark. 154.

50. HDA SBU, f. 5, op. 1, spr. 67988, tom 3, ark. 154–154 zv.

51. HDA SBU, f. 5, op. 1, spr. 67988, tom 1, ark. 102. To reiterate an important point, none of the rank-and-file investigators who fabricated cases did so in response to a direct order. Rather, they fabricated cases in an effort to avoid humiliation and punishment and also, it seems, to secure the approbation of superiors. See, for example, HDA SBU, f. 5, op. 1, spr. 67988, tom 1, ark. 103.

52. HDA SBU, f. 5, op. 1, spr. 67988, tom 3, ark. 171, 101; tom 5, ark. 324 zv.

53. HDA SBU, f. 5, op. 1, spr. 67988, tom 3, ark. 88. During the height of the Debal'tsevo mass operation, Kocherginskii demanded that investigators secure from three to seven confessions each day. See also HDA SBU, f. 5, op. 1, spr. 67988, tom 3, ark. 101–2.

54. HDA SBU, f. 5, op. 1, spr. 67988, tom 3, ark. 170.

55. HDA SBU, f. 5, op. 1, spr. 67988, tom 3, ark. 174.

56. HDA SBU, f. 5, op. 1, spr. 67988, tom 3, ark. 153.

57. HDA SBU, f. 5, op. 1, spr. 67988, tom 3, ark. 175–76.

58. HDA SBU, f. 5, op. 1, spr. 67988, tom 3, ark. 90–91.

59. HDA SBU f. 5, op. 1, spr. 67988, tom 3, ark. 130 zv.

60. HDA SBU, f. 5, op. 1, spr. 67988, tom 3, ark. 135, 88–89, 97–98; tom 5, ark. 3220b.

61. HDA SBU, f. 5, op. 1, spr. 67988, tom 3, ark. 186; tom 5, ark. 131. Kocherginskii first learned how to use *otstoiniki* to procure confessions while serving on the Mironov brigade. HDA SBU, f. 5, op. 1, spr. 67988, tom 5, ark. 322 zv. Due to the shortage of manpower, Kocherginskii mobilized unvetted Communists and Komsomols to guard prisoners in these cells, which resulted in rumors of their existence spreading among the general population. This represented a breach of NKVD secrecy norms.

62. HDA SBU, f. 5, op. 1, spr. 67988, tom 5, ark. 323.

63. HDA SBU, f. 5, op. 1, spr. 67988, tom 5, ark. 367 zv.

64. HDA SBU, f. 5, op. 1, spr. 67988, tom 5, ark. 367. Though obviously self-serving, it is worth noting the testimony of Debal'tsevo district branch office chief Ignatov: "[Our] employees didn't beat arrested individuals prior to Kocherginskii's arrival in Debal'tsevo." HDA SBU, f. 5, op. 1, spr. 67988, tom 3, ark. 181 zv.

65. See, for example, HDA SBU, f. 5, op. 1, spr. 67988, tom 4, ark. 1–3, 9, 11, 13–16, 20–25, 57–60, 61, 63–66, 75–76 zv, 80–80 zv, 82–87 zv, 89–90 zv, 92–95, 164–66. Efforts by the local procurator to investigate complaints referred from the central procurator's office were rebuffed by Kocherginskii with the backing of his superiors in Moscow. HDA SBU, f. 5, op. 1, spr. 67988, tom 4, ark. 61.

66. HDA SBU, f. 5, op. 1, spr. 67988, tom 4, ark. 63.

67. HDA SBU, f. 5, op. 1, spr. 67988, tom 4, ark. 63–68, 133, 135–42. Vyshinskii urged Ezhov to investigate Kocherginskii and the myriad complaints against him on 21 June 1938, 22 July 1938, and 10 August 1938. HDA SBU, f. 5, op. 1, spr. 67988, tom 4, ark.3, 61.

68. HDA SBU, f. 5, op. 1, spr. 67988, tom 3, ark. 4–5.

69. HDA SBU, f. 5, op. 1, spr. 67988, tom 3, ark. 19a.

70. HDA SBU, f. 5, op. 1, spr. 67988, tom 1, ark. 29–29 zv; tom 5, ark. 226–29.

71. HDA SBU, f. 5, op. 1, spr. 67988, tom 3, ark. 301; tom 5, ark. 5.

72. HDA SBU, f. 5, op. 1, spr. 67988, tom 5, ark. 294, 302–6

73. HDA SBU, f. 5, op. 1, spr. 67988, tom 5, ark. 337–41.

74. HDA SBU, f. 5, op. 1, spr. 67988, tom 5, ark. 373, 382.

Index

For the benefit of digital users, indexed terms that span two pages (e.g., 52–53) may, on occasion, appear on only one of those pages.

Note: Page numbers followed by *f* indicate a figure on the corresponding page.